THE STING OF CHANGE

THE STING OF CHANGE
Sicilians in Sicily and Australia

Constance Cronin

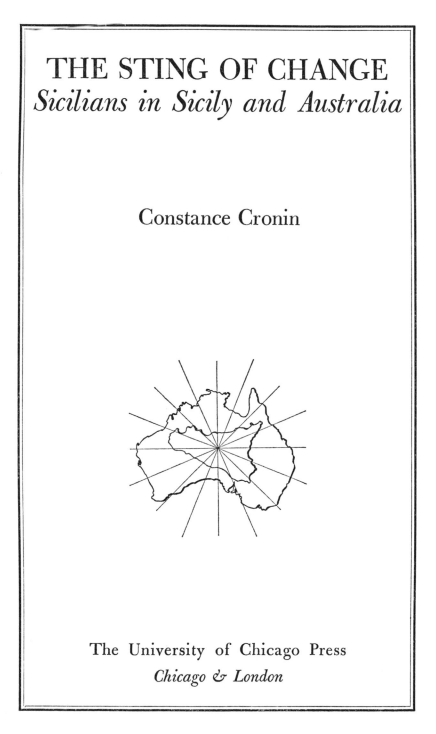

The University of Chicago Press

Chicago & London

International Standard Book Number: 0–226–12110–0
Library of Congress Card Number: 70–112707

THE UNIVERSITY OF CHICAGO PRESS, CHICAGO 60637
THE UNIVERSITY OF CHICAGO PRESS, LTD., LONDON

For the sting of change lies not in change itself but in change which is devoid of social meaning.

S. H. Frankel, *The Economic Impact on Underdeveloped Societies*

CONTENTS

ACKNOWLEDGMENTS

I WISH to thank the people on three continents whose help, co-operation, and friendship made this study possible. I am grateful to three foundations whose financial support enabled me to work full-time on this project: the Centro Studio per la Piena Occupazione in Sicily, the Fulbright Foundation for a Fellowship to Australia, and the National Institute of Mental Health for a Terminal Pre-Doctoral Fellowship.

My heartfelt gratitude to the following friends for their constant encouragement in good health and help in ill health during the Sicilian fieldwork: Dr. Vincenzo Borruso, Mariarosa Silvani Franco and Dr. Salvatore Franco, Cristina and Eyvind Hytten, Bruno Muratore, Marcella and Marco Marchioni, Mary Taylor Simeti and Cumpare Antonio Simeti, Fiorella and Giuseppe Viola, and Ingeborg Winkler.

My thanks to the following friends and associates in Australia who gave unstintingly of their time and talent: Dr. Charles Price, Dr. F. Lancaster Jones, and Dr. Jerzy Zubrzycki of the Australian National University; Dorothy Billings; and Salvatore Sudano.

In the United States my warmest appreciation for their years of encouragement and support go to Sally and Lewis Binford, my parents, Mr. and Mrs. James Cronin, McGuire Gibson, William Longacre, Katie and Edward Nash, Kathryn and Judd Sackheim, Murray and Robert Sumwalt, and Harold Youngblood. To Jane Bachman my gratitude and endless admiration for editorial services rendered in the name of friendship. A debt is due those University of Chicago professors who stimulated my intellectual growth and always had time to listen to my problems: F. Clark Howell, Arthur Jelinek, Paul Martin, and Eric Wolf; Clifford Geertz and Lloyd Fallers who, in addition, read and commented on this volume before publication; and Robert A. LeVine, advisor and friend, whose unfailing readiness to advise, counsel, and help was an important factor in the eventual completion of this long project. A special thank you to Rita Miller for typing an almost indecipherable manuscript. And, I wish to express my deepest gratitude to Alice and Peter Rossi whose years of friendship made this whole venture possible and pleasurable.

Lastly, I thank all those hundreds of Sicilians who must remain nameless here but whose sincerity, integrity, and worth are attested to by this study. Without them no amount of work or assistance would have been of value; with them, I have realized a goal, and I hope I have nowhere betrayed the trust they placed in me—
sunnu veru amici.

PREFACE

THIS study is based on the results of twelve months fieldwork in a Sicilian town, which I shall call "Nicuportu," and fourteen months fieldwork with Sicilian immigrants in Sydney, Australia. In Sicily I was employed as a researcher for a private development group, which greeted me when I arrived, paid me a monthly salary of 45,000 lire ($75), occasionally inquired how I was getting along, and sent me on my way at the end of my stay. It was the perfect position for a graduate student who wished to do independent research; I carried out my work alone, completely unhindered by the sponsoring group.

I lived in three different apartments in various sections of town and spent my days walking around, visiting and talking with people. Toward the end of my stay I planned a change of routine which involved structured interviews and collecting data from the *comune* (town hall), the priest, and various other officials. This had been put off because I did not want to risk antagonizing anyone early on and being forced to leave. I had completed interviews and genealogies with thirty-five families (many were seen more than once) when a case of hepatitis left me bedridden for the last two months of my stay. Therefore I did not have the opportunity to complete as many interviews as I had anticipated; I do not feel that the loss has been harmful or prejudicial to this analysis of Sicilian society because the notes gathered during ten months, plus the completed interviews, revealed such a striking uniformity that I believe additional interviews would have revealed only more of the same information.

Many people have asked how it was possible for me to work in Sicily since (1) Sicilians trust no one, (2) Sicilians never talk to anyone outside the family, and (3) Sicilians make it impossible for a woman to live alone there. The above points may be true but I had no difficulty whatsoever. I was accepted and even welcomed (as a pleasant diversion in the monotony) from my first week in the town, and I received the complete cooperation of every person I met. I embodied three features which Sicilians like—I am an American, a student, and a woman. Sicilians generally have the highest regard for America and anything American and feel real kinship with individual Americans since almost everyone has many relatives in the United States. My status as a university student writing a thesis on Sicilian customs gave me a reason for being in town, for spending vast amounts of time doing "nothing," and gave me prestige and respect as well. However, it was as a woman that I found it easiest to meet and become friendly with Sicilians of both sexes. A foreign woman is free to talk to Sicilian women and to enter Sicilian houses and is not suspect or dangerous to the women she meets. Therefore, the women certainly had no fear of me and the men often commented that it was fortunate that I was not a man because they could not have asked a man to their homes or felt comfortable with a strange man present. In addition, it was easy to use household activities as an excuse for sitting in a house for hours. I "learned" how to bake bread, how to make pasta and Sicilian pastries, and how to embroider. These activities take hours and during these times we talked in a free and relaxed atmosphere. I sat at work tables with the artisan men in front of their houses and was shown how to make shoes, paint horse carts, manufacture barrels, and make pom-poms and bridles for the horses and mules. The men thought it silly but commendable that a girl who came from such a modern tin-sealed society should be interested in such activities. As we sat we talked and usually others joined us in the street adding their comments to the topics under discussion.

I told people during these early months that someday I would come back to do interviews, which I did. I had been told in the States and in Sicily that this would be impossible with Sicilians, but these people, who had appeared so logical and sensible, were just that and in every case agreed to let me write down what they said. Many wanted it read back and then changed the wording or added something; others called their friends to hear what they had said; and many, when I came in the evening just to visit, insisted that I record conversations and sent children for paper and pencil. Most inhabitants took a great interest in the study and often would bring up previously discussed topics because they had thought of something else "important." Most saw through my topic "Sicilian customs" and would remark, "Why didn't you say you wanted to know about families and engagements and that kind of thing?" and then proceed to tell me with whom I should talk and what to ask. They proved themselves very good sociologists with a profound and subtle understanding of their own society.

The data from the Australian interviews do not correspond perfectly with the Sicilian data because the two field situations were so different. In Sydney the occupations of the immigrants, their time schedules, and their dispersion throughout a large metropolitan area made it impossible to see everyone more than a few times. I did see some families more often than others and I was invited to many parties, dinners, and picnics; but nonetheless when I entered their homes it was as a visitor and not as a close neighbor just walking by. When it takes two hours by bus to travel from your house to the respondent's one does not "drop in" or just "pass by" very often. However, the knowledge I gained in Sicily and the cooperation of the Sydney Sicilians made it possible to investigate their lives in a new country.

One researcher with a limited amount of time always encounters a problem basic to field studies in the social sciences: should he interview many people and concentrate on a few topics, or should he interview a few people in depth? Often the nature of the study itself dictates the answer to this question and so it was here. I went to Australia to investigate a great many problem areas in social change, and since this dictated several long interviews with each respondent it was impossible to see a vast number of immigrants. In one year in Sydney interviews were conducted with forty-eight immigrant Sicilians (the first generation) and fifteen adults born in Australia of immigrant Sicilian parents (the second generation). However, I lived and socialized with the immigrants and their families during this time, and while it is possible to speak with authority only of the respondents cited above, my conversations with many hundreds of other Sicilians in Sydney allowed me to check the results of the interviews. This study concerns only the immigrants themselves (although passing references are made to the second generation) because the analysis is concerned with change from one society to another and the children of the immigrants have not participated in this movement.

Sydney was selected as the site of the study because it is a large cosmopolitan urban area that had not been studied before and also because Melbourne, which has a larger Italian population, was at the time experiencing a series of riots among the Calabrians which had made Italians in that area suspicious of outsiders. A plan was made to select a nonrandom sample of Sicilian immigrants who were diversified in occupation, time in Australia, residential area (in Sydney), and age. A variety of techniques were utilized to find the respondents. The Sicilian family I lived with in Sydney supplied eleven of their relatives and *paesani* (fellow townsmen in Sicily); the mother of the husband in this family put me in contact with three of her friends; a non-Sicilian doctor introduced me to a second-generation woman who took me around the city to meet a total of nine people. I wrote letters to several professionals whose names I plucked from the yellow pages of the telephone book, interviewed them, and through two met another nine persons; for the rest, I asked the first respondents to give me names of other Sicilians who would talk to me. For a time I interviewed everyone whose name I was given, but eventually I became more selective asking specifically for "an old man" or "a professional" or "a prewar immigrant" in an effort to keep all the relevant variables balanced in the total sample. This rather cumbersome procedure was necessary because the only records that include all Sicilian immigrants may not be used by researchers for the purpose of contacting people.

Each respondent was interviewed twice. There were no refusals to my requests for interviews; in fact, toward the end many persons asked to be interviewed. All respondents were told that I was writing a thesis for the university about their experiences in Australia and how their lives have changed. There was extraordinarily fine cooperation from everyone. People often suggested that the respondent and I go off by ourselves because "that's the way you do interviews." They were all interested in the "book" I would eventually write and hoped that it would give non-Sicilians some idea of their lives and personalities. Almost all the interviews were done in the respondent's home though a few were written in offices and shops. Interviews usually included dinner and an entire evening or day of socializing, which was not only enjoyable but also extremely valuable for getting a taste of how the immigrants live. It is apparent that in Sydney, as in Nicuportu, the Sicilians were warm, generous, sincere, and cooperative in all respects.

Interview schedules were drawn up and duplicated and the same questions were asked of each respondent. The respondent was allowed to choose the language in which he wished to speak. Responses were taken down in longhand and no attempt was made to use a tape recorder, although in most cases this would have been acceptable on the second interview. The validity of the answers is always a problem of course, but there is no reason to suspect, with two exceptions, that the answers were biased by a desire either to hide information or to please the interviewer. The two exceptions were when men would try to appear much more authoritarian as husbands and when there was unwillingness to detail quarrels within the family or among relatives. Respondents would give negative opinions of relatives in general but would rarely cite examples of specific quarrels. This is in accord with the findings of most researchers who have worked in southern Italy.

The interview schedules themselves (see Appendix A) were long and detailed. The average interview lasted over two and one-half hours. Working in a city of two million inhabitants is very different from working in a rural town of 26,000. Sydney respondents were not available during the day, with the exception of three elderly retired men, and were not willing to interview on what they considered holiday time—Saturday, Sunday, legal or religious holidays, and the month-long vacation period at Christmas when the entire country virtually shuts down. I had originally planned to interview both husband and wife in each family, but because of these time limitations, it was in most cases only possible to interview one person; so I usually chose the husband because of his position as head of the household. On the numerous occasions when the wife was also present during the interview, her responses were solicited and revealed only rare disagreements, usually on matters of minor importance. So finally for the Australian study, forty-eight respondents (forty-five men and three women) were interviewed on two separate occasions, and genealogies of almost all the families were drawn.

In both the Sicilian and Australian accounts, all names and, where necessary, places, occupations, and personal stories, have been altered to preserve the anonymity of individuals.

1
THE STUDY OF
CULTURE CHANGE

ALTHOUGH studies of culture change are increasingly attracting the attention of sociologists, anthropologists, social psychologists, and historians, the problems of conceptualization and method are particularly great in this field. Many of these problems stem from the differing theoretical orientations of the disciplines, and to clarify much of the confusion which today prevails in the theories of culture change it is necessary to trace briefly the history of the subject within each of the two main divisions—sociology and anthropology.

THEORIES OF CULTURE CHANGE

American sociologists, as a result of the large influx of immigrants from the European continent just after the turn of the century, were the first to devote extensive amounts of time and energy investigating the effects of mass immigration on the receiving society and on the ethnic or national groups who made up this wave. They were also responding to the angry or concerned reaction of millions of "old" Americans some of whom saw their cities and their institutions threatened by the immigrants and others who saw the immigrants suffering under the effects of prejudice and poverty. But the situation in 1902 and the various "philosophies" designed to "do something with the immigrants" were only new manifestations of questions and problems which had existed in the United States since the colonial period. Somehow, it was felt, immigrants must be assimilated or taken into American society if each ethnic group was to be prevented from forming its own separate society with distinctive institutions, values, and behavior patterns.

The earliest assimilation theory is that of Anglo-conformity which holds "as a central assumption the desirability of maintaining English institutions (as modified by the American Revolution), the English language, and English-oriented cultural patterns dominant and standard in American life" (Gordon 1964, p. 88). This theory has been held by a majority of the American people throughout the history of the country and even today has not lost its potency. The agitation to assimilate the newcomers waxed and waned with the fortunes of the new country and reached its most extreme form in the Native American movement of the 1830s and 1840s and with the American or Know-Nothing party of the 1850s. An "Americanization" movement flowered during World War I as an attempt to cope with the millions of immigrants so recently come to the United States, many of whom were citizens of enemy countries. This was primarily "a consciously articulated movement to strip the immigrant of his native culture and attachments and make him over into an American along Anglo-Saxon lines—all this to be accomplished with great rapidity" (Gordon 1964, p. 99). However, by the early 1920s the movement had died down only to be replaced by a demand for legal restrictions on immigration. This was subsequently carried out with the effect of cutting down the numbers of immigrants and favoring northern Europeans, who were more easily assimilable. It is only today that some revision in the immigration laws is being made.

At the turn of the century another old theory gained many adherents who were disturbed by the elements of racism and forced change implicit in the Anglo-conformity idea. This new theory was eventually called the "melting pot" theory, from a popular 1908 play in which the Jewish hero is able to marry the gentile heroine because:

> America is God's crucible, the great Melting Pot where all the races of Europe are melting and re-forming. [quoted in Glazer and Moynihan 1963, p. 289]

Adherents of the melting pot theory believed that all the customs, ideas, and values brought into the United States by such diverse peoples (including the Yankees) would eventually melt and merge to form a new and American society. Thus everyone was adding his bit, no matter what his background, and the resulting society would not only be better than the old but would be agreeable to all since the distillation was a "natural" process which did not "force" anyone to give up his customs and beliefs.

American sociologists not only had the immigrant groups to use as a natural laboratory in their researches but they also had widely held ideas or theories of assimilation to investigate. Assimilation in the early days of sociology meant the total absorption of foreign nationals into American society: their traditions and values were, in one way or another, to be discarded and replaced either with Old American or with New American ideas and customs.

The numerous sociological and historical studies which grew out of the American environment were directly responsible for the eventual discard of the Anglo-conformity and melting pot theories because empirical researches showed that neither theory was working out in practice. Ethnic group identity and foreign national traditions were proving to have a firm hold on many immigrants and though most Americans continued to hold the belief that immigrants should be assimilated, the sociological studies were proving conclusively that many were not.

The early works of Park and Miller (1925), Thomas and Znaniecki (1918), Fairchild (1926), Foerster (1919), and others were instrumental in bringing before the American educated community facts "which provided clear evidence of the persistence of ethnic groups for generations" (Borrie 1959, p. 92). The change in ideas on the theoretical level was sweeping and the outstanding theory, after the abandonment of the earlier ideas, is that the modern industrialized society can and does allow a finite number of gradations in conforming to a cultural ideal. This is the theory of cultural pluralism which in essence says that "society is composed to some extent of different sub-systems allocated to different immigrant (ethnic) groups—groups maintaining some degree of separate identity" (Eisenstadt 1954, p. 15).

If the idea of cultural pluralism indicated some theoretical coherence and agreement among social scientists it also introduced a great many complications. The new theory is itself much more complex than the older models and necessitates a consideration of a far greater number of factors which can then be joined together in a bewildering variety of combinations. The following statement, which grew out of a UNESCO conference on culture change, sets forth the basic concept of this theory while revealing at the same time the possible complexities occasioned by its use:

> There was, however, general agreement on the concept of *plurality* plus *adjustment*, of a process towards uniformity at some levels but preserving differences at others. It was recognized also that the concept of *accommodation* was essential to the process. The process of adjustment was seen as one which is generally accompanied by sub-groups being accommodated within the total framework, while wholly or partially absorbed in various sectors or isolates of that framework. [Borrie et al. 1959, p. 94]

At this point we begin to see a difference between sociologists who are primarily concerned with theory but do not carry out many empirical studies and those who do field studies on immi-

3

grant groups but do not fit their data or conclusions into a theoretical framework. Thus today we have the theories of Eisenstadt, Gordon, Park-Miller, and Glazer and Moynihan, but aside from the illustrative examples of their originators no fieldwork has been carried out within these frameworks. On the other hand there is a vast body of field studies, some of which are Child (1943), Gans (1962), Lee (1960), Warner (1941), and Wirth (1928), but none of these have been placed into an existing theoretical framework (though the writers often develop a new theory themselves). The student of comparative cross-cultural research or the student who is attempting to fit all the field studies into a theoretical framework in order to find uniformities and differences is at a loss because "most of the works concerned were not written for that special purpose, and provide answers only by implication" (Eisenstadt 1954, p. 5). Other sociologists have concentrated on selected variables which always leave other variables, and indeed the over-all picture, in the dark. One always returns to the fact that "many of the systematic expositions of the processes in question are mainly demographic and economic in character, and although there are abundant social materials dealing with various specific aspects and instances of migration, they appear to have little unity or systematic interdependence" (Eisenstadt 1954, p. ix).

Anthropologists showed an early interest in culture change but they have, by and large, studied change in colonial situations in Africa and India, and among American Indian groups. They have almost totally ignored chance situations which result from migration or immigration. In a paper written in 1937, Herskovits (1958) stressed the importance of acculturation studies, but addressed himself entirely to problems arising from colonial situations. Spiro notes that there are less than thirty titles on "cultures of or the acculturation of ethnic groups" (1955, p. 1240) and that the knowledge anthropologists possess in this important area of research come from nonanthropologists.

Spiro's survey reveals that these twenty odd papers cover eight different areas of research interests, such as "impediments to acculturation," "religion and folklore in acculturation," and "personality in acculturation"; in addition, he notes that "some of the papers are too superficial to yield any general conclusions; some overlap with others in different categories; and some categories contain too few papers to allow any cross-ethnic generalizations" (1955, p. 1242). In summing up Spiro states the basic problem:

Although some of the studies are problem oriented, most of them are in the descriptive, "natural history" tradition of anthropological research. Hypotheses are seldom tested, but some emerge from an analysis of the data. [1955, p. 1242]

Even though some anthropologists have concentrated their efforts on change situations in colonial areas or in countries undergoing industrialization, many of the problems noted above for sociology and for anthropological ethnic studies are valid for traditional anthropological acculturation studies as well. Spicer sums it up admirably:

The growth of a general understanding of cultural change among anthropologists has seemed slow and unsatisfactory. There is a widespread feeling that we have no really useful concepts, that there is no theory worthy of the name, for comparing and understanding the many instances of change with which we are acquainted. [1961, p. 517]

Sociologists have been concerned with studying ethnic groups before they disappear while anthropologists have been turned away from comparative studies by the traditional belief that one studies cultures not individuals. The basic statement on acculturation studies was formulated by a team of four anthropologists and one sociologist for the Social Science Research Council in 1954 and remains today the basic formulation of anthropological thought in the field of culture change. It is elementary to an understanding of the cause of many problems in the field of change and is as true for sociologists as for anthropologists. The authors first define acculturation as "culture change that is initiated by the conjunction of two or more autonomous cultural systems," the latter being a system "which is self-sustaining" (Barnett et al., 1954, p. 974). After specifically including ethnic studies within the scope of acculturation they state:

The unit of analysis in acculturation studies is thus taken to be any given culture as it is carried by its particular society. It is recognized that individuals are empirically the culture bearers and that they are the mediators of any cultural process. Students of culture are, however, concerned with individuals as functioning members of a society and with the shared patterns of behavior constituting a body of customs. Consequently, while it is individuals who change their habits of doing and believing under the influence of alien forms, it is the body of custom of the society to which they belong that is said to be acculturating. [1954, p. 975]

The mist which today obscures the entire field of culture change has resulted from the exclusive emphasis on culture and whole societies. Anthropological and sociological studies of culture change are concerned with the outcome of acculturation and not with the process of acculturation itself: the works are descriptive not analytical. In other words, they investigate the structure and function of an ethnic society; they do not investigate the process which led to the result. This antihistorical or synchronic approach of anthropology may work well enough in static traditional, primitive, and peasant societies (though even this is open to criticism today), but it is the worst possible approach by which to study change. The most basic questions about the process of change and its effect on "cultures" or individuals are still unanswered because they have not been posed.

THE PROBLEM OF TERMINOLOGY

Another problem is particularly acute in the field of culture change—the terminology. The most common terms by which authors refer to social change are *acculturation, assimilation, absorption, accommodation, integration,* and *adaptation.* Gordon states that the terms assimilation and acculturation have sometimes "been used to mean the same thing; in other usages their meanings, rather than being identical, have overlapped" (1964, p. 61). He adds that in sociology there has been considerable confusion over the term assimilation particularly, but I would add that the situation is no less confusing concerning the term acculturation in anthropology studies. My own survey of more than twenty monographs on "acculturation" shows that most of the time the term is not defined and, in addition, other terms such as assimilation, adaptation, and absorption are used interchangeably (italics added throughout):

> the type of *culture change* involved is both one of *acculturation,* involving the continuous first-hand contact of representatives of two different cultures, and of *assimilation,* involving the gradual engulfing of representatives of one culture, and their *absorption* into the dominant group. [Barker 1947, p. 2]

> Studies in *acculturation* may well start with . . . then finally, an *adaptation* in which there is worked out a new equilibrium of cultural form and personality type. [Beaglehole 1937, p. 10]

> A number of studies have shown, indeed, that ethnic groups may discourage *acculturation* and social *assimilation.* [Martin 1965, p. 91]

6

Acculturation is viewed here as directed toward the ultimate *assimilation* of the ethnic individual in American society. [Broom and Kitsuse 1955, p. 48]

The generally held notion is that anthropologists use "acculturation" while sociologists use "assimilation"; yet it is apparent that both disciplines use both terms and many others as well. Which then are the variables which fall under acculturation and which are necessary to the study of assimilation? Let us examine some of the studies in the field from this point of view:

1. Child (1943)
   Social psychologist. An acculturation study as defined by the SSRC. Culture: language, eating and drinking, recreation, family structure, handling of sex, handling of aggression, economic life, religion, and superstition. Social organization: status of Italians in community, school, media, religion, politics.

2. Gans (1962)
   Sociologist. Looks at the impact of acculturation on Italian culture and of assimilation on social structure. Culture: food, eating habits, drinking habits, language, naming, identification with Italy. Social organization: social relationships, intermarriage, and the church.

3. Embree (1941)
   Anthropologist. Acculturation is concerned with changes in social organization, the network of social relations. These are measured by examining parties, language, food, household composition, neighbors, marriage, kinship, occupation, mobility, and values.

4. Honigmann (1941)
   Anthropologist. Contact is major term used. Examines technical culture, economic organization, dress, subsistence, band organization, religion, values, and sanctions.

It is obvious that a most appalling confusion prevails in both sociology and anthropology when change is studied. Siegel notes that researchers use

astonishingly unsystematic methods of formulating and reporting on research. In monographs, particularly, conclusion, implicit and explicit proposition, and even problem statements may occur anywhere in the body of the text. [1955, p. 4]

7

In discussing one monograph he makes the following statement which would apply to almost all anthropological and sociological studies of social change:

> In short one is left with a series of descriptive statements about the conditions under which groups are resistant or responsive to nativistic reactions. These statements, moreover, attempt to answer *what* happens, rather than *why* or *how* it happens. [1955, p. 8]

I personally reject all of these terms for the following reasons: *absorption, accommodation,* and *adaptation* imply very subtly that the host society is permitting the immigrant to be received into the new society; this, however, must be established empirically. *Acculturation* is concerned only with culture; *assimilation* has been so misused that any agreement on its meaning is virtually impossible; *integration* I reject because it too closely suggests the melting pot.

Cultural and sociological variables are mixed, making it impossible to compare studies and extremely difficult even to understand what is happening in any one study. The present confusion is a result of incompletely conceived field situations and a reliance on the old discipline-oriented theoretical formulations. It is apparent in change studies that there is little difference among the perceptions of culture and society because all social scientists are utilizing the same variables. It is time to drop the confusing and, in practice, worthless distinctions between culture and society, acculturation and assimilation, anthropology and sociology; we should instead apply ourselves to understanding what change entails, what variables must be examined, and what conditions promote or retard change.

PROBLEMS OF METHODOLOGY

In addition to the theoretical and terminological orientations of each social science discipline, the third problem area which has served to hinder growth in the field of change studies is methodology; theory and method are of course closely connected and act upon one another, but often fieldwork is carried out in a particular way simply because it is easier or because it has become standard practice.

There are four major methodological factors that deserve consideration here. The first is the overwhelming academic preference for working with visible ethnic groups. This trend is evident in almost all the extant monographs in sociology and anthropology and presets the nature of the data to be collected and the conclusions to be drawn. So long as ethnics are treated within a group structure, the investigation is limited to those ethnics who still conform to some traditional customs and who have retained many traditional values up to the third and fourth generation. The fact that they can correctly be termed a group, or a subgroup in reference to the wider society, should instantly indicate to us that they are different. We can properly study such a group in terms of their adjustment to a new society, but we cannot look to the group alone if we wish to study the process of change, for by its very nature as a group it is not being fully absorbed into the larger society.

Anthropologists who emphasize the group and the culture have by and large failed to realize that cultures or societies do not immigrate and they do not acculturate. Individuals or, at most, families immigrate—taking with them their values, beliefs, and a few material possessions. Their societal institutions do not follow with them, and although individuals may attempt to establish some of their pre-emigration institutions, circumstances force the alteration of these institutions and eventually the values which relate to them. There are no Lithuanian or Japanese "autonomous cultural systems" in the United States, Brazil, or New Zealand; there are, however, Lithuanians and Japanese, who after arrival set up national or ethnic institutions to care for their particular needs. These institutions which are never identical with prior institutions are the result of a common set of values or ideas about the way life should be lived. Irish immigrants in Boston may set up Irish voting blocks and may even, in certain localities, control a political party, but neither the individuals nor the political units are part of an Irish culture; they are American institutions in the United States and although the immigrants can vote "Irish" within the American context, they cannot vote Irish within an Irish context because they have left Ireland and its culture. Although more than four million Italians have emigrated to the United States, they came as individuals or as families—they were not picked up in a body and deposited in their new home as a group. These immigrants trickled into America over a period of sixty years and they did not carry Italian political, religious, or economic systems with them: they brought only themselves and their ideas.

The second major methodological factor is the use of geographic area in sample selection. Actually two criteria are utilized in the selection of a universe in most social change studies—common national origin and common residence in the new nation. There are studies of the Chinese in Chinatown (Lee 1960), the Italians in Little Italy (Gans 1962), and the Poles in Polishtown (Wood 1955). Each of these areas is an ethnic ghetto where the inhabitants can be studied in regard to the relative degree of change manifested, but to emphasize such studies of assimilation is more than misleading. It is obvious that a process of selection is operating on those individuals who are changing more rapidly or more fully or who are following quite different patterns in their change. It is these individuals who must be studied with greater interest, for they will carry change to its conclusion and reveal the full process which begins long before emigration.

Gans's book on second- and third-generation southern Italians in the West End of Boston is an excellent analysis of the group and its settlement area, but it does not permit us to see how these individuals and their parents came to be the way they are. And although Gans notes that numerous individuals or families had left the area to live in other ethnic communities or, more often, outside a ghetto, we are told nothing about these persons in his book or in any other studies. We cannot deduce all the elements in the process of change until we have a full range of studies which cover individuals in and out of the ghetto.

If the universe of study is determined by shared birthplace rather than shared residence in the host country, then the notion of group can be dispensed with because all members of any one ethnic group do not live together in ghettos (with the exception of a few ultraorthodox religious communities such as Hasidic Jews). The resulting study, rather than describing, for instance, the Polish community in Detroit with chapters on occupation, residence, language, kinship, and religion without reference to the process which transforms Polish immigrants into Americans, would instead be a study of all Poles born in Warsaw who now reside in Detroit and would take into account the effect of socioeconomic and Polish value orientations on the change of these individuals—individuals who came to the United States at different times, who live in different parts of the city, who are in different social classes, and who are therefore changing at different rates. Such a study would be areally based, but the area is the city of Detroit, a natural ecological area in all parts of which are found Polish immigrants. We cannot, with the present knowledge, even begin to estimate the effect of these and other variables on the process of change because such studies do not exist.

The third factor causing problems in methodology is that time (in years and months, not historical periods) is generally ignored in change studies. In any given year large cities in all major immigrant-receiving countries will contain individuals who arrived many years ago as well as individuals who arrived only weeks before. A study which ignores this fact, as the study of culture does, will never allow us to study the process of change because process is, by its very definition, a phenomenon which stretches over time. The perfect study of the process of change would of course be one in which a number of individuals are followed from the time they leave their homes until they die in their new country. This procedure is so difficult and time consuming that it has not been attempted, but the fact that immigrants arrive at different times as individuals allows us to use them as a controlled group, however contrived, for studying the effect of time on change. If there is any continuity to the process whereby individuals divest themselves of old ideas and substitute new ideas in their place as a result of contact, then it is incumbent to examine a range of such individuals to ascertain what changes take place, in what order, and whether variables such as age, marital status, sex, occupation, or education have an effect upon the change patterns of like-nationality ethnics.

The fourth factor is knowledge of the pre-emigration social organization and in particular its societal values. There is an assumption that most if not all immigrants place their highest values on ethnic solidarity, but when ethnic values are considered in conjunction with supposedly nonethnic values it can lead researchers such as Spiro to ask:

> if early experiences are of determinative importance, why do most ethnic groups prefer social mobility to ethnic integrity, and class-over ethnic-identification? [1955, p. 1249]

However, most ethnic groups described in the literature do not prefer social mobility to ethnic integrity; the Polish, Lithuanian, Irish and Italian groups have all been singled out over the years as prime examples of nonmobile groups, though this conclusion may be a reflection of the sociological concentration on nonmobile working-class ethnic ghettos. The main point is that the traditional values often included social mobility, but this value was, for the most part, inoperative in the European peasant world. Our knowledge of pre-emigration social organization is in most cases vague. Interviewing immigrants years after emigration to learn about their previous way of life may be the only way to know the world they left, but it is not a valid means of assessing a relative scale of values. Ethnic integrity may have a high value, but for some individuals social mobility may supercede it in value. One way to attack this problem is to investigate why immigrants left their homeland, which is a question most of the literature ignores despite the importance Eisenstadt (1954) places on it. The values of group or family solidarity, learned with the mother's milk in the old country, may be difficult to give up, but other values, even those learned much later, may eventually have greater importance for the individual. The most critical point is that there is variety between societies and within societies. Let us say for illustration that a society places its highest value on ingroup solidarity: many individuals do not emigrate because they wish to remain with their own people; others emigrate because their financial position is so precarious that it is the only alternative to the prospect of starving (some of these individuals remain loyal to the group after emigration, while the rest make money and advance in social status); still others emigrate because financial success or occupational advancement is more important to them than remaining with the group, and the immigrant country offers better opportunities than the home country. Thus, we can see very clearly that while one main value predominates in the "culture," individuals, as a result of personal experiences, differ in the importance they place on several values which are relevant to them. Anthropologists do indeed study individuals: they extract culture from them.

THE PRESENT STUDY

There are indications of a new trend in studies of change. The examples set by second- and third-generation adults in major immigrant-receiving countries such as the United States, Australia, and Israel have forced researchers to reexamine old theories and to formulate hypotheses based on new data. It is becoming increasingly clear, especially in North America, that immigrants, their children, and their grandchildren often retain a sense of ethnic identity which is complex, subtle, and not easily recognized when "cultural" factors such as differences in language and dress disappear.

A few studies in sociology, particularly political sociology, point out that though immigrants and their descendants may lose their "cultural" traits such as language, they do not necessarily become like native-born (Yankee) Americans in outlook, values, and identity. Glazer and Moynihan, discussing five ethnic groups, comment:

> In the third generation, the descendants of the immigrants confronted each other, and knew they were both Americans, in the same dress, with the same language, using the same artifacts, troubled by the same things, but they voted differently, had different ideas about education and sex, and were still, in many ways, as different from one another as their grandfathers had been. [1963, p. 14]

Gans (1962), in his discussion of second- and third-generation Italian-Americans, notes that cultural features such as language, gesture, and dress have been given up but that many features of Italian social organization, especially in reference to primary relationships, have been retained.

Anthropologists are not catching up as fast, but as long ago as 1955 Spiro noted that:

> What is of considerable interest, however, is another finding: external acculturation is not a reliable index of personality change. . . . In other words, cultural changes occur without corresponding changes in personality. [p. 1248]

Personality in this case often means ideas and values in connection with more psychologically oriented personality traits such as aggression. In other words, anthropologists are beginning to note the same phenomenon which sociologists have observed: cultural traits or customs often disappear quickly while ideas and values are proving extremely resistant to change.

Implicit in all these newer studies is the following: those areas of life which fall in the public sector (and are therefore controlled to some extent by the legal and moral sanctions of the country) are affected quickly and easily by conditions of change, whereas those areas of life which fall in the private sector (and are not controlled by societal institutions) are more resistant to conditions of change. If this is true for the second generation and even more obvious in the third (all the newer studies deal with descendants), then this duality is a feature of change situations which originates in the first generation; so it was this point which I endeavored to investigate. I wanted to know what changes and what does not; I wanted to know who changes and who does not; and I wanted to know why. I therefore decided to carry out a detailed study of change among a group of first-generation immigrants, basing my theoretical outline on the public sector–private sector distinction and hypothesizing that there would be habit changes in the public sector of life and value changes for some but not all immigrants in the private sector of life.

The assumption underlying the public-private division is that the immigrant must participate in the public sector of life and will probably show evidence of change which may or may not have any direct connection with his becoming identified with the natives of the country. On the other hand, the immigrant is free to pursue his own idea of the good life in private, and changes in this sector will have a direct connection with his person and with his life style becoming like that of the host country.

The public sector includes all those activities in which the immigrant is forced to conform to societal rules and regulations and in which deviancy is punished. Thus occupation, residence, language ability, and adherence to the laws of the new country are considered to be public sector variables. For instance, an immigrant must work to support himself and his family; in the work place he must obey the rules of the company in his tasks and the rules of the society in his interaction with fellow workers. If he insists upon doing the work in his own way he will lose his job. If, on the other hand, he does not care to work and turns to a life of crime, then he has transgressed several societal and legal norms and will be imprisoned. The job he takes or the job for which he qualifies and his success at that task may well depend upon other factors, such as language ability or education, and these too must be considered in this sector. Whether the immigrant's choice of occupation is free or forced and whether he is successful or not are questions which must be answered. Immigrant satisfaction with these factors, the dependent variables, forms what I call here public satisfaction, a sense of pleasure with the occupational, residential, linguistic, and government institutions he finds in the new country. Thus his experiences within the public sector and his satisfaction with these conditions form one category of change—habit change.

The private sector includes all those activities with their attendant values in which the immigrant has free choice, assuming always that he does not transgress the law. Some of the variables which come under this category are family patterns (relatives, extended family, nuclear family), friendships, membership in associations, home language, food habits, religion, and political affiliation. The immigrant may maintain a home and family which is as like the original in his birthplace as is humanly possible, and no one in the new society can force him to change in even one particular.

The natives may criticize and gossip, but there is no legal or moral sanction which will make changes mandatory. The immigrant's children may bring pressure upon the parents to change the way of life in the home, but this is another side of the private sector since they are in the home too. The satisfaction which the immigrant feels toward his own life style in the new country and toward the way of life of the natives (if these are different) is what I call here private satisfaction. His experiences in the private sector and his satisfaction with these form another category of change—value change.

As is obvious by now, habit changes are alterations in those customs that carry little or no value, and they will not seriously damage the more important values that the immigrant brings with him. On the other hand, value changes are those alterations which will drastically change not only activities but also ideas and beliefs and ultimately the way of life, outlook, and identity. I have ignored the acculturation-assimilation distinction in these formulations. To use concepts which, before the fact, cut up a whole and parcel out the pieces to various disciplines, is to distort and confuse an already complex situation. For example, language is always considered to be one variable and is usually, though not always, assigned to "culture," but in the present study language becomes two variables: language ability and usage in the public sector and language ability and usage in the private sector. An immigrant may learn English and use it in his job and in his institutional contacts with English-speakers, that is, in the public sector, and this informs us of a habit change, but when we also learn that the same man forbids the use of English in his home then we know that a corresponding value change has not occurred. This man has conformed to the institutional demands of the new society, perhaps because he wishes to "get ahead" and a knowledge of the native tongue will help, but he has not conformed to the general practice of speaking English at all times because he does not have to and he wishes to remain ethnic where it counts.

There are four factors which appear to be important independent variables in immigrant change situations: age at emigration, education, time in the new country, and occupational mobility. It should be possible, using these variables, to begin an analysis of different patterns of change between national groups and within them. If this concept has any worth when applied to Italian immigrants, then somewhat similar studies among other immigrant groups should reveal basic differences between, for instance, Italian immigrants and Polish immigrants, between occupationally mobile and nonmobile Italian immigrants, and also between the mobile Polish immigrants and the mobile Italian immigrants. Such comparative studies should also supply data on pre-emigration social organization as well as on changes occurring after emigration. I did not anticipate wildly deviant changes from traditional Sicilian values and habits among the immigrants; rather, I believed that any changes which did take place, whether habit or value changes, would be a direct outgrowth of the traditional organization. This implies inner-directed change, impelled by existing values and habits. Confirmation of this idea would indicate the necessity for a thorough understanding of the pre-emigration social organization and for a movement of social scientists to study, even now, the traditional European and Asian societies which have furnished most of the world's immigrants.

Using these theoretical formulations, I did fieldwork in Sicily for one year to study the pre-emigration social organization, with emphasis on the Sicilian family system and its values, and then in Australia for fourteen months to study Sicilian immigrants. Sicilians were selected, first, because I had long had an interest in Italy and in Italian society; second, because even though Sicily shares in the great Western cultural tradition, the literature indicates enough differences to claim for the island what Redfield termed a little tradition; and third, because southern Italians have constituted one of the largest immigrant groups in the world for the past sixty years. Australia was chosen because it is a recent recipient of vast numbers of European immigrants, and therefore it was possible to find many immigrants settled in a society very unlike their homeland.

I did not concentrate on a ghetto area in the city of Sydney but rather drew a sample from Sicilians residing all over the metropolitan area. In this way I avoided a sample which contained only working-class residents of a relatively homogeneous neighborhood and I was able, at the same time, to avoid the "groupiness" which is the unavoidable result of such areally based studies. The sample includes individuals who are from differing socioeconomic backgrounds, who have differing educational credentials, and who today exhibit great variety in their occupations, residences, and change patterns. I also attempted to stratify the sample by length of time in the country to provide a rough continuum from very recent arrivals to immigrants with thirty or more years residence.

2
SOUTHERN ITALIANS IN THE LITERATURE

THERE is overwhelming agreement in the literature on Italian[1] social organization in Italy and in areas of heavy Italian immigration on certain familial characteristics such as the importance of the nuclear family and parental domination of children. However, on other characteristics such as the nature of the husband-wife relationship and bonds among relatives, there is disagreement, contradiction, and more ominously, silence. An examination of this literature reveals why such a curious situation has developed.

ON ITALIANS IN ITALY

In comparison with the vast body of sociological and historical literature on Italian immigrants in America, writings on Italians in Italy are few, but if the comparison is made with the anthropological literature for any one tribe, it is abundant. Moss and Thompson note:

> The Italian family has long served as a classic example of family solidarity in the social literature. Actually, however, most citations in American sociology refer more often to the Italo-American family than to the Italian family in its original culture setting. [1959, p. 35]

There is not one full-length monograph on the social organization of an Italian village, town, or city in the Italian literature. Those works which do exist are: Pitrè (1913), twenty-five volumes on Sicilian folklore; Tentori (1956), a relocation study; Marello (1960) and Anfossi (1959), short sketchy works glittering with generalities and based on most inadequate fieldwork (the former was completed in one month); and Parca (1959, 1965), studies of regional values and sexual mores (both volumes are now available in English, 1963, 1966).

There is, however, an impressive number of articles in Italian social work journals, such as *Centro Sociale* published by CEPAS,

1. Unless otherwise indicated Italian here means "southern Italian" comprising the area south of Rome and including the provinces of Campania, Abbruzzi, Puglia, Basilicata, and Calabria, plus Sardinia and Sicily.

and many excellent bachelor's theses written for the Italian professional schools of social work. Many of these articles and theses are sound academic studies employing good field methods and the latest American theory as well as displaying an extraordinary grasp of the American meaning of social anthropology. The problem is locating such a body of widely scattered reports, but the results are worth the effort because this is without a doubt the only adequate literature in Italian which analyzes social organization in a modern and imaginative way.

In the absence of academic studies it is not out of place to note popular works of fiction and nonfiction (in Italian and English) which serve to place the available literature in a living social context. These are: Barzini, *The Italians*, 1964; Crichton, *The Secret of Santa Vittoria*, 1966; Douglas, *Old Calabria*, 1915; Lampedusa, *The Leopard*, 1961 (first published in Italian, 1958); Levi, *Christ Stopped at Eboli*, 1963 (in Italian, 1947); Vaillant, *The Law*, 1958. Each of these authors deals specifically with family and social organization in so penetrating a manner that their books are basic reading material for any social scientist interested in southern Italy.

Films should also be mentioned because this often frivolous industry has, in Italy, produced pictorial documents which faithfully depict current social problems and portray social custom. Their style is insightful and thorough, if ironic and humorous. Some of the finest examples are: *Il Bell'Antonio* on the Sicilian male and family prestige; *Divorce Italian Style* on divorce in Sicily; *The Mafioso* on family obligations; *Rocco and His Brothers* on migrants to northern Italy; and *Seduced and Abandoned* on family organization, ritual kidnapping, and honor. It is no accident that all these films are set in Sicily. The single American film of this calibre is *A View from the Bridge*, an adaptation of Arthur Miller's excellent play about southern Italian immigrants in New York.

Five studies treat Italians in Italy; all are good but only two are published. Gower (1930) carried out a detailed Sicilian village study with emphasis on social organization. It is an excellent and important work since it is the only full-scale Italian village study in existence which was carried out before World War II. However, it is still in manuscript form and can be found only in the anthropology department of the University of Chicago. Pitkin (1954) has a study of land tenure and family organization in the province of Latina which is not, strictly speaking, southern Italy. Banfield

(1958) published an important document on Apulian family organization. Though based on questionable fieldwork techniques, this work of a political scientist is undoubtedly the most detailed and accurate picture of the Italian nuclear family. Lopreato's dissertation (1960; published 1967) is a sound and imaginative study of the effects of emigration on the social organization of a Calabrian village, and McDonald (1958) wrote an excellent study of the correlation between emigration and family organization. The last two works form an extremely interesting and important source of ideas about the process of emigration itself. It is noteworthy that with the exception of the little-known Gower manuscript, none of the preceding were written before 1954. Only Banfield concentrated on the family and even his work is limited to the nuclear family.

ON IMMIGRANT ITALIANS

There are eighteen studies of the Italian family after emigration to the United States, Australia, and Great Britain; twelve were written before 1954 and none of these writers based their research on Italian field studies. To ignore the old world social organization is to deny the effects of the immigration experience itself and the subsequent changes which may begin the day the European decides he wants to leave his native country. Eisenstadt notes:

> Thus it is obvious that the analysis of the immigrant's motive for migration and his consequent "image" of the new country is not of historical interest alone, but is also of crucial importance for understanding his initial attitudes and behaviour in his new setting. It is this initial motivation that constitutes the first stage of the process of social change . . . this first stage largely influences the subsequent stages inasmuch as it decides the immigrant's orientation and degree of readiness to accept change. [1954, p. 4]

Of the southern Italian literature in English let us take first those studies which are not specifically oriented to social organization. These include: Mariano (1921), a statistical, somewhat defensive, and demographic study based on census data; Foerster (1919), a biased demographic look at Italian immigration; Park and Miller (1925), a polemic directed against the immigrants and their disorganization in a new land; Radin (1935), a series of unanalyzed interviews with immigrants in San Francisco and a long section outlining the evils of fascism (supported by the WPA); and Williams (1938), an inventory of "cultural traits" for the edification of social workers in the ethnic ghettos. This last is rather unusual and excellent in its treatment of cultural factors in Italy, mainly Sicily.

Australian sociologists have concentrated most of their recent efforts on immigrant groups in Australia in response to the heavy postwar influx of Europeans. There are seven major studies of Italians: four of these are statistical and demographic in nature and do not attempt to analyze social organization except as it bears on the major focus of each study. The four are: Borrie (1954) and Zubrzycki (1960), who both rely entirely on census data to trace postimmigration settlement patterns; Jones (1962) and Price (1963), who were concerned with the chain migration phenomenon. Three unpublished reports or theses complete the list: Bromley (1955), Gamba (1952), and Hempel (1959). Each studied a southern Italian community in Australia relying entirely upon published sources and their own fieldwork in Australia. Australian sociologists have not worked in field situations in Italy, and Australian anthropologists have ignored immigrants to study aborigines and New Guinea natives. The resulting situation is best stated by Price, the foremost Australian social scientist working with immigrant groups:

> Indeed the whole matter of southern European family life in Australia, and the extent to which the family customs and loyalties of each particular group survived amongst the second and third generations, requires considerably more research—if possible by anthropologists trained in matters of kinship and of family customs and values. [1963, p. 63]

The British literature contains a single study by Firth (1956) on Italians in London. This is a very small study which concentrates on an anthropological investigation of kinship through the use of genealogies and range of known and recognized kin. There is some slight attempt to study change through these media. As such it is a useful study, but no mention is made of other features of social organization and no published sources are used.

The American literature contains the most important group of Italian studies—the analyses of social organization that constitute the heart of the literature on Italians, both in Italy and in the United States. The group is composed of six books: Ware (1935), Whyte (1943), Child (1943), Covello (1944), Gans (1962), and Glazer and Moynihan (1963). The history of these monographs reveals a curious pyramidlike structure, which helps to explain some of the confusion regarding the southern Italian family. Ware, with the help of settlement-house workers, did a study of Greenwich Village in the early thirties. She interviewed Italians there, compiled data from the reports of social workers, administered a fine, though incomplete interview schedule, and using no published sources (at least none are cited in her book), analyzed the changing social organization. Whyte's early book on street gangs is frequently noted as a source of information about Italians. It is true that he worked in an Italian slum with second-generation Italo-American boys, but his study is in no sense an "Italian study" and he himself never makes this claim.

In 1943, Child published a book which has subsequently been much quoted as a source of southern Italian social organization and for the assimilation of southern Italians in America. On the first topic Child states that the practices referred to are as they were in the United States but adds that they accord with usage in Italy—thereby equating Italian and Italo-American customs on the simple and unproven assumption that no change has occurred. Regarding assimilation, Child set up three "types" of reactions to this process, which have been cited many times since 1943. But Child gives no information about the fifty-three boys interviewed except that they are second-generation Italo-Americans of New Haven who attend men's clubs. In addition, when Child set up his three reaction types he used only thirty-one of his fifty-three respondents—those who exhibited the "pure characteristics" of each type. The remaining twenty-two respondents were not included because they "did not represent predominantly any one type of reaction" (1943, p. 76). This crucial fact is mentioned in fine print in a footnote. Child used two sources: Williams (1938) and Ware (1935).

The next writer, Covello, was brought to the United States as a boy of nine from his southern Italian village. He lived in East Harlem and grew up to become the principal of a large high school in that area and a leading educator. He produced a doctoral dissertation (1944) which focused on education in order to study the assimilation of southern Italians in New York. Even though based on fieldwork in the United States alone, this weighty (three-volume) monograph is by far the most complete, most accurate, and least distorted picture of Italian social organization available.

Between 1944 and 1962 there is a gap in the literature. Immigrant, now called "ethnic," studies were out of favor with the academic community, and only in the last few years has there been a revitalization of change studies and a reexamination of the theories of social change. The first of these field studies is Gans's monograph (1962) on Boston second- and third-generation Italo-Americans. His primary source for pre-emigration Italian social organization is Covello.

In 1963 Glazer and Moynihan attempted a reexamination of the melting pot theory using examples of four minority or ethnic groups, including Italians, in New York City. Their analysis, based entirely on literary sources, rests mainly on Covello and Gans but also utilizes the work of Whyte and Child.

An examination of the literature on Italian family and social organization reveals that: (1) there is only a small number of sociological or anthropological studies of Italian social organization in Italy—these were written recently and are, for the most part, unpublished theses, secured only with difficulty; (2) there is a considerable body of studies involving Italians as immigrants to the United States, Australia, and England. However, judged against the premise that change studies must be firmly rooted in the preemigration social organization, these works are constructed on a shaky base and as change studies are open to serious question. Some are weak in methodology, presentation, and data (Child and Mariano). Others are entirely acceptable as studies of second-generation Italo-Americans (Gans), street corner gangs (Whyte), or the melting pot theory (Glazer and Moynihan), but not, however, acceptable as studies of the process of change. Gans's analysis of Italo-Americans is a picture of how they are today, not how they got that way. All of these studies describe one product of change, which is in itself of interest, particularly in the field of cross-cultural research, but not the process or its variables. The reason for this skew is, as already noted, the absence of good field studies, plus the reluctance of so many social scientists to execute depth studies of social organization and then present them in a systematic and quantified format.

ON THE NATURE OF THE FAMILIAL SYSTEM

The primacy of the family in southern Italy reaches a degree not known in parts of the world where it shares in importance with other societal institutions such as religion, politics, and economics. Thus "attachment to one's own family is the overriding loyalty to which all others are subordinate" (Boissevain 1966, p. 202). The importance of the family in Italian society is recognized by everyone writing about Italy, and all writers attempt at least a brief analysis of the kinship system even though they are more directly concerned with politics, the Mafia, *comparaggio* (godparenthood), or immigration. If the family can hardly be avoided, neither can it simply be included as a chapter in a general monograph because:

> scholars have always recognized the Italian family as the only funda-
> mental institution in the country, a spontaneous creation of the
> national genius, adapted through the centuries to changing condi-
> tions, the real foundations of whichever social order prevails. In
> fact, the law, the State and society function only if they do not
> directly interfere with the family's supreme interests. [Barzini 1964,
> p. 190]

The central place of the family in Italian society has been primarily attributed to the disturbed, precarious, and always unpredictable fortunes of invasions, wars, occupations, and the intermittent interest of the national government. Beginning about two thousand years ago with the Phoenicians and Greeks, followed by Arabs, Normans, and Americans, Sicily has seen a series of foreign peoples invade, conquer, and then abandon the island. The local people, defenseless and exploited, pulled into themselves and developed their own distinctive arsenal of weapons: outward ignorance, suspicion, servility, noncooperation, distrust, and physical withdrawal behind the walls of their houses. As Lampedusa so eloquently states:

> all those rulers who landed by main force from all directions, and
> who were at once obeyed, soon detested, and always misunderstood,
> their sole means of expression works of art we found enigmatic and
> taxes we found only too intelligible, and which they spent elsewhere:
> all these things have formed our character, which is thus conditioned
> by events outside our control as well as by a terrifying insularity of
> mind. [1961, p. 185]

In earlier times towns were generally small; all residents in one *paese* (village, town) were related and the combined forces of the extended family were brought to bear against the outsiders. It is no accident that the Mafia, begun by the people for protection, originated within families and that recruitment today still draws heavily on the relatives. The family came to the front as the one enduring institution within which "the individual finds consolation, help, advice, provisions, loans, weapons, allies and accomplices to aid him in his pursuits. No Italian who has a family is ever alone" (Barzini 1964, p. 190). And to very few Italians is it ever permitted not to have a family.

The family is the basic core of the social structure and the source of an all-pervading influence in the society. But the nature of this familial system, its structure and function in anthropological terms, is still to be explained since the written evidence is vague, general, and contradictory. It is implicitly, if not explicitly, agreed that three interwoven themes characterize the Italian family: extension of the family, service to the family, and dominant husband–submissive wife. Under other names these are the major foci of all Italian family studies. It is only with a complete understanding of each as a separate theme and of all three joined to form a trinity that this complex family system, wherever it may be, can be understood.

EXTENSION OF THE FAMILY

Before analyzing a family system it is necessary to define the subject, but here we encounter the first and probably most important source of confusion in the literature. There are two family units—the nuclear family composed of husband, wife, and unmarried children and the extended family composed generally of parents, children unmarried and married with their spouses and children, aunts, uncles, cousins, and grandparents. The disagreements concerning the southern Italian family do not lie in a disputation of these definitions but rather embrace two other problems: (1) which unit does the term "family" refer to, and (2) which unit is the most basic and important in Italian society. Consider the following statements:

1. *Pro extended family*

    the members of a family had a completeness of confidence and a oneness of interests in their relationship with each other. [Covello 1944, p. 243]

    . . . nor did the extended family disintegrate upon emigration. [Vecoli 1964, p. 409]

    To the Italian, "family" meant not only husband, wife and children, but also grandparents, aunts, cousins and godparents. [Williams 1938, p. 73]

    The family becomes almost a clan. Even the godfather and godmother are looked upon as blood relations. [Day 1929, p. 162]

    The Italian family was more than a married couple and their children. It included their parents, sibs and even in-laws, closely knit both in feelings and in organization. [Pisani 1959, p. 53]

2. *Pro nuclear family*
   the various households of a *famiglia* exercised a certain independence and resented interference of relatives with
   domestic problems of their own. . . . [Covello 1944, p.
   250]

   The most important grouping based on blood relationship
   is the family in the narrow sense, the household. . . .
   [Gower 1930, no page number]

   Relatives do not constitute an isolated unit and rarely
   act collectively, not only for situational consideration but
   for one reason or another members of one's kindred may
   be at odds with each other. [Pitkin 1954, p. 119]

   the overriding goal was the survival of the nuclear family.
   [Gans 1962, p. 210]

3. *Both units important*
   Even in areas such as Catania, Messina and Reggio
   Calabria—where the small nuclear family system generally
   prevailed—the wider kinship group still retained some significance. [Price 1963, p. 63]

   In the South, the nuclear, neolocal family, set in a multilinear kindred system, was the rule. [McDonald 1958, p. 97]

   It is the larger family that serves as the unit of orientation
   but, in most areas of the South, it is the neolocal nuclear
   family which serves as the primary focus of the family.
   [Moss and Thompson 1959, p. 38]

4. *No specification given*
   On the basis of field observations we have found the Italian
   family to be an extremely cohesive, closely-knit unit.
   [Moss and Thompson 1959, p. 38]

   The family has always been the central institution of
   Italian culture. [Ware 1935, p. 172]

   The American of Italian extraction comes from a race
   where family ties are strong. [Mariano 1921, p. 29]

There are two major points to notice here. The first is that
while authors contradict each other and sometimes themselves,
there is a pattern to these observations. The authors who most
definitely come out for a strong extended kin unit (with the exception of Gans who followed Covello) are those who worked
exclusively with first- and second-generation ghetto dwelling Ital-

ians in the United States. The writers who have done fieldwork in Italy, such as Pitkin, Gower, Banfield, and McDonald are much less emphatic in their assertions regarding the strength of the extended family. In fact, they state that the nuclear family is the primary institution in the society and has no equal in importance, power, and exclusiveness.

The second point is that writers who have worked in Italy, plus Covello who is in a category by himself, while declaring that the nuclear family is the main institution of the society, state that the extended kin group has an importance, but it is never spelled out or analyzed. The reader is left to sense that the relatives are doing something, have some meaning, and play some role in the society but that the exact nature of their function is still unknown. What is the meaning of "some significance" (Price), "multilinear kindred system" (McDonald), "unit of orientation" (Moss and Thompson), or "patri-sib" (Pitkin)? These are not phrases pulled out of much broader explications; these are the final statements of the authors on the role of the extended family.

The extended family, then, is either the basic unit in the society, or it is not. The literature does not reveal which point of view is the valid one, or if both are legitimate depending upon which segment of southern Italian society is under analysis.

SERVICE TO THE FAMILY

"Service to the family" is a phrase which in this case means the extent to which the individual—his desires, plans, and ambitions—is subjugated to the interests of the family. In most urban areas where a neolocal bilateral kinship system predominates, the main function of the nuclear family is the rearing of children who must one day take their place in society as individuals, not as family members. Other institutions aid in this weaning process and the societal values are directed to this end. The functioning of the system is not without its discontinuities and attendant pain and problems, but the ideal is held and recognized by all. In Italy the obverse is seen. There the individual does not count, does not even exist:

> Established on a definite but also narrow policy, the family was by no means a medium for the social training of its individual members: Rather, it precluded or at least hindered the appearance of individuals whose social outlook would transcend family interests and bring into life a more closely integrated community. [Covello 1944, p. 245]

The literature reflects this overwhelming orientation of service to the family. There is complete agreement on this theme in Italian family literature. Author after author reiterates the concept:

> an adult hardly may be said to have an individuality apart from the family: he exists not as "ego" but as "parent." [Banfield 1958, p. 107]

> aspects of the traditional Italian family include . . . the subordination of the interest of children to the welfare of the family group. [Ware 1935, p. 188]

> In Italy the individual to a large extent was subordinate to the welfare of the family unit as a whole. . . . [Pisani 1959, p. 160]

> Their mildness outide the peer group is due to the fact that they exist only partially when they are outside the group. [Gans 1962, p. 40]

Not only does the literature reveal agreement on the presence and structure of this theme in Italian family life, but there are, as well, excellent, corresponding accounts of how the system works:

> Individuals shared equally in fortune and misfortune and the whole family received credit or blame for the success or error of any one of its members. [Bromley 1955, p. 302]

> a child would be expected to sacrifice his own ambition and advancement to the interest of the family group—interrupting his educational or his professional career to aid the family, for instance. [Ware 1935, p. 197]

> The parents continued to keep the child in some form of filial dependency up to a mature age. No allegiances save those to the family were inculcated. [Covello 1944, p. 255]

This unanimity reveals a value system designed to train, socialize, and utilize the talents and efforts of family members in producing and maintaining a synthetic individual, a corporate person—the family. The distinction is between a family organized to aid its individual members and one designed to aid itself.

DOMINANT HUSBAND—SUBMISSIVE WIFE

The third major theme in Sicilian family life is masculine dominance, that is, the authority of male over female stated in societal values and expressed in familial role behavior—husband dominant over wife, sister subservient to brother, father wielding authority over daughter. The most frequently cited example is the first, since the place of the husband-wife relationship is central to Italian family organization, and probably also because it is, in theory, most removed from the northern European conjugal relationship.

Dominance-submission sets are implicit in the operation of any social system or power structure. The amount and type of deference or authority varies, but the existence of these elements in certain social dyads is never questioned. The most free-and-easy democratic organization has a certain amount of dominance-submission based on sex, age, or position, although it may be muted and appear more as deference (Goffman 1959). Certain autocratic social systems are rooted in a series of dominance-submission sets—a dictatorial government or a prison, for example. Family systems also, as one of their main structural axes, contain a varying number of dominance-submission sets. These are usually based on age, sex, and kin role, although other factors such as wealth, occupation, and marital status may also be relevant.

The cultural theme under consideration here is based on a cross-sex factor and flows always from the dominant male to the submissive female. Therefore, sets such as mother-in-law–daughter-in-law, older brother–younger brother, and father-son (like-sex pairs which do exist) are not germane to this theme.

The concept of a dominant authoritarian male and a yielding submissive female is well-known in Mediterranean countries such as Greece, Italy, Yugoslavia, and Spain (including its former colonies in the New World), and in the Middle Eastern Moslem countries stretching from Afghanistan in the east to Tunisia in the west. This *machismo,* as it is known in Spanish-speaking countries, is manliness in its purest and most refined form. The male

> jealously defends his independence. No woman submits him to her will. His pride is clearly visible . . . he is visibly the master of creation. And what is woman? She was obviously placed on earth to amuse and comfort him. When she does not become the victim of seditious propaganda, she can indeed be pleasant and useful. She is also happier when she is kept in her place. She knows it, too, and she is grateful to her master. She knows practically nothing of her husband's private life. [Barzini 1964, p. 201]

This opinion is echoed by the following:

> The man is the head of the house, and exacts obedience from his wife and children. He even has a say in the affairs of his grown-up sons and grandchildren. [Day 1929, p. 162]

> women occupied a definitely subordinate position except in washing, cooking, sewing and other matters considered to be purely

of female concern . . . women were subordinate creatures whose primary duty was to minister to the needs of their menfolk. [Price 1963, p. 63]

He does not discuss work matters with his wife neither will he listen to her problems. [Moss and Thompson 1959, p. 38]

A convincing picture is presented, one which is easily believed because it fits the American stereotype of the Latin male. But let us refer again to Barzini, who follows his previous comments with:

All this, of course, is mostly nonsense. . . . Do Italian men believe it? Many do. Most of them, however, harbour secret doubts and fears. . . . What is the truth? . . . The man is the titular head of the household but by no means the absolute monarch. He is in charge of general policy, definitely responsible for war and peace and for relations with the rest of the world. The wife is officially a subordinate figure, in charge of humbler duties, but her sphere is largely undetermined and wide-ranging. [1964, p. 202]

Many writers agree with Barzini:

In order to be able to do what they wanted, the girls thus had to learn early how to subvert the male authority by verbal means . . . and what they did not learn elsewhere, they learned from the mother's wile in getting her way with her husband. [Gans 1962, p. 48]

During much of the day, the father is away from the home working in the fields. The working decisions of the household are constantly being made by the mother during his absence. She handles all economic problems, metes out discipline to the children, and parcels out the weekly allowance to her husband. [Moss and Thompson 1959, p. 38]

. . . the woman wielded considerable influence. . . . Actually she enjoyed a prestige that contradicted her assumed subservience to the husband. [Covello 1944, p. 337]

All men rule over women, we Romans rule over all men, and our wives rule over us. [Cato]

Here again is the problem of contradictory evidence among authors. It is impossible on the basis of the written sources, giving equal weight to each writer, to determine which is the correct and which is the incorrect view, if, in fact, there is a clear distinction between right and wrong.

The contradictions on the first and third themes cause another problem, that of integrating the three themes into a smoothly functioning family organization. If each father-husband is absolute, then it is very difficult to imagine how a family system which extends the power of decision making to the extended kin group could operate. On the other hand, if the wife-mother shares authority with the husband-father in the rearing of children (and the extended kin do not form a viable group), then what are the exact perimeters of her sphere of authority? How is it possible for one woman to be equal to a man in one area of life and submissive to him in all others? The psychological gymnastics required of the woman would be interesting indeed. This and many other questions are raised by the incredible amount of confusion in the literature. The Sicilian family organization is a complex institution containing layers seen and unseen, voices heard and (equally important) voices unheard. It is not surprising that conflicting ideas have arisen if one considers the length of time covered by the literature, the scanty number of field studies, and the pyramidal effect caused by building hypotheses on a series of writers whose studies almost all in some way derive from Covello's. The basic cause of the entire problem is the intricacy of Italian social organization, which is designed to keep things hidden and has very effectively done so. The southern Italian skill at confusing the issue is nowhere better illustrated.

PART ONE
The Sicilians: Sicily

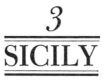

3

SICILY

In the livid light of five-thirty in the morning Donnafugata was deserted and apparently despairing. In front of every house the refuse of squalid meals accumulated along leprous walls; trembling dogs were rooting about with a greed that was always disappointed. An occasional door was already open and the cumulative stench of sleep spread out into the street; by glimmering wicks mothers scrutinized the eyelids of their children for trachoma; almost all were in mourning, and many had been the wives of those carcasses one stumbles over in the turns of the mountain tracks. The men were coming out gripping their hoes to look for someone who might give them work, God willing.

Lampedusa

BEGINNING with the first recorded occupation of the island by the Greeks (to 413 B.C.), Sicily has been conquered and ruled by fourteen different foreign governments, excluding the British and American occupation during World War II. The three most influential, other than the Greek, were the Arab (827–1060), Norman French (1060–1194), and the Bourbon (1735–1861). There is little direct evidence for the precise effect which these foreign governments had on Sicilian society because the social history of Sicily has yet to be written. However, there are a few references, and one can draw some evidence from vestiges in present-day Sicily. The Arab occupation, which was centered primarily in western Sicily, followed a policy of allowing the native people self-government; however the large number of Arab immigrants from Africa and the many conversions among Christians to Islam firmly established the culture of the Arab world in society. The Normans, with their capital in Palermo, also had an influence on the local people and proved themselves generally to be beneficent and just rulers who introduced cultural refinements and massive architecture and reintroduced Christianity to the island. Sicilian dialect which is based mainly on Latin contains many loan words from Arabic and from Norman French, and many place names in western Sicily still bear Arab and French names.

The Sicilians talk constantly of their Arabic heritage and use this as a reason (or an excuse) for everything they do which is even slightly out of the ordinary. They point out the terraced hillsides, Arab food, and Arab customs as proof of an enduring "Saracen" influence in the island. Hillside terracing, which still exists today, is attested to by history, but there is reason to doubt that Arab customs or food such as *cous-cous* are holdovers. It is likely that these are much more recent importations resulting from trade between Sicily and Tunisia. The other custom which is most often alluded to is the western Sicilian practice of keeping women in the house. Most western Sicilians are proud of the fact that the "harem" is imported from North Africa because they feel it sets them off from other Sicilians and Italians and proves their superiority. It may be that this is a relic of the Arab occupation, but more educated people claim, and this is borne out by stories told by respondents, that until the unification of Italy in 1861 and the redistribution of land, both men and women worked in the fields of large landowners and, having observed the upper-class custom of secluding women, the western Sicilians adopted the same practice when they received land of their own. Since so many grandmothers were cited as active farmworkers, one is more inclined to give credence to this version. However, it is fruitless to speculate on the origin of Sicilian customs. We must await the scholar who will undertake such a study.

Even today most Sicilians consider themselves to be in a state of foreign occupation since the Italian government at Rome appears to them as strange, dictatorial, and corrupt as any other they have known. The last island-wide movement to secede from Italy occurred just after World War II when many Sicilians, both high and low, led by the bandit-hero Giuliano petitioned President Truman to allow Sicily to become the forty-ninth state. While such thinking may seem ridiculous or at best quixotic, there are still Sicilians who tell Americans "you abandoned us after the war" and believe that they are ill-treated by the Italian government. It is true that Sicily and the south of Italy have been badly treated, past and present, but the fault often lies with local officials and administrators, not with the central government which has instituted a series of admirable plans for the development of the south.

Southern Italy, which includes the provinces of Campania, Abruzzi, Pulia, Basilicata, and Calabria plus Sardinia, and Sicily, contains 40 percent of the total land area of Italy and 37 percent of the national population. Sicily, comprising 9,830 square miles, is the largest island of the Mediterranean and it is separated from the European continent by the Strait of Messina which varies in width from two to ten miles. Near the coast the climate is warm in both summer and winter; the mean January temperature is more than 50 degrees on the coast and 40 degrees inland; in summer the mean near sea level falls between 75 and 95 degrees with extremes of 100 degrees. The coastal area is characterized by low rainfall which is less than twenty-five inches in the rainy autumn and winter seasons. There are no major rivers in Sicily, but there are seasonal torrents from the mountains which, in the absence of dams and irrigation schemes in most of the island, flow directly into the sea passing through arid treeless land which would be valuable for farming if the water was caught and stored.

The population of Sicily was over 4.7 million in 1961. In 1961 the province of Palermo had a population of approximately 1.1 million; in 1881 its population was just under 700,000. Although this indicates an increase, it is not large for a period of eighty years. Other towns also reflect the slow growth or decline of population: the population of "Nicuportu" changed from 21,452 in 1881 to only 25,119 in 1961; Roccamena rose from 1,855 to 2,772; and the population of Poggioreale fell from 3,468 to 2,698 (Italian censuses, 1882–1963). These figures bear mute testimony to the fact that Sicily, with the second highest birth rate in Italy, has barely managed to hold its own in the larger and more accessible towns while the population actually declined in many of the smaller and more remote *paesi* (towns). The reason for this relative leveling-off of the population is, of course, emigration—mainly to the United States but also to other European countries, Canada, Australia, and Argentina. The movement began slowly but quickly increased into a tide which is still one of the most important phenomena in the history of world immigration. There were 756 Sicilian emigrants in 1877; 1,093 in 1881; 7,015 in 1888; 25,579 in 1898; 58,820 in 1903; 127,603 in 1906; and 146,061 in 1913 (Renda 1963, p. 42, 48). During the period 1820 to 1955 the United States admitted 4,849,033 Italian immigrants (Pisani 1959, p. 5); between 1891 and 1947 Australia received over 33,700 Italian immigrants and has since taken in a much greater number (Price 1963, p. 11); over 40 percent of all Argentine immigrants have been Italians, who today make up almost one-fourth of its population. Italians are among the largest immigrant groups in the United States, Australia, New Zealand, and Argentina, and a large percentage of these Italians have been from Sicily. The effect on those remaining at home has been good in one sense because it

averted an intense population pressure, but it has allowed government and influential private citizens to ignore the problems of
the southern area because the crisis which threatens never reaches
a peak:

> On the basis of international units . . . the average income of
> Italy is one of the lowest in Europe and indeed, in the civilized
> world and, on the same basis, that of southern Italy is 60 percent
> below the average Italian income. [Dickinson 1955, p. 4]

Some comparative figures illustrate the underdeveloped state of
the southern Italian economy: in 1960 in southern Italy there
were 8.4 telephones per 1,000 people, whereas in northern Italy
there were 39 per 1,000; milk consumption was 117 pounds per
capita compared to 400 pounds per capita in the north; meat
consumption was 22 pounds per capita compared to 40 pounds.
Southern Italy had only 22 percent of all Italian state investment
and 16 percent of all private investment, compared to 77.4 percent
and 84 percent respectively for northern Italy (Lopreato 1960, pp.
28–31).

The Sicilian birth rate in 1961 was 22.1, the death rate in the
same year was 8.8, and the infant mortality rate was 47.0 (an
improvement over the 1951 rate of 55.4).[1] Illiteracy was double
the average for mainland provinces. A study of the town of Palma
di Montechiaro revealed that 74.9 percent of the children had
thread worms; that 90.2 percent of the houses were without running water and 86.4 percent lacked lavatories; and that only one
house in a total of 600 was entirely free of mice and rats (Dolci
1964, p. 302). Dr. Silvio Pampiglione, professor of parasitology at
the University of Rome, who conducted the study, revealed that:

> The average daily menu would consist of bread with some salted
> sardines, potatoes, cooked onion, tomatoes, figs or olives for break-
> fast; pasta with tomato sauce, cabbage soup, potatoes, or tomato
> and onion salad and, in some cases, more bread for dinner; and
> bread and vegetables or sardines, as for breakfast, or soup or
> pasta if these had not been eaten at midday, for the evening meal.
>
> Each person consumes on an average of one kilo of bread (about
> two pounds) and a good three *etti* (about 11 ounces) of pasta per
> day. Consumption of animal proteins is low. In some families meat
> is eaten only on important feast days. . . . Milk is looked upon
> unanimously as a food for invalids. [Dolci 1964, p. 302]

No one need speculate why Sicilians emigrate—the answers are
here.

1. For comparison, United States birth rate in 1963 was 21.6, death rate 9.3,
infant mortality rate 25.3.

THE TOWN AND ITS PEOPLE

Nicuportu, as I have named the town in which this study was conducted, is a medium-size market and administrative center about thirty miles from Palermo on a well-used road to Marsala. Little is known of the history of the town, which today has a population of over 26,000. It is somewhat unusual in that the lands surrounding the town have not recently been held in large pieces by landed aristocracy or by the church; the occupational structure, which has a high proportion of small-landed farmers, reflects this. Nicuportu is known by all Sicilians as "il paese dei delinquenti" (the town of the delinquents), a not undeserved epithet, although most other towns in the western zone would also qualify for the title.

A description of Nicuportu by an English journalist who lived there is gloomy:

> The place has a martyred look. In 1955 the only standard things about it were an abiding preoccupation with death and a passionate mistrust of the outsider. The town is spread flat white in a broad basin. . . . From afar the houses appear herded together, in the shape of a tuatara lizard, uneasily united under the shadow of nude ocher mountains. They are of white and stippled blue wash. . . . The Corso, the main street, is a mile long and dead straight. Every second shop seems to be a barber's and every third a bar. The rest are mostly butchers. In summer when the flies appear and alight on the blood-red meat hanging outside, the flies are sometimes sprayed with DDT. Paunchy, white-jacketed policemen stand about chatting in pairs, unbothered by the traffic jams of the mules, which outnumber the motor vehicles. Even today it is difficult to find a man about town who cannot produce a knife or a gun on demand. But for the absence of hitching rails, it is a classic Wild West setting.

This is a highly dramatized picture of what is, after all, simply a flat, ugly town. Nicuportu sits on the northern edge of a fairly large valley, surrounded by mountains on three sides and by the sea, seven miles away, on the fourth. As is usual in land-hungry Sicily, the town is surrounded by many small villages for which it serves as a government and economic center. It is isolated from Palermo by a low mountain range but there is a daily bus service between the two, and the main road from Palermo to the south forms the town's corso, thus adding to the incredible traffic confusion of Vespas, Fiats, trucks, horse carts, and mules.

The corso runs the length of the *paese* and contains almost all the shops, the piazza, the cathedral, other smaller churches, and the apartments of the middle-class. Social class is judged by residential distance from the corso. The rest of the town is a jumble of narrow unpaved or rocky streets containing, for the most part, one room, single-story houses. The majority of these houses contain a family, a mule, a cow, chickens, several dogs and cats, and at night the family Vespa, Fiat, or cart. The crowding inside is reflected outside. Houses are contiguous, streets little more than lanes, and greenery is reserved for balconies and roof tops. Day and night the streets are alive with people; children playing, women working, gossiping, or sitting at their embroidery, men wending their way in a constant coming and going on foot, bicycle, horse cart, or mule.

This is an agricultural area but the rocky, arid soil and the Italian laws of equal inheritance have combined to render farming difficult and unprofitable. In common with the rest of southern Italy, peasants live not on their land but in urban agglomerations. These are not the small hamlets with contiguous fields which are so common in parts of England, France, Spain, and Central America and which are designed for the conveniences connected with living together. Life in Sicily is neither convenient nor pleasant in character. Fields are miles distant, one man's holdings are often split and veer off in all directions, and the slowness of horse cart or mule means that most men spend from one to three hours traveling to and from the fields. There are no figures on the average number of pieces of land held by Sicilian peasants, nor are there figures on the distance of farm lands from town or from one another. Table 1, however, illustrates the fragmentation of farms. Though taken from a recent study for the *pianura* (flat plain) of the province of Palermo, the data are representative of farming in western Sicily. Most farms except the very smallest are broken into two or more tracts. For example, among farms of from one to two hectares (2.5–5 acres), over six hundred are composed of two pieces of land, over five hundred are three pieces, almost three hundred are four pieces, and over one hundred are five pieces. This means that the peasant proprietor who owns a total of five acres of land may have his acres split into five one-acre lots or one piece of two acres plus and three others of less than one acre each. The time required to go from town to the land and then from one piece of land to the other is great, and the energy lost using their primitive modes of transportation is incalculable. In addition these small farm owners usually hire out to larger landowners for wages and many sharecrop even other pieces of land.

TABLE 1
CLASSES OF FARM SIZE AND FRAGMENTATION IN CORPI DI TERRENO: PROVINCE OF PALERMO

Total Size of Farm in Hectares	Number of Pieces													
	1	2	3	4	5	6	7	8	9	10	11–15	16–20	21–25	25–50
0.10 or less	739	34	9											
0.11 to 0.5	3,304	810	188	35	7									
0.51 to 0.75	796	478	215	65	19	4	2	1						
0.76 to 1	488	373	192	65	31	8	8		1					
1 to 2	700	623	546	270	118	43	22	11	5	3	2			1
2 to 3	247	199	199	189	64	58	22	11	7	8	4	1		
3 to 4	95	74	121	92	52	33	27	16	7	14	3			
4 to 5	65	55	59	60	40	22	17	15	2	4	5	2		
5 to 7.5	60	49	52	58	42	41	14	8	8	0	6	1		
7.6 to 10	48	28	27	21	15	12	8	7	2	5	4	2	1	
10 to 25	53	32	24	32	14	7	7	9	7	10	7	2	2	1
25 to 50	18	4	4	1	1		2			2	1			
50 to 100	6	4	3	3	1			1	1	1				1

SOURCE: Istituto Centrale di Statistica, 1962, pp. 28–29.

In Nicuportu 21,485 persons are engaged in agricultural work: 10,696 of these are hired day laborers who work, on the average, 100 days a year and are paid about 3,000 lire a day ($5.00). This work does not include benefits such as insurance, health plans, or pensions (although some are provided by the government); nor are there paid vacations or raises. There are 10,817 farms in the commune of Nicuportu: 2,102 of these are 0.5 hectares or less; 4,535 are 0.5–2 hectares; 2,204 are 2–5 hectares; 923 are 5–10 hectares; 630 are 10–25 hectares; and the rest (approximately 500) are 25–99 hectares—there are no farms of 100 hectares in the commune (Istituto Nazionale di Economia Agraria 1947, p. 39). All acreage in the zone of Nicuportu (which includes an area much larger than the commune) is distributed as shown in table 2.

TABLE 2
ACREAGE DISTRIBUTION: ZONE OF NICUPORTU

Vineyards	53.3%
Grain	25.7
Citrus and other fruit	8.0
Market gardening	4.5
Pasturage	.4
Varied	8.1

SOURCE: Silvani 1965, p. 37.

It is extremely difficult to say how much the average *contadino* (peasant) earns in any one period because the few figures which have been published are widely criticized. However, one recent, acceptable study states that from a vineyard of 4.88 hectares in the Nicuportu area the net product per hectare (gross saleable product less costs of production) is 340,000 lire—about $560 per hectare or $2,683 total net farm income. The rate per hectare is lower as the number of hectares decreases (Istituto di Economia Agraria 1964, pp. 66–67). Gross income before taxes for this farmer would be less than $3,000 while the day laborer who earns $5.00 per day (for an average of only one hundred days per year) must work a great many days at other jobs if he is to support a family. Many men leave the fields for other work because farming is too exhausting and because the repeated division of land each generation creates pieces too small to support a family.

There have been attempts to lure the peasants out to live on the land. A series of self-contained farming areas with new houses, schools, and good free land have been developed by the government. The program began during the Facist regime and is being continued today by La Cassa per il Mezzogiorno (The Fund for the South), but to no avail. Thousands of these developments stand today, deserted and ghostly, each only inhabited by two carabinieri, and already beginning to crumble in the sun. The abandonment of these projects is partly the fault of the government, which did not furnish all the services essential to an isolated agricultural area, such as roads, electricity, water, and the promised schools. The peasants refuse to move until such necessities are provided, while the government maintains that it will supply these only when the peasants move. The *contadini* centuries ago gave up their last vestige of trust in government or authority of any kind and so they remain in their crowded towns while the new projects die. Many officials feel that the objection to the lack of utilities and schools is merely an excuse, since most people do not have or use these things in town. In any case, the peasants refuse to leave the populated areas where they have relatives, friends, shops, movies, bars, and above all the sense and feel of life over-brimming. Dirty, squalid, and uncomfortable as the towns are, there is no denying the activity and zest which constantly surrounds one. The Sicilian love and need for people, their whole-hearted enjoyment of modern amusements, and their utter disdain for the land and the way of life connected with it put them outside the world of classic peasantry. It is more accurate to categorize their way of life as urban; farming is simply the principal occupation, and that not by preference.

Nicuportu does not have any inhabitants who are titled or enormously rich, but it does have social classes and everyone is intensely aware of these gradations and individual changes in the social scale. However, "the old unified feudal view, in which there was a pecking order agreed on by all, no longer exists, especially as the possible categories have multiplied vastly. It is also hard to distinguish between social esteem and economic envy" (I Simeti, personal communication). The following is a tentative ranking of social classes today:

Upper	*Middle*	*Lower*
1. Very large land-owner	4. Various professions, priests	9. Artisan
2. Physician, arch-priest	5. Office employee	10. Builder
3. Nobility if rich or landed	6. Medium land-owner	11. Laborer
	7. Owner-farmer	12. Fruit vendor
	8. Merchant	13. Agricultural day labor
		14. Pushcart vendor
		15. Shepherd

Sicilian is one of the many dialects in Italy which are local variations of Latin. In Sicily the dialect has been changed over the years by the addition of words from Arabic, Greek, and Norman French, and its grammar has been altered, especially by the last. The dialect is not immediately intelligible to speakers of Italian, though in a short time one can understand it with some ability. The dialect is the same throughout the island though there are regional variations in words and more especially in accent. It is used by all classes of the population; Sicily is considered by Italians to be the only part of Italy where even the aristocracy speak dialect at home. Today all but the oldest people in Nicuportu speak standard Italian also, and even though many speak it poorly or mix it with dialect, it is recognizably Italian. Most working-class Sicilians are not proud of their dialect and feel that it sets them off from the rest of the population, putting them automatically at the bottom of the prestige scale. They are quite correct in assuming that other Italians look down on them, calling them *terroni* (people of the land), and pick them out by their accent even when they speak quite good Italian. Italian newspapers, radio, television and education are having an effect on the dialect, however, grandchildren often cannot understand their own grandparents who speak the old form of dialect.

Sicily is conservative in politics. The Communist and Socialist parties are active in the area of Nicuportu but have never had a huge or strong following. Most people vote Christian-Democrat because "we're Christians." They feel no need to change government in order to change the social order, because they believe that all governments are alike. There is still a positive feeling for Mussolini, if not for his party, because of the social changes which he, and he alone, managed to introduce into the island.

Most Nicuportese are nominal Catholics although there is an active and growing fundamentalist Protestant church which people join because "it's so orderly and life is always so confusing and noisy here." Very few people attend mass, even on Sunday, but all flock out for the many processions of the numerous Madonnas who circulate in the region. Most studies of Italy claim that although men do not attend mass the women do; but in Nicuportu the women stay home as well since they do not feel it is a sin not to attend mass. They do not go to confession, except at Easter, and even before the change in church rule did not abstain from meat on Friday, since Nicuportu receives meat only once a week—on that day. Apparently no one had ever told them the rules of the church, and most of the information they did have came from relatives in America. There is great disdain for priests, who are not noted for their pure moral lives, but a great deal of respect is accorded the local clerics on the street and in the piazza. The Nicuportese, except the anticlericals and Communists, consider themselves devout Catholics and display enormous love for the pope, the Madonna, and various saints who are popular locally. They would be scandalized if anyone told them that since they did not attend mass they were not good Catholics; for them, that has nothing whatever to do with being a Catholic. The most frequently used phrase of commendation is "he is a Christian," and when a woman was asked if she was a Christian (synonymous with Catholic) since she did not go to church, she replied, "Of course, what do you think I am, a Turk?"

Few people in Nicuportu go to school beyond the fifth grade, the end of elementary school, and even though the school-leaving age has recently been raised to fourteen and books and fees are provided by the state, few working-class people keep their children in school. This fifth-grade termination means that though most people learn to read, they become functional illiterates within ten years. Many people have never attended school, and the laws of school attendance are not enforced by the state in this area. Schools are run by the state (there are few religious schools) and are staffed by lay teachers. The school day runs from 9:00 to 1:00, six days a week. Education is considered a tool which enables a person to advance himself occupationally, financially, and socially, but few peasant children are able to take advantage of this all-important tool. Parents maintain a policy of not helping children with their school work and not broadening their cultural horizon since "learning" is done in school. It is virtually impossible for most children in Nicuportu to do their homework at home, because home is a crowded one-room building which affords neither quiet nor privacy. The schools are locked tight in the afternoons, and no provision is made for disadvantaged children. The teachers display preference for the children of the middle- and upper-class families and make a point of berating children who come without shoes, homework, or a nice bearing. Few working-class children want to continue in school beyond one or two years and are only too happy to leave the hated institution to work or stay around the house. Boys go to work in the fields with their fathers, in construction gangs, or as attendants in the coffee bars while girls are put to work on the embroidery which will form part of their dowry.

THE SICILIAN FAMILY SYSTEM

Every Sicilian community is a network of related families. This is more apparent in the smaller towns where few if any strangers—such as police, civil servants, and teachers—reside. And with the exception of these representatives from the central government, even the larger towns are kin-centered. The very large Sicilian cities such as Messina, Catania, and Palermo are exceptions to this rule, but even there it is probable that neighborhoods or *quartieri* contain a high percentage of related families. Every *paese* is, therefore, structured around the principles which govern the recruitment and maintenance of kin.

The Sicilian kin group is, in its widest extension, composed of all persons related by blood or by marriage. Visualized as a series of concentric circles, three major divisions are perceived; the nuclear family composed of husband, wife, and unmarried children—the real relatives; the extended family consisting of married siblings and their spouses and children, married children with their spouses and children, parents, and one's own nuclear family—the intimate relatives; and *"i parenti"* (the relatives) including all other kinsmen irrespective of genealogical distance. The distinctive feature of the extended family is that from the point of view of one individual, or one set of siblings, the roles and the individuals change. An unmarried person describes a kin group as a core composed of parents and unmarried siblings (the nuclear family of orientation), encircled by the families of married siblings, followed by parents' siblings and families, then parents' parents, and finally all other relatives. The married individual describes kin groups somewhat differently: spouse and children (the nuclear family of procreation) are at the core, surrounded by both sets of parents, married siblings and families, followed by parents' siblings and families, then parents' parents, and finally all the rest of the relatives. Unmarried persons thus count five levels of kin while married persons number six. This re-formation of groups is one of the most elementary principles of the Sicilian kinship system.

After marriage, there is no distinction between the rights and obligations of cognates and affines. The parents and siblings of both spouses assume equal importance in the eyes of the newlyweds and, conversely, the parents and siblings do not distinguish between the rights and obligations of the spouse who is related by blood and the spouse who is related by marriage. One respondent commented:

> When my uncle married a stranger she became an aunt. She is like my uncle from the moment when she married the brother of my father.

The bride is now formally equal to her husband and his parents; his siblings and all his relatives are now her relatives. For the husband, his relationships with his own kindred change as the result of his marriage, and he now adds on the kindred of his wife although he does not make the two kindreds one; they remain separate. Therefore there should be no difference between husband's siblings and wife's siblings for either of the spouses. The two sets of kindred are not joined or related in any formal way; however, some slight recognition is made of the fact that a member of each group is related to the other through the married couple.

The structural inclusion of an affine in the kindred does not preclude an affective and behavioral exclusion, or at least differentiation—affines are "like" blood relatives. However, cognates are excluded as often on personal grounds as are affines, and in theory as well as in practice there is no difference between them. The same respondent in discussing the preparation for his sister's engagement said:

> I went to talk to my uncles, that is, to my mother's two brothers and a little to my mother's sister's husband. Brothers are intimate and this relative is a relative by marriage. But I didn't go to talk to my father's brother, even though he is an uncle by blood, because we don't like him. I get along much better and see much more often my mother's sister's husband.

Residence is based on the rule of neolocality. A newly married couple never lives with a relative of either partner, and no relative lives with them unless there are grave circumstances which force joint residence. For instance, aged and infirm parents are cared for as are unmarried, parentless siblings, particularly females. Other relatives are almost never brought into the house since in most cases they have a member of their "family" who will care for them, although certain considerations of charity and pity will sometimes come into play and a "distant" relative will be found in the household. If a dependent relative lives with a nuclear family, he or she resides in their house but is definitely considered an outsider. If, as occasionally occurs, since housing is scarce and expensive, the nuclear family moves into the home of one of the parents, a sale takes place which transfers property ownership to the nuclear family and places the parent in a dependent position. Many aged widows and widowers who value their independence live alone in preference to intruding upon their married children. In my earlier study of one *quartiere* of Nicuportu, I found that in a sample of sixty-nine families, only six had relatives outside the nuclear family living in the home. These relatives, three mothers, one father, one unmarried sister, and one aunt who had raised the respondent were all very old, ill and had no other relative who could care for them. Several of the women reported that they had lived with one set of parents or the other before finding a house of their own, but all considered this to be a poor solution necessitated by economic circumstances and one which was changed at the first opportunity.

The new nuclear family is therefore spatially cut off from both families of orientation and from all kinsmen. The only people who belong in the house are members of this nuclear family and relatives in the house are there on sufferance. A well-known Sicilian proverb states "i veru parenti sunnu chiddi dintra la casa" (the real relatives are those inside the house). Further questioning of the speaker reveals that the proverb might better be, "the real relatives are those who should be in the house," since non-nuclear-family members are specifically excluded, and no one but parents and their children can ever be a member of that family.

Sicilian rules of inheritance follow the 1861 Italian law. It is of more than incidental interest that this law reflects precisely the primacy of the nuclear family in Italy and the equality of its members (when viewed as members of the family and not as actors in dyadic situations). All children must share equally in one-half of the estate, known as the *legittima* (legitimate), while the other half, the *disponibile* (available), can be given as wished. The widow gets no property outright but has usufruct of a part of it. The size of this portion is determined by the number of children in the family. In a family with one child, the wife receives one-third. With two or more children, the wife receives one-fourth. She may not alienate this portion nor may her children sell it without her consent. The wife is therefore protected from her own eccentricities and the sometimes selfish interests of her children. In practice, the children usually receive their share of the *legittima* plus the *disponibile,* all of which is divided as equally as possible under conditions where all real property is in land and buildings and very little money, either cash or investments, is available. Surplus income is normally put into more land or real estate, the only safe form of investment. It is impossible to divide such property equally, and if there are many children or a small estate, or more usually both, then the task of the father is difficult indeed.

If, for example, the father has three pieces of agricultural land of equal size and three adult children he can give each child one of the plots, but since it is extremely rare that all three pieces will be equal in quality, one or two of the children will receive a less valuable inheritance. But if he divides each piece into two halves, and distributes these halves as equitably as possible, the result is still not satisfactory because plots of land are small in Sicily and one half here and another half many kilometers away will serve no useful purpose to the owner. Fights, arguments, and bitterness against parents and sibs is the result.

There are two exceptions to the rule. First, if a daughter has been given a very large dowry, her portion of the estate may be reduced by that amount. However, often the expectation of a normal share of the paternal estate is worked into the dowry agreement. Second, invalid children of either sex and daughters who for some reason seem destined never to marry will be bequeathed a larger than legal share out of the *disponibile* so that they will have an adequate income for the rest of their lives and thus not be a burden on married siblings or other relatives. Fairness, equality, and common sense are the guiding principles in the disposition of an estate; the parents make an earnest effort to divide the estate as fairly as possible among all the children, taking into account age, marital status, and sex.

There is a patrilateral bias in favor of the group of father's kin. This is reflected in the biblical or Arab use of the term *house,* as in "house of David." People frequently speak of their "house" as being honorable, or absent, or important. Surnames are the hallmark of a house and are frequently invoked. One respondent on being asked if he included his father-in-law in his family, since the old man lived with him, replied, "No, of course not. He is a La Bella, I am a Sovaco, he has his house, I have mine." This does not mean that this man felt an allegiance to the members of his house or that he frequented kin with his surname as opposed to the kin of his mother or his wife. In fact, he was very attached to his wife's relatives and had nothing but contempt for his own kin, especially his brothers with whom he had no contact. Women legally change their surnames at marriage but rarely do so in practice. Others may refer to a woman as Signora Puccini, her married name, but she refers to herself as Arnetti, her maiden name.

However, a patrilateral bias has a double edge and usually produces a seemingly inconsistent result. There is more contact with and affection for the mother's relatives than the father's kin. Since descent is traced equally on both sides of the family each parent has a paternal house to which the children should refer. The way in which the nuclear family of procreation slowly turns toward the wife's kin group is one of the most important features of this kinship system.

Another subject eliciting unanimous opinion regards frequency of contact with relatives. The general rule is: more contact, more relatedness. If a kinsman is not frequented, he is usually placed in the category of "the relatives" or is completely dismissed with this sort of statement, "Some cousins are not relatives, I know them, greet them and that's enough. When you don't have frequency of contact, you don't have a kin relationship." This denial of kin ties is the logical consequence of a kinship system which does not structure kin relationships but which organizes a series of rights and obligations between all kin who are in the category of kin. A denial of their relationship, and its reciprocal duties, thereby removes many people from the structured sphere of kin and frees an individual from an odious task. A cousin who is not considered a relative is therefore a nonrelative, and future interaction between the two can be placed on a footing of stranger, friend, or enemy. But in these relationships it is the two actors in the dyad who set the limits of the relation, and it is quite possible to have a cousin as a friend who is much more valuable in this role than in his more structured role of cousin.

In this vein Sicilians very frequently deny kin status to those who have moved away from the *paese*. Knowledge of deceased relatives is considered to be "superfluous information." They are dead and gone and hold no interest for the living. The extreme emphasis placed on the importance of those persons with whom one has frequent contact, and its correspondingly strategic importance for an understanding of social structure, probably force people to deny all relatives who are, literally and figuratively, out of sight.

Nonrelatives are those persons who have no direct kin-based tie with a person or who are related but so remotely that they are considered to be nonkin. The inherent tendencies for friction and splitting in most bilateral societies often drives individuals or families to nonkin, there to create friendships and affective ties which are based on individual closeness. However in Sicily it is difficult to make a friend and it is even more difficult to keep one. Many people have friends but since loyalty to the nuclear family is paramount, it is almost impossible to achieve a degree of intimacy which is necessary to the fruition of a real friendship. Respondents questioned on this point gave answers such as:

> One can have friends but usually they can't have very close friends. In confidences or familiarity this often doesn't exist because you can't tell these things out of the family.

> There are friendships sure, but here they are family friendships. The whole family goes to visit another family and while there you might find someone to talk to for awhile and you call them a friend, but it's always with the family.

The only person who does manage to have a friend outside the family is a married man or, much more frequently, a woman who has formed a friendship with a neighbor; the two may exchange informal vows of San Giovanni, which makes them *comare* (godmothers). This is a practice unrelated to baptismal godparenthood. In Italy it is possible to be *compari* and *comare* through witnessing an engagement, a marriage, or simply on the basis of friendship. This is a very important means of formalizing friendships into quasi-kin status and thereby show the community that an always suspect friend is really like a brother or sister. It is the one valid way of legitimizing a nonkin relationship. The tendency to change friends into relatives or at least to formalize the relationship on a kinship basis is certainly not restricted to Sicily. The American habit of teaching children to call close friends of the parents "aunt" and "uncle" or to classify elderly neighbors who behave as relatives as "auntie" or even "grandma" is one instance of this.

The practice of baptismal godparenthood is another example of this custom. A godmother or godfather or godchild is placed in a fictitious kin role. Christian countries of the Mediterranean and their New World extensions carry this practice one step further by altering the terminology: the Italian child, for instance, calls his baptism sponsors *madrina* (little mother) and *padrino* (little father) and these adults use the complementary terms *figlioccio* or *figlioccia* (little son/daughter). The godmother and godfather terms, *comare* and *compare* (literally, co-mother and co-father) are reserved for the adults in the setting. The real mother and the godmother employ the term *comare* with each other.

Comparaggio (godparenthood) in southern Italy is not nearly so strong or so important as it is in Spain and in Spanish Latin America where it appears to have a place almost equal to real kin relationships. Usually relatives are used as baptismal godparents in Sicily and when outsiders perform this role they are rarely seen afterward unless they already happen to be good friends. Most people never see their godparents and even more do not care if they see them or not. However, the *comare* who unite themselves informally, though no less bindingly, through San Giovanni are usually neighbors and over a period of years had formed a close friendship before validating the relationship with the tie of fictitious kinship. With this one exception, friendships in Sicily are rare because outsiders are regarded with distrust and suspicion. Freeman states:

> Indeed, the development of the institution of friendship is marked in bilateral societies, for the formation of personal friendships is not impeded by loyalties to this or that segmentary descent group. [1961, p. 212]

The formation may not be impeded by segmentary descent groups because they do not exist in bilateral societies, but there are other groups which demand loyalties, and in the case of Sicilian society the nuclear family is just such a group.

4
THE EXTENDED FAMILY

UNDERSTANDING the place of the extended family within the kinship system and its interconnections with the nuclear family demands an understanding of the central values and the societally patterned actions resulting from them. The primary value is honor—family honor and individual honor. Honor involves being brave, strong, virtuous, unified, and respected. Since an individual does not exist socially apart from his family, any blot on his honor is a stain on the family honor. The man who is betrayed by the adultery of his wife is automatically *cornuto* (cuckolded) and his family has lost its honor. Likewise, a girl who is not a virgin at marriage is *disgraziata* (disgraced) and the family honor has a stain upon it. These two circumstances are the most serious (and most common); there are no other derelictions which will so completely tarnish the purity of the extended kin group.

The concept of honor rests upon the virginity and purity of the women. The impure woman is *vergognosa* (shamed), but her circumstance is understood because when a man and woman are together "everything will happen" and the especially weak and naive woman must "fall." It is the duty of the man, father, brother, or husband to so arrange things that such a temptation will not occur. If it does, it is the fault of the guardian male, and since he is the public representative of the family, he and the family suffer. The impurity of one individual stains the whole group and the kin then are responsible for retribution if the worst has happened, or more happily, controlling one another so that this disgrace will not occur.

The extended family is the only viable kin group outside the nuclear family and it is called into action on only one occasion—the marriage of one of its members. The nuclear families or the individuals who make up the extended family may or may not have some importance for another family or individual, but this significance is not societally prescribed. When a decision is to be made regarding the sale of a piece of land or whether someone should emigrate, the decision is made in the nuclear family without any necessary recourse to the extended family.

The "relatives"—aunts, uncles, and cousins of the parents and grandparents—play no part in the lives of the more closely related kin. They have their own "families," and no more than an occasional greeting on the street and an invitation to baptisms, weddings, and funerals is considered necessary. There are no occasions on which this entire group gathers and no expectation of aid or assistance is held. Reciprocal rights and obligations belong exclusively to the extended family group, and *parenti* who manage to exist in a state of amiable indifference are considered exemplary since bitter and prolonged arguments are possible. If a disowned relative presumes to reactivate a kin relationship in order to ask a favor or if a family member is "insulted" by one of the *parenti,* the offense is never forgotten; and even sixty years later it may be the excuse for having nothing to do with *quelli* (them). The bilateral extension of the kindred fosters such a feeling because the Sicilians are correct when they declare "I have my family, she has hers, and we have nothing in common." Minding one's own business, or rather the business of one's own family, is one of the qualities most highly prized by Sicilians. Boissevain notes that the "supreme accolade of a man's character is 'Christu fa i fatti sui' (Christ minds his own business)" (1966, p. 204). The only occasion on which relatives are approached as kinsmen is when a favor is needed, such as a recommendation for a job, a scholarship, or a place in an overcrowded city hospital, and only one person can grant it. So patron-client bonds are forged between distant kinsmen, but the patrons are usually individuals with some standing and prestige in the community and are thus beseiged with requests from kin and nonkin alike. There are only a few distant *parenti* with whom the kin tie is occasionally activated in order to maintain one's family in a nation underwritten by the institution of *clientelismo.* For the rest, the distant *parenti* are the consanguineal and affinal kin whose affection and help is neither asked for nor given. A Sicilian proverb best expresses this feeling— "amicu pruvatu è cchiu di lu parintatu" (a proven friend is worth more than a relative).

SOCIAL CONTROL

Sicilian society is controlled by customary sanctions and for this reason legal sanctions applied by the state are not disgraceful. In one sense, the entire *paese* is charged with protecting its good name and by extension the reputation of everyone residing there. After a crime against custom the community administers its own punishment in the form of avoidance, scorn, ridicule, or teasing, the last two being the most effective and most serious. A widow living alone with her children has transgressed if she takes a lover, but since she is alone and weak, the less hurtful sanctions of silent scorn and avoidance are used. The husband whose wife is suspected or known to be guilty of adultery must avenge this "crime" or else he will suffer as an eternal object of ridicule, teasing, and verbal scorn. Pressure is also applied by the members of his extended family. The only way in which a stain on honor can be avenged is by washing in blood—*sangu lava sangu* (blood washes blood)—so homicidal acts against the woman or the other man, or both, are performed. The victim's blood has washed clean the reputation of the extended family, and honor is restored.

Usually when the husband learns of the adulterous situation he immediately arms himself with a pistol or *la lupara* (the shotgun favored by mafiosi) and takes his "just" vengeance. But sometimes the husband is not willing to kill his wife, whom he loves, or the other man and thereby incur a sure and heavy prison sentence. (The belief that the Italian courts look leniently on *affari d'onore* is false. The Italian legal system operates smoothly and efficiently for the entire country, and no exceptions are made for customary law.) Then it is the obligation of his extended kin group members to force him to carry out his duty.

For example, a newly married man in Nicuportu heard from *gli altri* (the others) that his wife was receiving her young unmarried cousin every morning after he went to work. One morning the husband left the house and returned in about an hour. He found his wife and her cousin sitting in the kitchen drinking coffee. He told them why he was there and they explained that they had been friends for years, that each was the only friend the other had, and that they felt a need to talk to each other. The husband knew of their previous relationship and was aware that he and his wife had not yet developed this companionable intimacy. He loved his wife, was happy in his marriage, and decided to believe them. The cousin was sent away from the house and promised never to return since he knew that being in the house alone with a woman was prima facie evidence of sexual relations. The married couple patched things up and life resumed its normal course.

However, *gli altri*, who were not swayed by emotions of love and happiness, were very unhappy. His extended kin still had a blot on their honor, and if the husband did not care about this, they did. A succession of relatives—his father, brother, mother, various aunts, uncles, and cousins—began to insist that he must do something to wipe out this stain. They appealed to his sense of group loyalty and to his understanding of the source of their shame. His father offered his gun for the killing. The pressure might not have been effective except for the fact that the community was not idle. Every time the husband left his house he ran a gauntlet, *alla Siciliana*. "Cornuto" was murmured by the women as he walked down the side streets; giggles and snickers followed him everywhere. In the piazza men removed his cap as he walked by "to see the horns." Tablecloths in the bar were used as matador capes to cries of "ole, eh toro, toro." Ridicule so direct, constant, and painful could hardly fail to have an effect; before long the husband took his father's gun, shot his wife, turned himself into the carabinieri, and was sentenced to six years in prison. Peace again reigned in the *paese*. The potentially disruptive figure had been jeered into conformity and the honor of the extended family was restored. A real threat to basic values and the continuity of life had been dealt with by the relatives, the community, and eventually the state.

A court case in December 1966 in the town of Alcamo showed a dramatic reversal of this pattern and is one instance of change in Sicilian social organization. A girl was abducted by a boy and his twelve cousins. She was taken to a remote mountain hut, beaten, starved, and raped by the boy. She was then returned to her nuclear family. Since marriages by abduction are common, the girl's family and relatives customarily would have forced her to marry the boy to restore the family honor. However, Franca Viola did not want to marry the man who raped her, and her father, presumably out of love for his daughter or disgust with the local custom, upheld her wish. The father went to the carabinieri and made a legal denouncement against the boy and his twelve cousins. The thirteen were tried on seventeen counts ranging from rape to kidnapping and sentenced to a total of 155 years in prison. The townspeople of Alcamo sent a petition to Rome asking that the father be made a Knight of the Italian Republic for his courage and valor. Thus *omertà*, the Sicilian code of silence, was not upheld and it seems that the Violas have not suffered for their unusual stand.[1]

These are examples of the process of social control and social sanction applied by the extended kin and the community. But

---

1. In 1969 Franca Viola married a soldier from northern Italy who was stationed in Alcamo.

these are not everyday occurrences, even in Sicily, and the more usual and preferred solution is prevention before the crime. For instance, the kin group becomes active when it appears that violations of the sexual code might at some future time occur because of current mistakes in one of the member nuclear families. A mother who allows her daughter too much freedom or a husband whose wife has, even once, overstepped the limits of her role will be spoken to. The fault may lie with the daughter or the wife, but the blame is placed on the stronger guardian figure. Let us take the mother-daughter situation as an example. An act of the daughter is noted by a neighbor who comments on it to the mother's sister. This relative will see that the word is passed on to other members of the kin group, again in an unconcerned reportorial way. One of the relatives, often the one closest to the mother, will visit and mention that this act has been observed and commented upon. It is usually not necessary to point out the implications of the statement, but if the mother should not understand or not wish to understand, then the relative will have no hesitation in putting the matter in much stronger language.

Two important points emerge from this example. First, there is nothing the relatives can do if the culpable relative refuses to heed their advice. The extended kin can warn, advise, and even threaten, but they cannot apply real restraints to the offending kinsman. However, this form of social control is highly successful in Sicily. The second point is that the relatives do not gather together for discussion. The news passes from person to person in a seemingly haphazard fashion, and the opinion of each relative travels in the same fashion back to the original courier. This person then takes the "group decision" to the offending relative and in the midst of other news and gossip comments, "Oh by the way, Franco said that he saw your daughter Maria out on the main street the other day." The mother then knows that everyone knows and can mend her fences by replying, "How could that be, I'll speak to Maria," or "Oh yes, I sent her to the pharmacist for me." The latter statement may or may not be true. Truth is irrelevant in Sicily; appearance is all. Even when the extended kin produce a group decision there is really no group as such and Sicilians vehemently deny that any such body exists.

If an offense is repeated or if a scandal occurs as a result of an offense, the extended kin cannot ignore the offender. The community will not allow them to do so. Society long ago laid down the rules for the society and individual exceptions are not allowed.

The extended kin must admit their relatedness, announce their intention to have the crime avenged, and then defend the group. A proverb heard almost daily is a succinct expression of this attitude—"o tortu o gridu, difenni i to" (right or wrong, defend your own).

The Mafia is but a microcosm of Sicilian society, and anyone who has even a surface knowledge of this institution will see unmistakable resemblances between the operation of the society as a whole and the operation of the Honored Society (*Società Onorata* is the Sicilian name for the Mafia). The Mafia grew out of the *contadino* class of Sicily and reflects almost perfectly the societal values and practices of the group from which it grew. The Old Mafia, prewar style, is not a tightly knit organization of vicious gangsters who wantonly kill and destroy but rather a bounded network of members who, following a rigid set of rules and regulations, bring order and peace to a troubled land. This old style Mafioso is silent, humble, clean living, and orderly in his habits. His chief characteristic is taciturnity and he obeys the code of *omertà* unquestioningly. His family is orderly and precise, and he administers it with justice and an iron fist. Many of his qualities are virtues in the eyes of more ordinary Sicilians because they themselves have not a hope of ever attaining such a degree of orderliness and stability. The term *mafioso* can be used in a pejorative sense, but it can also be used as a compliment. (For the same reasons the Germans, the Fascists, and the Evangelical Church are viewed as good things—they are calm, orderly, and organized.)

MARRIAGE MAKING

Since Sicilian familial honor based on the concept of feminine purity is retained or lost through the sexual code, marriage should be the central act which will ensure continued honor for the extended group. Members of the extended family play an active vocal role during the period of betrothal and marriage whereas they play an inactive role as observers most of the time.

Unfortunate and drastic consequences can be avoided if individuals control themselves and others properly. The best way to accomplish this is to ensure that a marriage is good and that the arrangements for the marriage have been *corretto* (correct). There is a set procedure for making a marriage, and allowing for certain class differences, it is believed that by following this procedure a person or a group is doing all that is humanly possible.

A boy chooses a girl he wishes to marry, his nuclear family approves his choice, and then the boy and another adult visit the nuclear family of the girl to ask her hand, returning after eight days for the decision. These eight days are the crucial period in making a marriage, especially for families without land or wealth. Sicilians say that at this point it is a *dovere* (obligation) to go around asking the relatives about the advisability of the engagement even though "their advice doesn't count."

The nuclear family consults with the extended family about an engagement because the members in both families share almost equally in the responsibility for the ultimate marriage. The family and relatives of the boy must be assured that the girl is a virgin and that her family is correct, while the family and relatives of the girl must be convinced that the boy is steady and hard working and that his family is respectable. There are general concerns of wealth, dowry, inheritance, and stability—but these are secondary. If a bad marriage is contracted, then the blame and loss of honor falls on all the relatives though the nuclear family of orientation is most guilty.

In most families it is the job of the mother to go around asking about the family of the prospective spouse; yet there is a great deal of variation in this. She initiates a round of public visits to her extended family members, plus neighbors and acquaintances of the other family. At the same time, the relatives are consulting privately with one another in the round-robin manner described above. The mother visits relative A and says that her son is thinking of marrying a certain girl and asks what the relative thinks about it. Relative A brings forth what information he or she has on the other family and gives a general approval or disapproval. The mother then moves on to relative B, relative C, and so on until all the families in the extended family have been contacted.

The relatives in the meantime initiate their series of consultations. Relative A goes to relative B, they mention the engagement, and A says "Yes, she is a nice girl but you know her uncle is said to be a gouger of the poor." Relative B then goes to relative C saying "Yes a nice girl, but you know her uncle is a sponger and the mother's brother died of tuberculosis." The round continues from relative to relative, each one adding to the weight of evidence for or against the other family. The decision is then carried back to the nuclear family. The parents have by then accumulated rather complete information about the other family, and their decision, weighted by this information plus their affection for their child and concern for his or her desires, has been tentatively made. Often the two sets of decisions are the same, but the relatives, who are not swayed by affection and intimate nuclear family ties, can arrive at a conflicting decision. A boy from a wealthy family who is generally conceded to be a vicious brute will frequently be turned down by the nuclear family while he is approved of by the extended family for the money and prestige he will bring into the group. Kinsmen seek status and prestige and do not have to live with the often disastrous consequences of the mating. But a marriage with a wealthy boy who is decent and hard working may be vetoed by competitive, envious relatives since it will add to the prestige of one nuclear family at the expense of the others.

Parents are of course quite free to accept or reject the decision of the extended family, especially when the decision has been motivated by jealousy. When some really unsavory news has come to light about the boy, his family, or his relatives, then the final decision is much more difficult to make. A Sicilian does not lightly admit a potential source of trouble into his family as a member of that family.

However the matter is resolved, the relatives do count. In this case again, the group does not function as a group but as a bounded network of related nuclear families—the "invisible clan."[2] The extended family influences a decision, the most important decision in the life of every individual and every family. They act in concert to protect their reputation and honor by ensuring that the marriage of a kinsman or kinswoman will be good and will not eventually reflect badly on them. Their reputation as persons and as families is intricately tied in with the fortunes of the other families, and they fear that if adequate precautions are not taken at this stage, dire consequences may arise later.

The main reason why they act as a network rather than as a group is to preserve their autonomy as nuclear families. The fierce independence of the nuclear family would be challenged and weakened if there were a semicorporate body which was recognized as possessing greater authority and power than it. The Sicilian way therefore preserves the independence of the nuclear family while it provides an effective form of social control through the secret activation of the extended family.

2. I am indebted to Dr. Salvatore Franco for this term and for many insights about the Sicilian family.

DECISION MAKING

There are few major decisions in the life of a working-class Sicilian. There are set formulas (customs) for regulating daily life, and change in social organization is minimal (though material culture has changed rapidly in the postwar years). Sicilians perceive their lives as essentially boring and closed. Major decisions concern education, occupation, marriage, emigration, and the use of capital. Of the five decisions, marriage is by far the most important, and the role of the extended kin in that decision has been described already. The others might never occur as conscious decisions; the pressure of necessity dictates what must be done.

Education is largely class determined. The working class has from zero to five years of schooling (elementary school), the lower-middle or white-collar class goes on to the lower high school (*media*), and the upper-middle or professional class attends the classical *liceo* and the university. There is today some mobility from the white collar to the professional class, and it is of course possible for a working-class child to go through the school system to the university, but it happens very rarely. Therefore, among the *contadini* and *artigiani* (artisans) the children leave school almost automatically at the end of fifth grade, if not before. Relatives are not consulted about this decision.

The girls stay home until marriage because the period from puberty to marriage is the most dangerous to her virginity. Women do not work in Sicily, there is no industry, and the farmlands are out of bounds; so there is no question of a decision regarding occupation for them. Formerly boys were sent to work in in the field with their fathers or as hired day-laborers. Today it is possible to secure employment in other lines of work. As this is preferred, the ten- or twelve-year-old boy is apprenticed to a mechanic or a construction gang or he is sent to work in one of the coffee bars. There is still little choice involved, although the range is much greater than it was in the prewar period. Most parents, with or without the boy's wishes in mind, simply decide which of three or four possibilities will bring the most money to the family. This is a decision which is made entirely within the nuclear family.

Emigration is one possible major decision in a person's life. Since so many millions of Sicilians have emigrated since the nineteenth century, they are well versed in all the factors which must be considered. Information and statistics about jobs, housing, climate, industry, indigenous people, and foreign governments are common knowledge even among people who have not the faintest desire to move. The actual decision itself is thrashed out in the nuclear family and if any outside help is needed, returned immigrants or experts are consulted, not members of the extended family.

The existence of excess capital is more common today because it is possible to migrate seasonally to one of the flourishing common market countries. Men leave their homes in order to amass savings. If other factors such as "making a new life for oneself" are involved, then it is more common for the entire family to go overseas. Since this accumulation of money is a new phenomenon for working-class Sicilians, many people seek advice from others on the best way to use it. The traditional method, still favored by many, is the acquisition of farm land because it is a secure investment which cannot be taken away or destroyed and which provides one's family with food. However, men who emigrate to northern European countries for a season learn new skills, and it is increasingly common today for a trained industrial or construction worker to continue in this trade, investing money in a new and very modern house in town. Husband and wife discuss these considerations for months and usually the husband seeks out an "expert" to advise him. If a relative is consulted, it is because he is an expert or more commonly he is asked to recommend an expert whose advice he has found trustworthy.

Such decisions for most men are in reality a series of related subdecisions based upon the first decision—education. If a boy is not sent to high school, he will be of the working class all his life and his choice of jobs—all very similar in pay, hours, and advancement—is extremely limited. He will at some time probably consider emigration because his job is limited: an illiterate construction worker will never move up to "master craftsman" because he must have the basic skills of reading, writing, and arithmetic. If he chooses to seasonally emigrate, he is not really changing anything; his life is the same, his opportunities are the same, he is simply working in another place for more money. The only change is that he now can afford a house of his own. Rents are low in Nicuportu and the house represents a form of emotional security which will raise his status somewhat within his own class.

Most people stated that they would not seek advice from a kinsman and in fact would try to conceal from the relative that a decision was being made. Relatives are always envious, jealous, and duty-bound to help their own families, and therefore advice from a relative is suspect: "Who knows why he gives this advice. Maybe it's bad advice so as to injure me." Even though a relative will usually not profit directly from the bad advice he gives, he will increase his prestige in proportion to the loss of the other's prestige. Asking advice is placing your faith in another; people generally will betray you easily, but a relative will betray more easily because he has more prestige to gain from the failure.

However, since outsiders, nonkin, are even more untrustworthy than relatives, kin are sometimes consulted. There are also many extended families in which two of the nuclear families have good relationships, and these will consult together. Such advice is always compared against that given by outsiders. Relatives, however, may turn the tables and refuse to give any advice, on the grounds that this makes them responsible for the outcome of the decision. Responsibility for the actions of others is avoided at all costs.

In sum, of the five major decisions in the life of a man, the extended family participates fully in only one—marriage; they are rarely consulted about education, occupation, and emigration; on the use of capital the relatives may give advice but it is accepted only provisionally to be checked with other relatives, nonrelatives, and experts. The most frequently consulted kin are: spouse, parents, wife's parents, husband's brother and wife's sister and their spouses. The person most frequently cited as the preferred relative for advice on major decisions was spouse.

ADVICE AND AID

The role of the extended kin group in major decisions of its members is limited, but advice and help on minor concerns can be freely solicited—as on choosing a new dress, weaning a baby, finding a medical specialist in Palermo, or deciding the correct time for sowing a new crop. It is true that some of these problems are not minor, as, for instance, the season's crop, but they are old problems which can be solved with set formulas. Life exhibits remarkably little variety in Sicily. Experimentation is frowned upon, women's clothes are made according to the continental styles, jewelry has a traditional form and appearance, farmers are reluctant to try out new agricultural methods. To be different is to be eccentric: eccentricity of this kind is not sanctioned. However, these matters are discussed freely with everyone. For the most part people are not really asking for advice, but just wanting to talk about whatever it is that interests them most. For example, one young woman who was quite ill during her pregnancy talked of nothing else for months. All day she and her neighbors discussed her medical problems and almost every evening she and her husband strolled around to the relatives to talk about remedies. When her medical troubles became severe she went first to the *ostetrica* (midwife), then to the doctor, and finally decided on her own that she would not take medicine for fear it would injure the unborn child. Nothing would have budged her from this stand, but the conversations and advice given by others served two purposes: it made her the center of attention, and it was something to talk about.

There are other kinds of advice and aid which are more important. Financial aid, assistance during an illness, and help during a time of great sorrow are examples of meaningful assistance. Coming to the bedside of a bereaved mother or a critically ill cousin are forms of assistance which the relatives can and do offer. This not only costs them nothing except time, but it fits in with their very real feelings of sympathy for anyone in trouble, particularly through illness or accident. These events are meaningful in Sicily because the loss of a family member can ruin a family and the loss of a son can ruin a person. The more distant relatives merely pay their respects and ask if there is something they can do while members of the extended family move in for a time. The women take over cooking, shopping, cleaning, and sitting up with the afflicted family, and men will work in the fields of another so that a father may stay at the bedside of a dying child. Godparents, friends, and neighbors also participate in these rituals. This is not a time to be alone and those afflicted are drawn out of closed rooms into the light of day and the sympathy of those who care.

Financial aid, which may be crucially needed, is not so easily secured. The extremely precarious nature of life in Sicily plus the central value of advancing one's own nuclear family preclude any form of economic assistance. Sicilians were unanimous in stating that one should help a close relative in time of need but that this is rarely possible. One respondent, speaking of his married sister, stated:

> For financial things, help, there is none of that. Oh, there can be, but . . . well you see it depends on the economic situation. If I am in limited economic circumstances and can only live for my

family, and my sister finds herself in even worse economic straits, it is evident that if I can live only for myself and my family, I can't give money to her.

There is no expectation of financial aid from married sibs, who are members of the extended family, because at marriage the economic solidarity on which the parental nuclear family rested stops. Each new family has a primary obligation to look out for itself, and in an economically depressed area such as Sicily this is never easy.

Sometimes, especially more recently, families are able to save a bit of money, but it is felt that this wealth belongs to the family and should not be dissipated through loans to relatives. Another man said, "Sure you can go to the relatives for help, but if I have one hundred lire and I give them to my brother, then there will be nothing for my family if they need it, and what if my brother doesn't return them?" Anticipated need of one's own family is as important a factor as actual need of others.

A third point is that when factors of need are not relevant there is still personal feeling which may, and very often does, deter one relative from helping another; for instance, "If I am well off and my sister is not, I can give her economic help but it all depends always on the relationship we have—and I would give my sister nothing." The relationship between married sibs is usually so touchy because of past wrongs and arguments that they are not kindly disposed to help each other. In fact, prestige is augmented by comparison to others, and the advancement of one married sib over the others is one very good way to appear much more prestigous in the eyes of the community.

In these circumstances a man may try to borrow money from the bank or a wealthy patron, but without collateral or good evidence of future repayment this avenue is rarely successful. The only thing left then is to take his son out of school and put him to work, set his wife to embroidering for money, and secretly send his daughter to work in someone's house. Failing these efforts the only thing a man can do is emigrate, if this possibility is open to him.

Even under the most dire conditions relatives are not censured for neglecting to aid a kinsman. The refusal may be deplored but it is normal and natural. Many people will not approach their relatives for financial help because their pride will not allow it; many others cannot ask money of a kinsman because they are not speaking. There is a deep-seated reluctance to allow any news of approaching calamity to leak out to the relatives. The neighbors know of course and with them one can be oneself, but the relatives should believe that all is well. A well-organized family is a great tribute to its members, and sometimes enormous pains are taken to maintain this facade. Covello gives an interesting account of this, speaking of his own family in their southern Italian village:

> In Avigliano there were times when there was no food in the house. Then we bolted the door and rattled kitchen utensils and dishes to give the impression to our close neighbors that the noonday meal was going on as usual. After the *siesta* everyone went about his customary tasks and the outside world never knew exactly how it was with us. The intimate things of family life remained sealed within the family and we created for ourselves a reserve both as individuals and as a group. [1958, p. 36]

Contact among Kin

Amount and quality of contact is an important indicator of the depth and breadth of relationships. Relatives assemble only for the major occasions of weddings, baptisms, and funerals. All relatives must be invited to these *feste* (feasts), and their attendance is mandatory unless they wish to risk giving offense. A legitimate reason such as a sick child is, of course a valid excuse for not attending, but anything less urgent is an *offesa* (offense). If a relative absents himself from a formal occasion without reason, nothing is done and nothing is said, but when the offending kinsman has a similar event in his family, the offended family does not attend that. The matter is then formally closed although it is never forgotten.

The distant relatives are seen only at *feste* or by chance in the street. They are referred to as the "wakes and weddings relatives" and are almost never nominated as kin in ordinary affairs and are rarely placed on genealogies. Their lapses from good form are viewed somewhat tolerantly though never with complete objectivity. Close relatives must attend all formal occasions. Other festive days such as Christmas, Easter, *Carnevale,* or the feast day of Saint Antonio may or may not bring the extended kin together. The very poor families never unite in a group though they usually go around visiting on religious holidays. Those families which are somewhat better off sometimes attend parties together on these holidays, but many do not. Two factors play a role in determining whether one visits or whether one joins in a party. The first factor is the presence of a slightly more wealthy nuclear family within the kin group. This family will have a larger house and be better able to afford refreshments. The second factor, which overrides the first, is the kind of relationship which has been established between the nuclear families in the extended family group. One middle-class family saw their close relatives only on duty visits every six months, while one artisan family joined with the married sibs of the wife at the house of their most prestigious member to celebrate Christmas and New Year.

There is a difference between a visit and a party. An invitation into a home for a visit is accorded anyone who comes to the house, but invitations into the house for a party or a dinner are rarely given. Most people go from one year to the next without participating in any group activity with the exception of the formal events such as baptism and wedding, which thereby assume an even greater importance because they are the only opportunity to display fancy clothing, jewelry, and the nuclear family as a group.

When considering amount of social contact two factors must be taken into account—the organization of societal institutions and economic resources. *Contadini* are absent from the house six and a half or seven days a week for twelve to eighteen hours a day depending upon the season. Artisans work long hours over their crafts. Women who do embroidery for sale must work even more hours on this activity, in addition to normal housework and child care, if they are to make appreciable profit. Most white-collar employees work six days a week and the siesta of three hours in the middle of the day means that work is not finished until about 7:30 P.M. and then supper is eaten. There is, therefore, little free time for socializing, and after fourteen hours labor on any job no one is inclined to do more than sit in front of the house and chat with neighbors. In addition, working-class people earn very little and prices for many things, especially foodstuffs, are high. Therefore it is a sacrifice to offer coffee to visitors, although this is always done. Entertaining a group of people with coffee, liquors, and cookies is usually out of the question. Feeding outsiders is, needless to say, almost unheard of. Christmas, for example, is celebrated within the household, and if there is meat on the table, it is an exceptional treat to be saved for those who do count.

Unless there have been serious and prolonged rifts within the extended family, some contact is necessary, otherwise one risks giving offense. The usual pattern is to pay visits on religious holidays, on Sunday during or after the *passeggiata* (promenade), and on summer evenings. Until 5:00 P.M., Sunday is reserved for work or family; then everyone dresses up and goes visiting. They may go to only one house or they may make a series of visits, but in any case gossip is exchanged, opinions on local and world affairs are aired, and an obligation has been met. These rather formal visits are not the time or place for serious conversation. The frequency with which any one related family is visited depends on many factors, primarily relations established in the past, although other things such as a death or a birth in the family, the age of a couple, or their aloneness are taken into account. If an elderly couple have seen all their children emigrate, they may well be visited more often because loneliness, one of the worst misfortunes imaginable, is understood and pity is an impetus to help.

Almost everyone claimed that visits were much more frequent in the past when, before the advent of automobiles, motor scooters, movies, and television, they were the principal source of entertainment. More money circulates today and people are freer to indulge their desires, to ride to the sea for an ice cream, for instance, or to attend a film on Sunday evening after the *passeggiata.*

The most usual form of contact is accidental meeting: on the street, in the piazza, at the town hall, or in church. Here the network operates, revealing again the private level of society on which almost all important conservations take place. Men meet their close relatives on their way to and from work or in the evening: "I see my uncle Giovanni every day in the piazza on my way to work. We talk and in that way I keep seeing my relatives"; or "I see my aunt every day as I pass her house on the way from school. I stop and we tell each other what has been happening in our lives." Women usually must rely for news on men who pass their house or wait until evening to hear from husband and sons. However, other lines of communication are operating at the same time and a women very often hears news of her kinsfolk through a network of neighbors and *comare.* These meetings are essentially private, and information of a secret sort that would not be mentioned in a public visit or *festa* may be passed here.

A child learns the values and rules laid down by the parents. If the parents are not on good terms with their married siblings, then the child will have little contact with and even less affection for his aunts and uncles. His first cousins are extensions of their parents, and if good relations between the adults do not obtain then neither do they develop among age-mated first cousins. These kinsmen were almost never nominated as friends or "close" relatives and many respondents stated that it is easier to be on good terms with one of the distant relatives than it is with a first cousin.

The extended family has been examined in some detail. In summary it is a bounded network of nuclear families related through the sibling tie. The function of the extended family is to ensure that familial honor, based on the purity of its women, remains untarnished. This is accomplished in two ways: prevention and reparation. Marriages are approved by the extended kin in the hope that this will bring into the network only those persons who will never disgrace the family. In the event that this is not successful and a member of a nuclear family commits a dishonorable act, it is the obligation of the extended family to exert their special type of social control on the errant individual and to see that the stain is washed in blood—the only course which will restore honor. This form of control is made more effective and in fact is made possible by the backing of the *paese,* which activates the Sicilian social sanctions of teasing and ridicule.

5

THE DOMINANT HUSBAND AND THE SUBMISSIVE WIFE

DETERMINING the true characteristics of the husband-wife relationship depends primarily on a recognition of public face and private face. Goffman's (1959) work on the presentation of self, which utilized role, actor, and stage variables, recognized this duality. The examples in his book are drawn from societies such as Victorian England, Mandarin China, and contemporary United States. The concept is not limited to Sicily though it appears that the Sicilians have developed its use to their natural limits. Goffman's concluding statement expertly sets forth the conceptual framework of what he has called "impression management":

> Within the walls of a social establishment we find a team of performers who cooperate to present to an audience a given definition of the situation. We often find a division into back region, where the performance of a routine is prepared, and front region, where the performance is presented. Access to these regions is controlled in order to prevent the audience from seeing backstage and to prevent outsiders from coming into a performance that is not addressed to them. Among members of the team we find that familiarity prevails, solidarity is likely to develop, and that secrets that could give the show away are shared and kept. [1959, p. 238]

For the Sicilian husband and wife there is a division between those qualities which are permissible in public, outside the house, and those which must be reserved for the private sphere, inside the house. We could say that the husband is authoritarian outside the house and permissive inside, but this is not the true picture. Or we could state that the submissive wife in the piazza becomes a dictatorial harridan in her own home, but this again is not the case. Reality is much more complex than these simple statements allow for. Each enduring role has qualities which are internalized by the actor. This pool of role attributes contains many qualities which are inconsistent with one other: the actor dramatizes the appropriate qualities for specific stage settings according to socially determined patterns. Responses must be in tune with the demands of the society in which the individual lives; otherwise the strain could become unbearable. Some societies are very lenient in the amount of deviancy allowed, but Sicily is not one of these. Sicilian cultural values and norms demand a high degree of conformity to role expectations, and deviancy in this sphere is censured. Therefore, it is not correct to say that some authors are right and others are wrong when they take sides on the issue of whether a Sicilian wife is submissive or authoritarian. In one sense they are all right, in another sense they are all wrong; the wife is both submissive and dominant. As one Sicilian man put it, "A wife obeys her husband but she knows when to say certain things and she knows how to say them."

The basic problem of whether the wife is submissive or not exists because social scientists have not investigated other roles which both male and female play, nor have they tried to inter-relate social context, social norms, kin roles, and other institutions. Within an over-all analysis, it is quickly apparent that it is almost impossible for a wife to be always submissive and a husband to be always dominant. Some women may be more submissive than other women, and there is probably a higher percentage of sub-missive women in southern Italy than in areas of the world where a more egalitarian ethos pervades the society. But to conclude from these hypotheses that all Sicilian women are always sub-missive or "slavish" to their husbands would damage our under-standing not only of this role but of the entire society.

Society defines the values, norms, and behavioral components for the wife and husband and in addition spells out their interac-tion. One respondent described it thus:

> The function of man is to work and bring money home. The func-tion of woman is caring for the money and not letting it go for non-useful and dispensable things. The husband has the obligation to guarantee the wife in all and for all. The wife has the obligation to obey the orders of her husband.

The husband administers the family and its affairs and is respon-sible for providing the security of the family through his work. The wife on the other hand submits to the administration of the *capo famiglia* (head of the family) and is responsible for main-taining the security of the family through her administration of the household. The husband commands, the wife obeys.

The working-class husband labors in the fields or over his workman's bench for ten to fourteen hours a day in order to secure the funds to keep his family. He expects that when he returns in the evening the household will be in order: the wife will present a clean house, orderly children, a hot dinner, and clean clothes. After dinner she remains at home while he goes to the piazza for conversation and relaxation with other men. The wife must be pure, submissive to the will of her husband, obedient to his orders, modest, and in general be unobtrusive and humble. The husband on the other hand is proud, virile, commanding, and free to satisfy his every whim and desire. The girl who is dishonored before marriage never marries, and the girl who openly rebels against the dictates of society may have other satisfactions, but she will never know the satisfaction of being a wife. The daughter of a white-collar family who worked in a public utility office in Nicuportu had been engaged, but the boy broke the engagement because:

> his family objected to the fact that I work, that I leave the house every day, and that I have contact with men during the day. Girls like us can never get married because we work. We must resign ourselves to being spinsters the rest of our lives because we are finished in the eyes of others. Maybe it seems like a sad future to you, but it's better than the other alternative. I'm not a slave for any man. And I'm not going to stay in a house all day washing and ironing so that he can come home, dress up, and go off to the piazza looking handsome. Not me. I prefer to stay alone and do as I please. There are different values in the world and for me these are the important ones. It's just unlucky for me that they are not the important ones in Nicuportu.

However, the society has other, equally important values. Some of these touch directly on husband-wife interaction; others touch only indirectly but nonetheless significantly affect it. The values are four: (1) the nuclear family must operate as an integrated unit; (2) the nuclear family must get ahead and if necessary it must advance itself at the expense of other nuclear families; (3) the husband must earn enough to maintain his family (in an occupational structure dictated by the society); (4) legal, moral, and social obligations must be met—visits must be made, bills must be paid, doctors and lawyers must be seen, children must be cared for, and daily emergencies must be dealt with. The first and second points have been discussed in chapter 4; the third and fourth will be taken up briefly here.

Sicily is classified as an underdeveloped area and as such the primary occupations are agriculture and related activities, such as wholesale produce distribution, grain and implement marketing, and small-scale manufacture of agricultural equipment (horse shoes, straw sacking for mules, etc.). White-collar jobs outside the large cities are for the most part government connected, for example, income tax collector, utilities office worker (electricity, fuel, telephone), policeman, city hall clerk, and farm inspector. Farms are several hours distant and men who work the land plus the men who work with or for the men who work the land are away from the town all day. Town workers are away from home from 8:30 A.M. to 7:30 P.M. except for the three-hour lunch period in the middle of the day when all shops and offices are closed. Therefore, with few exceptions, men are not available to carry out the myriad activities which must be handled if the household is to function at all.

Several half-solutions to this problem have been found. (One must always bear in mind the fact that women are not supposed to leave their houses except for church and the Sunday *passeggiata* with the family.) Children can be sent on errands but they are not capable of performing complex tasks. Older daughters are definitely not allowed out of the house alone and sons are either working or are in school. Stores remain open in the evenings so that men do most of the daily meat marketing, and traveling vendors wind through the streets of town supplying linens, hosiery, dress lengths, and some foodstuffs such as fresh vegetables and dried fish.

But the more complex and important tasks remain. Paying bills, never a simple matter in Italy, consulting professionals such as doctors and lawyers, gathering the constantly needed documents at city hall, and visiting the school when summoned are matters which cannot be delegated to children or the very old. The only adult in the house during the business day is the wife and she is the business agent of the family. She is discreet about her errands, never showing herself on the corso or in the piazza. But during the morning and late afternoon hours many women are seen, black mourning veils pulled low over their faces, scurrying along on important jobs. Women say they feel *vergogna* when they must venture out of their houses because one should not and because everyone stares. Part of the furtiveness they display in the street is caused by a very real feeling that they are doing something wrong or shameful. But part of this is assumed as in keeping with the role-determined behavior. Actually, they usually enjoy their excursions. They stop and talk to other women, collect news, gossip, and glimpse store windows and other people's houses. A chance to do and see something different is always welcome. They never stay long but they do enjoy these visits.

The timid, cowed creatures of the street scene are very different once they arrive at their destination. There, women are *furbe* (crafty), insistent, and good businesswomen, no faint praise in Italy where dealing with bureaucratic officials and professionals is a job for a saint. They display the intelligence and quickness of wit which alone allows them to carry out these tasks. Constant practice sharpens these qualities, and repeated success at complex jobs gives them a sense of self-assurance and competence which is quite out of keeping with formal role demands. Therefore, in order to be a good wife a woman must be at one and the same time: meek and aggressive, intelligent and stupid, equal to educated men and less than men, reasoning and irrational, trustworthy and untrustworthy.

Gower's comments, based on fieldwork in Sicily in 1927, are valuable here, not only as corroboration but also as revealing that the prewar traditional village was not so different from the *paese* of today:

> At the same time the cooperative aspect of marriage is recognized, there is an equally explicit pattern against the equality of the partners. The man is the head of the house. . . . At the same time it would be improper to represent the Sicilian woman as a much abused creature. She may be the occasional victim of her husband's displeasure, even when she herself is not the cause of his ill-humor; yet on the whole the relations between married persons are friendly and harmonious. . . . [1930, no page given]

The husband is the *capo famiglia* and as such it is he who commands. He must be consulted on all decisions and his word is law. He can be cruel, brutal, and insensitive to the needs and personalities of others. He rules with an iron fist, and it is not unusual to hear of wife and child beatings. He represents the family to the outside world and bears the final responsibility for all decisions taken in the family and for the actions of all its members. A child or wife who goes astray is criticized, but the husband is blamed. He must be very careful in delegating any of the authority which is rightfully his. A gentle kind man in the home is considered weak by others and is scorned for not fulfilling his duty, even when no scandal has taken place. The assumption is that weakness on the part of one person in a role pair necessarily reinforces and strengthens the other person. This idea is basically correct because husbands who do not display a certain amount of dominance and authoritarianism are intimidated by their wives who then take the opportunity to run roughshod over their spouses.

Women are normally very careful to foster the image of the

husband as the one who commands. In public places they are timid and withdrawn. When strangers visit the house, the wife is respectful and deferential to her husband. When the husband barks orders such as "Wife, get us coffee," she instantly runs to prepare the refreshments. The wife behaves in this manner partly out of fear of a man who really does lose his temper, who beats her, who ignores her, but she also observes the form because to do so is to increase the prestige of the husband, the wife, the children, and the family. A good husband commands, a good wife obeys, and couples who act this way are praised and commended. The private face is different, but not in the way that most people imagine, for even here with certain exceptions the wife continues to act submissive. Her deportment is submissive, but under this guise she is doing things which no wife should do.

Submission implies unworthiness. The Sicilian man is better than the Sicilian woman and she must therefore obey him. Statements concerning the innate attributes of women abound in Sicily and in southern Italian literature. A woman is weak and must be protected; a woman is stupid and so talks too much; a woman is naive and does not know the ways of the world; a woman is ignorant and does not know how to conduct herself in public; women, as a class are not complete individuals, but creatures who serve men only as bed partners and domestic servants. It is said that upper- and middle-class women more nearly approximate this cultural image because there are servants to attend to the needs of the family and the house. Among working-class Sicilians in Nicuportu, the usual estimate was that 10 percent of the families follow the stereotype and at the other end of the scale the same percentage was projected for the families in which the wife dominates.

Although women as a class are perceived by Sicilian men as incomplete human creatures, an individual woman may be very intelligent, verbal, and crafty, and men perceive this. A wife who displays these qualities is fulfilling the demands of society that the family be cared for, and the husband of such a woman recognizes this and takes pride in the fact that his woman is different. Gower notes that "apart from the sexual code there are no important differences in the moral standards for men and women. Amiability, industry, generosity, cleverness, loyalty and reticence are admired in anyone" (1930, n. p.).

People recognize that men often play out the commanding virile side of their role too well. They make hasty judgments and are frequently not competent to make certain decisions, at least not by themselves. Therefore statements concerning the command of the husband and the obedience of the wife were tempered with clauses such as:

> The husband is obliged to give orders, but they must be just orders. The wife is obliged to obey the orders of her husband, if they are just orders.

> If the husband is not intellectually capable, the wife commands, but it is a secret command, because legally he commands.

The secretness of all this is actually quite open and visible in some settings and with some people. With strange men the wife would never contradict her husband. But when the strangers leave and only the family and neighbors are left, she then speaks her mind openly and eloquently. With these intimates she maintains the appearances when it does not matter but is vehement in her opinions when it is a matter of some importance to her. An example conveys this: Franco was asked where he would go if he could go anyplace. He said America. When asked the same question, his wife replied, "I would go wherever my husband wants to go because he makes all the decisions. He's the important one, it's up to him. I have nothing to say about decisions." A few minutes later he was asked how many children he wanted. He shrugged his shoulders, smiled, and looked at his wife. She said, "It's not up to him. All he has to do is work as usual. I'm the one here in the house with all the extra work of the babies, the washing and cleaning and worrying if they are going all right and not learning bad things, and if they are speaking good Italian, not only this dialect. No, it's my decision."

In addition, men often referred to women as being smarter and better able to handle certain jobs. Peasants especially feel this way because as they say, "I'm out alone in the fields all day. I only have the mule to talk to. What do I know about such things? My wife has more experience, go ask my wife." A number of men refused to participate in this study on the grounds that they did not know how to talk correctly but that their wives would be excellent respondents. Gans, speaking of second- and third-generation southern Italians in Boston, states:

> At social gatherings I attended, whenever women initiated conversations with men, the men would escape as quickly as possible and return to their own group. They explained that they could not keep up with the women, that the women talked faster and

more readily, turning the conversation to their own feminine interests and that they tried to dominate the men. The men defended themselves either by becoming hostile or by retreating. Usually, they retreated. [1962, p. 48]

A woman has neither physical strength nor societal values to uphold her in dealing with a man: she must rely on her wits and her ability to out-talk the men. Sicilian women are "fast talkers," and their ability to argue and often confuse the real issue is their only defense. They can be nagging and stubborn—two unpleasant attributes. Men characteristically say that "it is women who make peace in the family—and it is women who make war in the family." Men are said to be more yielding and compromising. A man is peaceful. A woman is more tenacious and when she wants something she almost always gets it. She talks and talks about it until the husband gives in to keep peace. His home is a quiet sanctuary from a hostile world, and if his wife persists in her arguments, then he is ready to do almost anything to keep her quiet. She usually does not yell and scream for that provokes a violent physical reaction from the husband. Instead, she wears him down by a never-ending flow of words which, like the Chinese water torture, finally produces the desired answer.

There are men however who are never swayed by such methods and even more men who will occasionally stand up and say no. A certain tone of voice shows the wife that this time he means it; but instead of giving up her idea she goes off on another angle of attack. One very usual means is "being cold in bed." A cool, if not frigid, response to her husband in this sphere is claimed to be the ultimate weapon which no man can resist. Another popular method is to give in to the husband, do as he wishes, and then ignore the effect produced. It works this way:

My mother was a typical submissive Sicilian woman, always following her husband's wishes, but with a twist of her own. When the fifth child, a son, was born, my father wanted to name him Giuseppe after his brother, while my mother wanted to name him Salvatore after her brother, who lives in America. Since the father had the right to choose, he won naturally and the child was baptized Giuseppe. However . . . he has always used the name Salvatore and is called Totò, the diminuitive. As an adult he uses Salvatore even for legal documents and never in his life has he used or been called Giuseppe.

Generally, however, the wife uses her hidden weapons with the full but unacknowledged support of the husband to advance the family even though this runs counter to the values of the society.

Men, for example, have the ultimate responsibility for money and wives must account for every lire they spend, but it is common knowledge that wives spend family funds in unauthorized ways:

> There is a proverb here—"Don't give an accounting to your wife, because there will always be debts remaining." Sure they all do it, they have their little jokes and we all know it. Like I see tonight that there is not a 1,000 lire bill in the money drawer and I ask my wife about it and she answers me like this: "Well, I bought thread for 100 lire, and needles for 40 lire each and I bought three needles, and pins for 55 lire and buttons, eight of them for 35 lire each . . ." and when she is all finished it all adds up, if you added it up, to much more than 1,000 lire and yet the total value of all the goods is much less than 1,000 lire. So now, what really happened? Well, she bought some things and saved the rest and then makes my head swim with her accounting. So I let it go because I know my wife is a good woman and will not waste the money on jewelry or other foolish things, but will buy something for the children. All the men do this and all the women.

Let us see now what she actually did with the money, noting first that a peasant family can not spend hard-earned money on frills such as fancy clothing but that on the other hand they must be well dressed if the prestige of the family is to be maintained:

> My wife, for instance, often buys a dress for Calogera and brings it home and hides it because we haven't enough money in the house for this kind of expense and I would be furious if I knew. Then some time later we are going out to a grand *festa* and Calogera comes out in her new dress and I say, "But how beautiful you look, how the others will all look at you," and only after that do I remember to ask where the dress came from. Then my wife admits that she bought it one day but isn't our daughter beautiful. Well, I should get angry but how can I? It is so important to us that we are well dressed for Sundays and *feste* and it would be impossible to let my children walk up and down the corso for the Sunday *passeggiata* in their everyday clothes. Look at my shoes, how terrible they are. No, it would be impossible. Instead my son goes out like a prince and when the others see him they all say "But who is that?" and others answer "That is the son of Salvatore DiSera." And so the wives often do these hidden things.

One important aspect emerges from this example: the husband knows his wife is a good woman. He can trust her because over the years she has proved herself. The time element is very important because when a couple marry they do not really know one another and the husband is not disposed to allow any freedom to his wife until she has proved herself. Some tasks she must carry out from the beginning because of his absence during the day. But he keeps a careful check on everything she does and on every penny spent. The slow process of trusting each other begins at marriage, accelerates with the birth of children, and is fully developed by the time the first child is five or six. Children are the means through which the family receives its greatest acclaim and they are the respository of familial prestige. Therefore, the wife who can balance the family budget, maintain appearances with her husband, and still give children all the love, protection, and material possessions necessary to maintain a certain style of life is respected and trusted. As one man said, "The husband is like the government at Rome, all pomp; the wife is like the Mafia, all power."

THE POWER OF WOMEN

Some married couples share almost equally the tasks allotted to them. It is not necessary for the wife to hide the fact that she saves money, nor is it necessary for another wife to sell farm produce secretly to neighbors in order to have a bit of spending money for herself or the children. Wives in the families which function cooperatively can and do talk things over with their husbands, who are generally understanding and sincerely wish their wives to develop into individuals on their own. In these cases it is not necessary for the wife to scheme her way to power because it is given to her. She, accordingly, has less in actual practice.

But the more common case is that of the wife who over time has beaten down the opposition—her mother-in-law—and has finally achieved a position of true power within the structure of the family. This does not happen overnight and it is not a pleasant process to observe, but it is effective precisely because the husband must, at some point early in his marriage, throw his lot in with his mother or with his wife. The families in which this power struggle takes place are those in which the wife has an early and positive means of proving her trustworthiness to her husband, always at the expense of his mother. The husband is in many ways irrelevant in this all-out war; he is the ostensible object over which the controversy develops, but in actuality he is merely the pawn used by two women who face each other in this crucial battle.

The mother-son bond is the strongest affective tie among all the dyadic possibilities. A mother will sacrifice all and even die for her son. The son has no one who is so selflessly devoted to his welfare. "Mamma" is a byword in southern Italy for total love. Even a man's wife and children will not give him the full and uncritical devotion that he received from his mamma, because they too have outside interests. The mother, of course, has a husband and other children, but *figghiu miu* (my son) is irreplaceable. The open demonstrations of affection which the mother has never been able to display with her husband are reserved for her son; in his eyes, whatever his age, she can do no wrong. Even old gentlemen often cry when they speak of their mammas.

Parsons (1960), on the basis of Thematic Apperception Tests administered in Naples, states that "the mother-son tie acts primarily as a centrifugal one, in that it maintains itself in such a way as to make for an unbroken continuity of the primary family" (p. 59). Women, responding to a mother-daughter picture, "expressed resentment" and demonstrated "a classic pattern of internalized but ambivalently accepted authority" (p. 40). Parsons's most important and far-reaching conclusion is that:

> in many ways the mother-son relationship is qualitatively different from that of our own society or that of Freud, most notably in the continuation throughout life of what might be referred to as an oral dependent tie, i.e., a continual expectation of maternal solace and giving rather than a gradual or sudden emancipation from it. [p. 50]

These observations are extremely important because it is all too easy for an American or Britisher to assume that the Italian mother-son tie is just a rather absurd extension of the relationship as it exists in the German or Anglo-Saxon world. This would be a gross error. The Jewish-mother syndrome in American society does not appear too far removed from the Italian complex. The same themes of love, devotion, service, and sacrifice that have produced the classic mother-martyr are there also. In Italy, mamma is a martyr, but only for her son.

Sicilians must marry and most do. There is no place for bachelors or spinsters in the society, and it is the duty of the mother to marry off her children. A good marriage is a source of prestige for the family and of pride for the mother. But the mother who sees her son leave her for another woman is a sad creature indeed. She does not give up and accept her loss; instead she attempts to keep her son, at the expense of his new wife. His love, the rock on which she has built her life, must not be transferred to another woman. The formal engagement precludes intimacy between the engaged couple, and so during this long period the mother still has the son to herself; but once the wedding has taken place and the son has moved into another house, then she must fight to retain his love:

> For the mother of the boy, she must get him married, that's for sure. But she doesn't really want to because she thinks he will stop loving her. So she tries in some way to keep his love, and to do

this she tears the girl apart, the wife. She fights with her *nuora* (daughter-in-law) because the *nuora* knows about this and she expects it.

The relationship between *suocera* (mother-in-law) and *nuora* is really bad, there are even fights when they hit each other. The mother cannot let him go, cannot stop interfering in their lives, she regards the *nuora* as an outsider or worse and resents her so terribly. If the *suocera* lives far away then it's all right and the two women get along but if she is fairly close then she never lets up and tries always to come between the couple.

This is a battle which is found in all parts of Italy, though perhaps in a more attenuated form farther north. In Tuscany, the curving oil and vinegar bottles that are joined together in the middle are called *suocera* and *nuora* because "they are stuck together and yet face in different directions."

In the beginning of a marriage the mother has the upper hand: she knows her son, and as a woman she can claim to know about women in general and about this wife in particular. She begins

by finding everything wrong in the girl's behavior: the son is not treated as he ought to be, she does not know how to cook for him, she does not send him out looking well with his collar in place. In short, there is a whole series of these little things which often bring about enormous family dramas.

The mother instructs her son in his handling of a wife: "Teach her to do like this, teach her what matters, you must give her so many of these blows that she learns it." The mother also keeps track of the wife's activities so that

when the son goes to see her each day she tells him little things about his wife. He begins to resent this but still he fights with his wife telling her what he has heard. He doesn't say where he heard them, but she knows because he knows things that only a *suocera* can know.

So he begins to resent his mother, but she is always his mother. The mother also informs others about her *nuora*. I was told, "Everyone knows that Signora A. is having an affair with her cousin while her husband is in Switzerland because her *suocera* is going around telling everyone." The mother rarely resorts to a blunt statement that the wife is no good. She prefers to find fault with her, to instruct her son in making this woman a good wife, and always to compare the wife's faults with the mother's corresponding virtues.

The husband's sisters carry out a similar but much milder form of harassment. One wife bitterly remarked, "She calls me 'la signora' in that tone of voice telling everyone that I put on airs. She never visits but complains to everyone that I do not visit her." Sicilian men explain this by saying that women always interfere.

The wife for the first year or so is in a very difficult and precarious position. She is being tested by her husband, which would be bearable by itself, but at the same time she is being criticized and vilified by her *suocera*. She knows well the hold the mother has on her son and she is too wise to put up any show of resistance. If she does not behave and speak properly of his mother and his other family members she will be punished—"Sometimes when there is no respect toward the relatives of the husband, the husband to stand up for himself forbids the wife to see her mother." So, for a time the mother "wins" because the husband is more attached to his mother and because "la mamma è sempre la mamma."

But a time comes, usually about a year after marriage, when the wife begins to pull her weight. She has by now begun to demonstrate her worth as housekeeper, cook, buyer, accountant, and mother. When this begins to be evident to the husband, then it is time for her to start hitting back. In this she is supported by the societal value which places the nuclear family above all else. She makes constant references to the fact that "you never ate like this in your mother's house; they are not so *gentili* [fine]." She sews better; she irons better; she does everything better than his mother. It is easier for her of course. She is younger and there is no one but the husband in the house who must be cared for. She then attacks the husband at his most vulnerable point—his mother's love for him. A male respondent told me, "She begins to provoke her husband against his mother, saying that the mother has not treated him like the other children, that she does not love him as she loves the others, that making the division of her love she gave less to him than to the others." This is a particularly effective argument because the inherent antagonisms in the sib bond make it much more painful.

The end comes "since we men are weak and we are often pulled by the women where they want." A crisis occurs when the fighting between the two women becomes so intense that the husband cannot stand it any longer. He must choose between them, and the victor is invariably the wife:

> In my house I was between the fire and the frying pan. I had to kick out my mother or my wife. A neighbor of my mother put my mother up to all the trouble by telling her that I spent more

money and time on my wife than on her. . . . So I had to keep
my mother and my wife away from each other for more than six
months and during that time I had very little contact with my
mother.

The wife eventually "wins" in the war because . . . well, there
is a proverb about it: peace inside, war outside. That is what
the husband thinks, and he must live with his wife and he wants
peace in his house so he begins to side with her against his mother
and finally the wife has won.

It's a funny thing, with time the husband goes over to his wife,
away from his mother. She begins to pull him more than his
mother. She has the force to habituate him to her way of life.
Women do this to men, men don't change women, but women
often change men.

Another result of the wife's victory is that the husband begins
to favor her side of the family, and eventually a matrilateral bias
is formed which extends to the children. They maintain respect
for the family of the husband, but intimacy is with the wife's
family only. Visits are paid to his family but they are formal and
stilted. If there is ever exchange of aid or pleasurable meetings at
a social gathering, it is with the wife's siblings and their families
and her parents. There is a proverb which says, "I parenti ru
mugghieri su duci comu u meli; i parenti ru maritu su aghiri
comu l'acitu" (the relatives of the wife are sweet like honey; the
relatives of the husband are bitter like vinegar).

The most interesting fact is not that the wife won, but that she
is able to amass and solidify her power through her handling of
the argument. She has forced the husband to recognize her good
points, and on a psychological level she has made him feel guilty
for doubting and betraying her. Without such a focal point it
might have taken years for her to fully convince the husband that
she has sterling qualities, that the family is all-important to her,
that she will defend him from outside enemies, and finally, that
the peace he craves is possible only through her good services. As
time goes by, the wife's position is reinforced by her expertise in
getting the best for her family. Through her successful socialization and training of the children and by bringing about good
marriages for them, she assumes a position of importance and
power within the nuclear family.

Increasing age aids in this process because her work load is
lightened; as an older woman she is no longer a symbol of sexual
purity and is allowed much greater freedom outside the home.
She is regarded by her associates as an authority on household

problems and more importantly as a source of information on families in the *paese*. When a man or woman does anything out of the ordinary these old women can "explain" why this particular person would act in such a way; they know if his father, grandfather, or some of his relatives acted in similar ways. The past is inextricably linked to the present and to the future, and it is important for younger people that old women with their stores of information are available. By the age of fifty, they are experts in the social relations of the community. Pitkin notes, "in the adult women's groups there is little differentiation according to age, for elderly women often have more to relate than younger ones" (1954, p. 185).

Normally, there is little respect for age in Sicilian communities. An old person is usually accorded some show of respect, but he is not truly respected. He is a "has been" who has outlived his usefulness. This attitude is especially noticeable toward men who are old and no longer work. The father-son relationship is structured in such a way that when the son takes over the father must resign completely. Since the old man's life, up to that point, was spent at his work, he has no other resources and says of himself that he is *sciupato* (run down, worn out). This is a common southern Italian characteristic. Lopreato noted it in Calabria: "The problems of the aged in Stefanaconi are probably due, at least in part, to the loss of prestige which they incur when they cease to produce" (1960, p. 72). Pitkin says of central Italy, "Among men, however, there is greater discrimination, for those who have ceased to work and no longer participate in local affairs are not felt to have much to contribute to the discussion of the younger men" (1954, p. 185). Gower, who did fieldwork in a small Sicilian village, concludes:

> In forms of address, great respect is paid to old age. . . . Sometimes this verbal respect is real and accompanied by other manifestations of regard. More frequently the attitude toward the aged is one of slightly contemptuous commiseration. . . . Old people do not have precedence, and they are often rather frankly treated as burdens. There is no attempt, however, to shirk the responsibility of caring for them. [1930, n. p.]

Thus old people continue to maintain their position in the community only so long as they continue to work at their customary tasks. The instant they give up these activities, often against their will, they are regarded as and treated worse than children, who after all have their lives ahead of them. The prestige of a working-class man is based on his ability to support a family and when this activity ceases so does his prestige. The *contadino* depends on brute force and physical strength; knowledge of the land and crops is tied in with this but these are not complex sorts of knowledge and the ebbing of his strength presages the diminution of his male role. Other men, younger and stronger, have replaced him, and since they have worked in their occupations since childhood they too are knowledgeable.

The woman accumulates prestige and status through her role as housewife and mother, and so long as she maintains a home of her own she retains her position in society. Her knowledge of house and children is common to younger women also, though her advice in an emergency can be important, but her knowledge of the community and its inhabitants is unique to her and other old women. In addition, she is skilled in problem solving, and a younger woman who has an old woman as her friend and confidant is fortunate. Questions such as how to handle a husband, how to treat a bitter *suocera,* how to bring an erring son back home are all matters on which an old woman is experienced. She, therefore, is in a position not only to maintain her status but actually to increase it.

Another point of importance here concerns the *capo famiglia.* There are actually two senses in which this title is used: it can mean the head of a nuclear family who is always the husband, and it can mean the head of the extended family. I am referring to the latter in this section. Most middle-class respondents named a *capo famiglia* for the extended family, but most working-class respondents denied that such a position existed. When there is a *capo famiglia* it is always a man—father, uncle, grandfather—who is responsible for representing the family to the outside world. Closer questioning, however, reveals that the person to whom relatives go for advice, the person responsible for maintaining the lines of communication between sections of the kin group, the individual considered wise and perceptive is a woman—mother, aunt, grandmother. An educated middle-class Sicilian in Australia describes it best, although his account does not differ from that of others:

> My mother's brother is the chief and is consulted because he is the eldest male: not to do so would offend him. They go to him because he has greater education and more contact with the outside world and as a man can do a lot women can't do, for matters which require knowledge of the outside world. He is an unofficial head and it's true to say there is always an unofficial head who at the very

least is acquainted with all that is going on, whose advice is listened to but quite freely departed from, whose help is taken for granted, who has more duties than powers, who is often informed or consulted out of vague and confused feelings of a necessity to help the family—my uncle.

My mother is the real chief. She is the intellect, the heir to my grandfather, she is recognized as having intelligence and clear sightedness. She is the one who has character and who is the ultimate arbiter of what is right and what is wrong. People go to her for real help and advice and she is the go-between for the various groups.

Working-class respondents who denied the existence of a *capo* for the extended family very often admitted the existence of a "kin center"—an unofficial counselor operating both within the kin group and among neighbors and friends. This figure was almost invariably a female. Intelligent, perceptive women carve a position of authority not only within the nuclear family but also outside the family. Male figures, such as husband, uncle, and brother, are the couriers who pass between the family and society, and their main function is that of carrying information.

By the time a married couple reach their sixties, death looms and here again, in this final event, the authority and continuing importance of the woman is evident. A very popular proverb says: "If the father is dead, the family suffers; if the mother dies, the family cannot exist." The impact of death on the spouse is variable according to sex. A man who has spent his life out of the house working alone has forged solid bonds of companionship and affection with his wife and with no one else, not even his own children, who often refer to their fathers as "outsiders." When she dies, when the relationship crumbles, he crumbles too. When the husband dies, however, the widow continues with her normal daily activities in the house and outside it. People depend on her; children, neighbors, and perhaps relatives have come to view her as a personage in their lives. She may well feel a terrible sense of desolation at the loss of her spouse, but she can survive.

The popular stereotype of the Sicilian woman as a meek being who submits to the harsh commands of an authoritarian husband is false. The Sicilian wife assumes a pose of submissiveness and meekness in order to pay respect to the ultimate authority of the family—her husband. But she is also cooperating with her husband in all the many tasks which must be carried out if the family is to survive and increase its prestige. Most decisions are made openly by the couple together; some other tasks, such as maintaining contacts with institutional authorities, are carried out by the wife with the knowledge of the husband, but her role is kept secret from the public. Other activities, such as saving money to spend on a prestigious but nonessential item, the wife must keep secret even from her husband. The wife, starting from a lowly and untested position as a bride, slowly consolidates her position in the family until finally, years after her marriage, she is an acknowledged source of authority, wisdom, and strength. The societal value which places the nuclear family at the pinnacle of the society, the occupational structure which necessitates the husband's absence from home during the daytime, the strength of the mother-son bond which the wife is forced to break, the values placed on active participation in the community and its corresponding devaluation of any individual who cannot maintain such activity—all these factors combine to place the wife at the heart of the family and therefore at the heart of the society. Barzini, as usual, has the last word: "Men run the country but women run men" (1964, p. 202).

6

SERVICE TO THE FAMILY

The individual's attachment to the family must be the starting place for an account of the Montegrano ethos. In fact, an adult hardly may be said to have an individuality apart from the family: he exists not as "ego" but as "parent."

Edward Banfield

BANFIELD's statement is as true in Sicily as it is in Apulia. It is clear by now that the nuclear family is the cornerstone of Sicilian social organization and the most fundamental of Italian institutions. It is difficult for a non-Italian to understand the importance of the family because it is not, as it must appear, a British-type family system writ large; the structure of the family is similar but its function is different. The Sicilian, or southern Italian, nuclear family is an entity composed of its several parts which exist for the sole purpose of furthering the interests of the family.

Although no one has studied the family in detail as it exists in Italy, spelling out roles, role dyads, and interrelationships between roles, all observers of the southern Italian scene have agreed on the values governing its operation. Some of these values are: the family is the base about which the rest of the social organization revolves; the family is the means by which individuals gain prestige and status; the family is the sole source of comfort and security; family members, their interests and wishes, are sacrificed for the betterment of the family.

The term *nuclear family* refers only to the structure of a particular kin grouping, it does not indicate the function of the family, the familial roles, or the value orientation. The nuclear family in the industrialized English-speaking world has become primarily an institution for the socialization of children—children who must one day take their place in society as individuals, not as family members. Other institutions aid in the weaning process and the societal values are directed to this end. Independence, personal liberty, and a sense of self are inculcated early into the growing child, and adult deviants are those who were not "successfully" socialized and who remain "mamma's boys" or "daddy's little girls." Phrases such as "stand on your own two feet" and "experience is the best teacher" reflect the values of being successful and independent. The emphasis on social mobility, on education for the masses, and on job opportunities for all are manifestations of the ideals and openness of American society. Rich natural resources, advancing technology, and freedom from oppressors aid in fostering these values, which in turn permit, or demand, the existence of independent individuals who know how to make use of such resources.

Sicilian society, on the other hand, is closed, fixed, and family oriented. The nuclear family is given the responsibility of maintaining itself and its members, with no expectation of financial or moral help from outside. The main task of the family is to keep itself functioning by holding fast all its members and by creating an ethic of conformity so strong that no one of its members will "betray" it. All societal values and socialization techniques are geared to utilizing the talents and efforts of family members in producing a synthetic person—the family. Since the combined labors of all are necessary to the fruition of the family, deviants and deviancy are severely censured. The individuals in the family "shared equally in fortune and misfortune and the whole family received credit or blame for the success or error of anyone of its members" (Bromley 1955, p. 302). The distinction then is between a family system designed to aid its individual members and one designed to aid itself. This is accomplished by the socialization of the child as a family member; the family is rewarded by other families and by the society at large for success in this task. The society in rural Sicily is the community, and it is significant that community approval of dependency training actually sacrifices the development of the community:

> Established on a definite but also narrow policy, the family was by no means a medium for the social training of its individual members: Rather, it precluded or at least hindered the appearance of individuals whose social outlook would transcend family interests and bring into life a more closely integrated community. [Covello 1944, p. 254]

The issue of "individualism" is often a confusing and complicating factor in discussing southern Italians. Individualism can mean either the exhibition of personal idiosyncracies that mark a person as being different from his fellows or the inability to look beyond personal and family interests. The term can be used in a disapproving, though amiable, way when applied to eccentrics and deviants; it can also apply to the strong-minded person who, with his principles solidly grounded, follows the course he believes is correct. Northern Europeans and Americans often refer to Italians as individualists, meaning eccentrics, on the basis of behavioral symptoms which are not approved of in the more northerly countries, such as singing in the piazza, laughing loudly, gesturing wildly, arguing at full voice, and spouting poetry. The fact is that many of these actions, such as gesturing and arguing, are culturally patterned and approved, but others, such as singing and declaiming in the streets, are discouraged even in southern Italy. However, they are allowed to occur and are even applauded if the actor is good enough. These actions do not mean that southern Italy has an open, free-swinging society in which each person can do just exactly as he wishes; quite the contrary. Southern Italians are severely restricted in matters of personal liberty and freedom, but these restrictions in the "important" areas of life are not operational in a few minor "unimportant" spheres of personal activity. The individual is restricted and protected by rigid societal values and rules when he takes socially meaningful steps such as marriage, choosing a job, or selecting a house, and for his compliance with the demands he is rewarded with approval and praise. A sense of group security allows him to "act out" in the piazza because the action is socially neutral and he has obeyed the dictates of society when and where it matters. This syndrome is found not only in southern Italy, but in other societies as well:

> It is usually, but not always, the case that considerable leeway is permitted for individuality within the confines of the definitely fixed customs which gemeinschaft groups require for the ordering of human relationships. Individuality and individualism are both results of attention being given to the autonomy of the individual, but they are vastly different concepts, and significant nuances of meaning are lost when, as is so often the case, they are either confused or equated. There is actually less opportunity for a truly spontaneous individuality of expression in an individualistic society than in other, more fixed and firmly regulated, social orders. But, on the other hand, the man in an individualistic society need not remain in a fixed position and need not so often bow his head in acceptance of a dominating authority. He is much more "free to be like everyone else." [Kluckholn 1958, p. 68]

Therefore the southern Italian is freed by the group to perform some spontaneous acts only so long as he conforms to the norms of society in all other matters: the American is more restrained in his behavior, but the restraints are self-imposed thereby permitting an incomparably greater amount of personal freedom. These reflections have important consequences on social mobility, the development of strong nonfamilial institutions, and social change.

The autonomous nuclear family which sacrifices individuals to promote the interests of the family is paralleled in the case of the nuclear family versus the extended family. In both cases there are values calling for unity and goodness among the members, but overriding these is the value that the nuclear family must be nurtured, protected, advanced, and defended. Relationships between the nuclear family and extended family members on the one hand and among nuclear family members on the other hand are contingent upon their effect on the nuclear family. Sicilians constantly speak of sacrificing: "I had to sacrifice my education (my marriage, my job) for my family because they needed me." But as a result of mutually held values and the effective socialization of children, these "sacrifices" are not perceived as onerous burdens. Sacrifice is part of the Sicilian way of life, and while a denial may often be referred to, the purpose of the sacrifice is more important than the object sacrificed, and the sense of satisfaction derived from the benefits to the group more than adequately compensates the individual for his personal loss. This does not mean that the individual is always praised for his action. The usual practice is to ignore him completely and concentrate on the group gain. For example, the son who gives up an opportunity to attend a university is not told that he is a wonderful, courageous person; no comment will be made to him or about him because he has done the expected and the father will say to everyone, "Well, now we will have enough money to buy the house in one year." The general pleasure when the house is finally purchased is compensation for self-denial.

It is almost axiomatic that groups, especially kin groups, which present a united front to the world outside the family are very often torn by friction inside. The members of a Sicilian nuclear family (hereafter in this chapter called "family") are always careful to exhibit complete cooperation and unity when facing the community, but when the group turns in on itself then the strains inherent in this type of tightly knit, multipurpose unit come to the surface. Societally dictated patterns of authority and ranking, intra- and inter-sex divisions of power, and concepts of feminine purity all serve to create dissent within the family. The Sicilian family is not democratic; however, there are no clear-cut authoritarian figures. Power, prestige, and deference patterns are ambivalent because the person officially but insecurely in power is harsh in his application, while the subordinates are rebellious and may refuse to accept their lower positions. These conditions make for what the Sicilians call "family dramas." Relations between and among family members seethe with conflict and rebellion, occasionally breaking through the surface into vicious battles, and then recede again only to smoulder until some incident, some trifling word is spoken, and the old antagonisms are again released.

These conflicts and sentiments are not peculiar to Sicily, but in many societies they are handled differently; one leaves the family, or authority is tightened so that rebellion is not possible, or affective distance separates the actors, but this is almost never the case in Sicily. Sicilians in and out of the family sphere seem to relish conflict and incidents and appear to deliberately fan minor events until they grow into major battles. For instance, when a dog was hit by a car on the main street of Nicuportu a crowd of about a hundred gathered. Everyone saw it and everyone had a different version which was related to everyone else. The very stern police arrived and instantly began screaming at everyone, totally ignoring the dog while the motorist was trying to convince everyone that it was an accident; the entire incident lasted over an hour, tying up traffic, ruining schedules, appointments, and waiting dinners. These "psychodramas," as one Italian called them, are lifeblood in Sicily; they liven up an otherwise routine day and provide several hours of conversation. Incidents of this sort are usually harmless and, if one is in the right mood, are quite a bit of fun. Occasionally such a gathering is actually helpful and renders aid. The only exception is an incident involving "honor" when *omertà* renders the homicide invisible to bystanders, and the crowd quickly, silently, efficiently disperses. This is an affair which rightly belongs to no one but the participants.

SOCIALIZATION OF CHILDREN

A child is socialized or trained to become a normal member of his society partly by the injunctions of his elders and partly by the world he observes around him. A Sicilian child is born at home, attended not only by the doctor or midwife but also by his two grandmothers, sisters of his two parents, and often his father. Immediately after birth other relatives and acquaintances in the community begin visiting the mother and child. The child in his expensive (60,000 lire), swan-shaped crib and the mother, pale and wan in her trousseau finery, receive the visitors, who are offered *confetti* (candy) and liquor or champagne.

The child's name is predetermined by rules which govern the

naming of infants. These rules are very strictly adhered to. Women sometimes expressed the desire to be free in the choice of a child's name, especially when the required name was not to their liking, but they accepted it because not to do so would give offense to the relatives and so "si cammina sempre la ridda" (the wheel keeps turning). The first and second males are named after the paternal and maternal grandfather respectively. Similarly, first and second females are named after the two grandmothers. Males born after this are named alternately for the father's brothers and the mother's brothers, and the same procedure, using sisters of the parents, applies to additional females. The only exceptions allowed are (1) the use of names of deceased brothers and sisters of the wife before those of the husband who are living and (2) the use of Maria or a saint's name when the child is born on a special feast day or when the parents wish to make a vow. Two reasons, other than the usual one of custom, were given for the existence of the naming rule. The first is that it reminds parents of their deceased loved ones:

> If you don't do it you lose your heredity, and this is true even today. There is a history in the names. It makes you think of the person whose name you or they carry. For instance, one of my grandchildren has the name of my mother, and now my mother is dead so when I call my granddaughter by this name I also think of my mother. In this way no one is ever dead.

The second reason refers to identification with the family, or more exactly the "house." The system places each person in a family, an extended kin group, and a social class:

> You know here everybody doesn't know everybody. But everyone knows someone in your family. When they meet you and someone says "This is Salvatore's eldest son," they say "Eh, you must be Vittorio, I know your father's father and you must have his name." Or the other way, "This is Vittorio X" and they say "Eh, you are Salvatore's eldest son," and they know this because of your name.

On the day of birth the father goes to the home of two chosen friends to ask if they would do the honor of being the baby's *padrina* and *madrina*. Later in the day, the godparents arrive with their presents: gold rings, earrings, and bracelets for females and gold plates and cups and tableware for males. The persons requested may, in theory, refuse the honor on grounds of insufficient knowledge of the parents, for financial reasons, or on the basis of atheism. However, only the latter reason is ever activated and then rarely. Communists often participate in the church ceremony. The financial burden of godparenthood is heavy. The total cost of the gifts should run about fifty or sixty dollars, and it is often necessary for the godparents to borrow for this expense. Visits continue for several days and the baby is brought more gifts, in which there is little variety. One child received seven hairbrushes, four plates, nine silver cups, twelve silver or gold spoons, eighteen pairs of earrings, and eleven rings. Gifts may not be exchanged for something else because that would give offense.

The baptism occurs about a month later and some sort of *festa* always accompanies it. The parents may decide to invite only the godparents for an elaborate noon meal and then go to the church, or the immediate family and the godparents will attend the church service first and then return to the house or a rented hall for a large party to which all the relatives, friends, and neighbors have been invited. Food and liquor or, if possible, *spumante* are served. The parents give gifts to the godparents usually in the form of jewelry. These gifts are supposed to correspond in value to the godparents' gift to the child, but they never do and a sense of injustice always remains: "You buy all that jewelry for the baby and it costs between 30,000 lire and 35,000 lire and that's a lot. Then the parents give you a present back and it costs about 4,000 lire. How do you like that, 4,000 lire for 35,000 lire."

From this time until the child is about six and begins school, he is the object of love and attention from everyone he encounters. Anyone who sees a small child immediately picks it up, smothers it in kisses and fondles it. It was strange to see rough or sophisticated teen-age boys uninhibitedly fondling and cooing to children. Parents are very permissive, allowing children free rein in and out of the house. Discipline is unheard of and a set schedule, while in theory approved of, is never followed. Children soon learn that they can do as they please and, for a time, become demanding and smug while they seize every possible opportunity to show off. Sicilians do not reason with children. They scream, curse, and hit them but with little or no conviction behind the punishment, and children ignore it.

Very bright or precocious children are trained to perform for visitors. They rattle memorized phrases, sing and dance, and very often at the age of one and a half are accomplished entertainers. During a one hour visit the child will be made to perform his routine six or even ten times. His adoring parents and admiring relatives and friends shower him with adulation:

However, it would be a mistake to conclude from this that they simply receive that much more of the "security" and maternal warmth which are currently so highly valued in the United States . . . the handling of children is very rough and unsubtle and includes a very high aggressive component. [Parsons 1967, p. 377]

Although a child is surrounded by people, given an overabundance of physical affection, and is constantly shown by word and by deed that he is the star in the house, the show is not for his own glory. A child performs to increase the status and prestige of his family, and credit for his performance is reserved for his parents, particularly the mother. He is the means by which the parents accomplish a family goal; he is not learning skills which increase his own prestige. "From the very beginning, there is an almost complete lack of concern for the baby as an autonomous individual" (Pitkin 1954, p. 214). Therefore, very early in life the child begins to learn that he is a representative of his family and that all his accomplishments reflect credit on the parents, who trained him. Children who are shy, diffident, or untalented are sternly reprimanded for their refusal to live up to the expectations of the parents. Nonperformance, in a young child, is never seen as innate inability but instead is viewed as recalcitrance. Even at this early age he has a task to perform for the family; inability or unwillingness represents failure to live up to the demands of his role.

Responsibility for carrying out the demands of any role, be it mother, host, or guest, rests heavily on Sicilians. Rigid role structuring and compliance with all the demands of any role each time the role is called into action ensures that the individual makes no mistakes and therefore receives constant rewards. One instance of this is the host's obligation to feed his guests. It is not enough that the guest be offered food or drink, which he may then refuse on one pretext or another; it is necessary that the guest eat or drink. Only then are the situational demands met, and both actors can feel satisfaction in having performed their roles properly. Good form demands that the proffered food or drink be refused at least twice before accepting. Sicilians in Australia recounted tales of hungry evenings spent in Australian homes because they refused once and the refusal was, of course, accepted as final. In this situation the visitors needs are unimportant; it is the satisfaction of the donor which must be met.

At about the age of four, children begin to take their place in the normal routine of daily life. They are no longer *picciriddi* but become *piccuteddi*. Sicilian dialect has three terms for "child," which distinguish three stages of childhood: a *picciriddu* (new-born to about four years), a *piccuteddu* (from four to about nine), and a *piccioto* (from nine to adulthood). An adult is an *omu* (a man), and this term is not used until a man is about twenty-one. Italian only distinguishes between a *bambino* (baby) and a *giovanotto* (young person). The Sicilian usage is much more in keeping with Sicilian social organization.

Little boys "help" their fathers in the fields or at the work bench. This is a form of play, but at the same time it indoctrinates the child into the world of work. He hears conversations around him and though little will be comprehensible some rudimentary understanding of social relationships and community activities is fostered. The little girl begins learning embroidery at home. This is an essential skill since the personal trousseau which forms part of the dowry consists almost entirely of linens and personal lingerie which the girl works herself. It is not an unusual sight to see little girls of four, working on tattered pieces of muslin, seated in sewing circles of women. Their work, of course, is very poor, and embroidered strawberries cover drops of blood. The child may be told that she is improving and the mother shows her work to every passerby, but direct praise is withheld until her work reaches the standard set by adults.

These forms of activity for both boys and girls serve also to keep children off the streets where they will learn "bad things" from less well-educated children. This is a constant preoccupation with mothers who, irrespective of social class, fret about the child learning bad things. Bad things may be anything from speaking dialect to sexual instruction. It is difficult to determine who these "rough" children are because in fact no one is allowed to run wild in the streets.

Young children are taught that it is dangerous to leave home, and the many activities manufactured for them in and around the home serve the purpose of keeping the child content. The poorest quarter of town borders on idle fields planted in grass. The children who live next to the fields never go there, preferring to play in the dirty, noisy, garbage-laden streets. When questioned about this, the residents replied that anyone could go in the field because the owner did not care but it would be too dangerous for their children to go so far away. (The fields, however, were visible from the houses where the women sat.) The children merely replied, "What would we do there?" Children in Nicuportu do not play games, and toys and dolls are almost nonexistent. There are enough babies to take care of the maternal instincts of the girls, and the boys roughhouse.

The effect of this practice is that children just out of infancy learn that the world away from home is a dangerous place filled with strange unspecified "types" who will teach one "bad" things. Security and safety are to be found only at home with one's own— *i miei* (mine). The home is not necessarily a pleasant place, but the other world is made so unpleasant that any alternative is preferable.

At five or six years children begin school, which meets from 8:00 A.M. to 1:00 P.M., six days a week. This leaves their afternoons free. The habits they began as four-year-olds are continued now with some intensification of the work role. Many children leave school by the age of eight or nine, and this advance training may not be a bad introduction to a hard life. Children are loaded with homework every day, but the crowded living quarters of most preclude any real study. Homework is dispatched in a slipshod manner, if it is attempted at all. Once the boys begin to work with their fathers they are of course busy all day and part of the evening and are less frequently seen on the town streets. They begin to act like little men and in public, except for teasing by older men, are accorded the respect due a working man. The only difference between the boy and his father is that, if salaried, the boy receives a fraction of the adult's salary for what is, very often, the same work. These little boys age rapidly, their faces become grey and lined and their undernourished bodies droop with fatigue, but they have a sense of manliness and pride for they are contributing to the household coffers. They occasionally break out into boyish laughter or wrestling play, but most of the time they are frighteningly like little men, as they strive to be.

Girls are often allowed to remain in school through fifth grade, the end of elementary school. Men often mention that their wives are better educated, although in terms of actual performance ten years after leaving school there are no observable differences in general knowledge, reading, or writing. Girls are seldom permitted to continue past the fifth grade for a number of reasons: they are needed at home to help with a large and growing family; they must begin to work on the *corredo* (trousseau); there is no money to send them any further; the middle school is coeducational and it would be dangerous for a girl to be in a room with boys all day; it is enough for a girl to be able to read and write. Lack of money or need for earnings of children must have been at one time very pressing, but, except for a few cases, this is no longer true. The family which uses this as a reason is usually the family which buys a new television set.

Many parents are of course genuinely saddened that their children could not continue in school because they recognize this as the one path to a better life. But often one spouse is not in agreement or the children have done so poorly in school that it seems ridiculous to force them any longer. Most *contadino* and *artigiano* (artisans) parents, however, do not see the value of education beyond the most elementary level and often take the children out of school against their wishes. In one family I asked the middle daughter, about twelve, if she was returning to school in the fall. She said no and the mother said they had no money, although a few days before she had told me that the girl did not want to return. I asked what the money was needed for and she said "books and things." I told her that books were free. She argued that books are not free, but when her daughters backed me up she dropped that and said the school didn't give them even though they were supposed to. Both daughters said "Mamma, that's not true." The mother just stared at me. Then the daughter very quietly said, "I would like to go back to school. I enjoyed it and I was second in my class." The mother then said that the father had decided she had enough schooling. He had decided the same thing for the elder daughter. I asked the mother if she had discussed this with her husband. She replied, "Oh, no, it wasn't important enough to talk about."

The girls then stay around the home doing embroidery, a little housework, talking with neighbors, taking an occasional childlike run up and down the street but usually wandering around the street near their house doing nothing. In very poor households with many children, daughters are put to work at jobs which are as physically taxing as the field work of their brothers. Internal injuries are common among these young girls. But most girls today have very little to do, and the mother handles all household chores herself. So they become like little women around in the street gossiping over embroidery with the neighbors. These groups, with which all the side streets are dotted, number about ten women each, though the number fluctuates constantly. For most of the day they sit together talking, sewing, and watching the activities of *gli altri*. The age range is from 7 to 107 and almost no distinctions based on age are noticeable. Girls who can converse like middle-aged women are treated as adults and most young girls sound like their mothers. Conversations are not changed just because adolescent girls are present. The most common topics of conversation are other neighbors, people on adjacent streets, relatives, and happenings of interest outside the neighborhood, such as an accident in the piazza or the latest fashions from Rome. Very little of international or even national scope filters through to them and during 1964 the death of President Kennedy was the only topic of this kind on which they had any opinions. (Most believed his killing had been arranged by his younger brother who coveted both his office and his wife—so much for sibling solidarity.) Conservations are often sexual in subject but this always takes the form of jokes or puns. Women are extremely adept at this joking and some are acknowledged "experts" though such things are never mentioned when men are present.

This habit contrasts sharply with the taboo on seriously discussing subjects even remotely connected with sex. A conversation about pregnancy, birth control, or menstruation is absolutely forbidden. One feels *vergogna* of the most extreme kind about these topics. The closer the actual relationship between two women the more *vergogna* each will feel. Thus it is all but impossible for a mother and daughter to talk openly about these matters. A study of working-class women in Palermo revealed that many mothers "do not give the indispensible explanation at the moment of menstruation . . . for the most part, upset and confused, [they] give this task to a neighbor who then furnishes the daughter with a superficial and confused explanation" (Franco 1960, p. 150). The girl eventually learns the facts of life but usually in such a scattered fashion that her comprehension is never complete, and the beginning of marriage can cause severe trauma. Women feel this is wrong and harmful, marveling at the American habit of openness between mother and daughter, but they feel themselves incapable of changing their own feeling enough to surmount the *vergogna*.

Adult women do talk to one another about these topics but not in public. In a country where not only birth control devices but the dissemination of birth control information is illegal, "family planning" is carried out through various abortion techniques which the women learn from one another. Abortion is extremely widespread in Sicily and some women proudly stated "I have never had an abortion." A study in Nicuportu by a physician-sociologist revealed:

> Provoked abortions among the patients who have been subjects in my study are 95, referring to 50 women, with a frequency of 1.9 abor-

tions per person; and referring only to the 30 women who effectively aborted, there was a frequency of 3 abortions per person. And this number does not seem excessive. [Borruso 1966, p. 25, my translation]

These "sewing circles" are primarily learning situations for young girls. Here they learn the ways of the world through the stories of the women after whom they will model themselves. Here they pick up a wide variety of those "little jokes" which will be useful in their married lives. Here on their own street, surrounded by neighbors and family, they pass their childhood, adolescence, and young adulthood.

Since Sicilian parents are the repositories of all wisdom they have the final responsibility for children and it is therefore their task to set "the children on the right road." This concept is acted out primarily in the area of decision making. Children are never allowed to make decisions on their own—they must be "controlled." If one word could be said to represent the parent-child relationship it would be control. Self-control is unheard of; someone other than the child must have power over him because a child cannot be trusted to control himself. Even adults must be controlled by an outside agency. Women are controlled by men and men are controlled by the sanctions of the community. A child brings all his problems to the family where the matter is thrashed out by the parents and older siblings; a decision is made and is handed down to the child. The child may have ideas of his own about the outcome of any problem and these may be heard by his elders, but they are given scant consideration. A child is selfish and will usually prefer to make a decision on the basis of his own wishes and desires, whereas his parents, who "understand things better," place much more importance on factors which may affect the reputation of the family and its individual members. A child is never told "you decide for yourself and then you must take the consequences" because this is not true in Sicily; the entire family and often the extended family must share in the blame for transgressions of the social mores. The child learns that not only may he not make his own decisions but that he is not capable of making decisions by himself. Decision making, judicial weighing of pros and cons, is a learning process which must be started early in the life of an individual. In the United States most parents begin teaching their children with minor problems whose outcome will not have serious consequences. In Sicily, however, the individual is never allowed to get started on his own, and he is finally incapable of making decisions for himself. There is always someone older or wiser to lean upon and to share the responsibility for a decision.

The major concern of the adults is with the family; individuals and their problems are considered in the light of how their actions will affect the family. A family will take a child out of school so that his earnings can go toward buying a house or a piece of land. The property will show the community that the family has the proper values well in hand: everyone in the family is working for the family, and the possession of real property immeasurably raises the esteem of the family and of the members of the family. The child who leaves school to work on a construction site has his reward in the society's approval of the purchase of property. The immediate needs of the family are of prime importance, and any thought of delaying the gratification of these needs to attain even greater prestige through a profession in the family is unimportant. Although some adults highly value education and muse over the thought of a lawyer son, the prospect of buying land or a car in the immediate future is overwhelming.

A Sicilian child obeys his parents and is kept in a deferential childlike position until his marriage. Decisions regarding his education are made by the parents. He may be taken out of school early or he may be forced to stay in school because the family has decided that an educated son will be of value to them. The hundreds of lawyers and doctors who fill every small Sicilian town are testimony to this practice. The man, as a boy, may have had no interest whatever in law or in medicine as a profession but his family did. This practice is much more common in the middle-class families who either are willing to wait for their prestige or who have money enough to buy property and send a son to the university as well. In the occupational sphere the final result of dependency training is the inability to leave family in order to advance career. With a promotion in the offing, either the entire family goes or the man does not accept the new position.

The working child gives all his money to the parents who allow him a very small sum for personal expenses and retain the rest to be used at their discretion. The items purchased with money partly furnished by children are, of course, partly the property of the children. Land and houses remain in the hands of the parents until their death, then children inherit the property. Other items, however, may never be used by the child. An automobile or a motor scooter is used by the father exclusively: this is his right.

Ownership of a car adds to the prestige of the family, but a young person is not considered capable of driving it. Very few boys and no girls are allowed to drive even though they may know how and possess a license for their jobs. If the parents decide that it is too "dangerous" to allow their son to drive, then he does not drive.

A child must always ask permission to go out of the house, and adult sons are frequently refused this permission by their fathers. No child is ever given a key to his own home. His hours are set by the parents and infractions of the rules are very sternly dealt with. His friends are not chosen for him, but if his choice is not agreeable to the family then the friend must be dropped. A twenty-one-year-old unmarried man from a traveled middle-class family commented, "I have no authority at home and I'm not working so I'm still under my father's authority. But he is pretty good; if I'm home at a decent hour he doesn't say anything, but if it is late then he is very angry and will be very severe and strict with me." The final decision to be made in the parental home is the choice of a spouse and that is made by the individual, although the family has the right to veto his choice. There are few arranged marriages today in Sicily and these occur most frequently in the landowning class.

Just as the host is more concerned with his own social function than with the personal needs of the guest, so "the concern of the parent is more with the child's social behavior than . . . with his development as a unique personality" (Pitkin 1954, p. 219). The child as an individual with personal problems and desires is of little interest to the parents, but in his role as son or daughter he is. Children often complained that their parents were not interested in them. Writing about second-generation southern Italian sons in the United States, Barrabee and Van Mering state, "neither parent shows interest in his personal problems" (1953, p. 51). Parents do not sit down and talk with children or listen to their confidences; intimacy through communication is never established. *Vergogna* prevails: neither parent nor child is able to reveal his innermost thoughts to the other. Parents are perceived as being distant, autocratic, and self-centered.

Activities and spheres of action are rigidly compartmentalized. Parents do not take an interest in what the child is doing and learning in school and do not attempt to help with homework or to supplement teaching at home because learning is the job of the school. There is no PTA in Sicily. Fathers do not take their sons to the soccer games because leisure time is spent with other men of similar age; there is no father-son baseball team or annual banquet. Mothers and daughters do not speak of intimate things for that is the responsibility of the individual; in Sicily there are no books which explain sexual matters to adolescents. If the child has a friend to whom he or she can talk, that child is fortunate.

Young boys have friends but more usually they are acquaintances with whom one talks in the piazza and with whom one goes to the movies. But even here it is very difficult to open up to another. First, the other person is an outsider and as such is never completely trusted, and second, for working-class young men there is little time or opportunity to cultivate friendships. The demands of work and family are so great that the *contadino* or *artigiano* has little more than a half an hour to spend in the piazza in the late evening. Even with middle-class boys, friendships tend to be superficial and fragile because the family is ever fearful of betrayal through the influence of an outsider on one of their members.

Young girls have even less opportunity to form friendships with other girls their own age. When they are still in school they must return home immediately after classes, and when they have finished school they never leave the immediate homesite. The situation is somewhat better in the early years for middle-class girls, but by the time they are fifteen or sixteen the demands of family increase and protecting their purity becomes more important so valuable friendships must be reluctantly dropped. However, working-class girls often make friendships with older women neighbors as do their mothers. The mature woman is not a close relative and so need not be avoided; she is wise and experienced and she is available. The *comare* of whom women speak in a surprising number of cases prove to be older neighbors who are linked to the women through bonds of friendship; they are not *comare* in the usual sense of a baptism or marriage sponsor. Cousins, who would be logical choices for friends since they are close relatives and could be seen often, are frequently not available for the friend role because the two nuclear families within the context of the extended family are not friendly with one another.

This discussion of dependency training of children is paralleled by the fusion of the world of children and the world of adults. In Sicily, there is no distinction between the two. Children interact with adults much more frequently than they do with other children, and no activities take place from which children are excluded. Sicilian society is, in effect, one world in which there are first-class citizens—the married adults—and second-class citizens —the unmarried children. Their values, ideas, activities, and actions are virtually identical, allowing only for sex differentiation and some minor alterations necessitated by physical weakness. This practice allows children to feel they are different from adults only on the basis of inexperience, which can eventually be corrected.

The family participates together in all special amusements. Parents never go out and leave the children at home. Babysitting is unheard of. Dinners, dances, weddings, parties, picnics are all family occasions whatever the hour. Restaurants contain family groups, and if two young people are seated alone, they are automatically recognized as tourists. Parents say that it would be no fun to go without the children, that enjoyment consists of watching and vicariously participating in the children's activities. Wedding receptions usually count more children than adults, and they are the stars of the show upstaging even the bridal couple. A dance takes place in Nicuportu each year for the more educated young people in town. Each young person arrives with his entire family; the parents and often grandparents sit along the wall with the younger children and watch while the young adults dance in the center of the room. The little children run all over, playing games, screaming, and getting in everyone's way (though this is a phrase which no Sicilian would ever think of using in this connection). By ten or eleven o'clock the young children are cranky and sleepy, but they stay on, finally falling asleep on the floor or in the arms of their parents. There are no special children's or young people's parties of any kind. Birthday parties, a recent innovation, are held within the family with perhaps some of the extended family in attendance.

Children get up in the morning when they feel like it unless they have school or work. They eat whenever they are hungry and often refuse a large meal which the mother spent hours preparing. Children remain up until they want to go to bed or until they fall asleep on the floor. There are no naps unless the child himself initiates it. Children know no regular discipline though they are sporadically reprimanded and receive a great deal of physical punishment. They participate fully in the conversations of adults and often elaborate at length on topics on which they feel knowledgeable. In small children this is considered "cute" and in older children it is praised and admired by all. It was often very difficult persuading parents and children to allow me to carry out an interview with an adult when a child had taken over. (The answers of eight-year-olds, however, were exactly the same as those of their parents.) They have an early and complete grasp of customs and traditions and of very comlicated genealogical problems. In American terms they would be spoiled, overbearing, and pesty; in Sicilian terms they are intelligent, cultured, and a constant source of joy and pride.

To inculcate in a child a central value of service to the family, the Sicilians certainly have found the best possible method: make the home the only safe place in the world; present family members as the only trustworthy people; give the child a place in the world of adults; remove the child from the influence of school; put him to work so that he labors as men labor; always make him subject to the dictates and commands of the parents; place all decisions in the hands of the adults; and foster a dependence on the group which makes him unable to survive alone. The same system has been noted in three different sections of southern Italy:

> The family solidarity was the basic code of such family life and defiance of it was something akin to a cardinal sin. [Covello 1944, p. 238]

> Even within the family solidarity is not complete or symmetrical. Until they are ready for marriage, the children are expected to subordinate their wishes to the *interesse* [interest] of the family. [Banfield 1958, p. 116]

> The members of a family are responsible for each other's behavior and welfare. It is in the home that a child learns to conform to the essential standards of behavior. . . . Children owe their parents obedience, respect and affection. . . . A child may not leave the family circle without permission. . . . As long as a child remains in the household of his father, which is customarily until his marriage, he cannot in any sense be financially independent. . . . [Gower 1930, n. p.]

A person learns that he cannot manage alone in this world: he must refer all his problems to others; he must remain in the physical confines of the family home; and his main satisfactions come from the accomplishments of family members which add to the prestige of the family. Southern Italian society is neither socially nor physically mobile, and it can be seen from this discussion that there are more reasons for this than simply industrial underdevelopment.

THE KIN ROLES

Every society has a number of statuses which are assigned to individuals or earned by them. The individual occupying a particular status is said to be playing a role. Assigned or ascribed roles are based on sex, age, and blood or marriage relationship to others. Earned or acheived roles are in the occupational, political, or religious spheres of life. There are many other roles, of course, and the number varies according to the need of the society. The society and the individual together determine which roles are important to each person. Much greater personal choice is allowed in the United States than in many other societies. In Sicily the family kin role or roles cut across all other roles in the society. The way the kin role is perceived and acted out is determined to a large extent by culturally patterned relationships with actors in other kin roles. A son in his nuclear family of orientation must interact with his mother, his father, his brothers, and his sisters, and these interaction sets are not determined solely by the free choice of the individuals occupying the roles. The society, its structure, its culture, its norms and values will predispose each person in one kin role to act in societally determined ways toward each person in another kin role. All brother-brother dyads have particular societal restraints and obligations which must be met if the individuals are to be socially acceptable as brothers. Feelings such as love and hate do enter, but they must be kept within accepted bounds unless both actors are willing to restructure the relationship. These personal factors are always a complicating feature of kin relationships and often have far-reaching and important repercussions on other roles within the same unit. A society may, and usually does, dictate that a mother love all her children equally, but the mother may in fact love her sons more than her daughters. If this occurs in a statistically insignificant number of families in the society, then we can conclude that personal, emotional, or psychological factors are responsible. But if 90 percent of the mothers in the group prefer sons to daughters in spite of the societally held idea of equality among children, then we can conclude that something in the social organization which may have nothing to do with the individual sons and daughters is predisposing mothers toward sons and is discriminating against daughters. In a Sicilian family, husband and wife should honor and respect one another; parents should love and protect all their children equally; children should love and obey both their parents; and siblings should love and help each other. Sicilians hold these ideals, but they recognize that the exigencies of life often prevent their realization.

Until children begin to take their place in the world (at about ten years for girls, often several years earlier for boys), there is little differentiation according to sex in the parents' treatment of them. Generally speaking, sex is not important: sons and daughters have the same rights and duties, they play together, and both parents display affection equally. If any bias is present it is usually cross-sex, fathers preferring daughters and mothers preferring sons. But this is not very noticeable in the early years of a child's life.

The mother is in charge of the children and is solely responsible for their early training. Though her authority is subject always to the higher authority of her husband, he seldom interferes because this is not his work and women are the acknowledged experts in caring for small children. The sexual division of labor between the sexes noted in the preceding chapter is extremely important in this context, because through her expert handling of the children, the wife is finally able to consolidate her position of authority and equality in the home. The process which began at marriage and was intensified during the battle with the husband's mother is now finished because the wife has proved herself. She is competent not only to care for the house, manage the family finances, and represent the family in the outside world, but she is now expertly caring for the family treasure—the children. If she carries out this task properly, and there are very few women who do not, then the husband can, in effect, relax and allow the wife a position of unofficial equality with himself. This does not mean that the married couple has the intimate companionship taken for granted among middle-class couples in the English-speaking world, because this kind of communication rarely develops between spouses. The years of sexual segregation before marriage, marriage to a virtual stranger, and the watchfulness necessary until the wife has proved herself all contribute to the formation of a pattern of affective distance between husband and wife. During the early years of marriage the wife has really no one to whom she can confide unless she is especially fortunate: she consults her mother on practical matters, but *vergogna* prevents any intimacy; sisters may be in competition with her; brothers are scorned as ex-masters;

and her husband keeps his distance, often by choice but sometimes because of an inability to get close to another human being.
If the wife has a sympathetic neighbor, this woman, her *comare*,
becomes her closest friend and confidant. The husband is in no
better position, for identical reasons; the very real bonds which
once existed, except the one with his mother, have been broken
in favor of his new family.

From the time children are about ten until they marry at
about twenty-four, certain role dyads form and construct themselves in a way far different from the pattern favored by the ideals
of society. The nature of these dyads is the result of the formation
of individual kin roles.

The Sicilian father is a demanding, domineering autocrat who
expects and receives blind obedience to his orders. His authority
in the house is final and there is no official redress to his commands.
Children are afraid of their fathers and display a servile manner
in front of them. In actuality, fathers are seldom in the house
since they work all day and spend leisure time with their male
friends in the piazza or in the street playing cards. But the position and the figure of father is unchallenged. One respondent,
forty-seven years old, remarked:

> A father is always a father and he must have maximum respect.
> As a Catholic I believe in God, I see the sun, I know there is a
> higher being; so, I know my father. Even if the father is old and
> ill and his mind is not good any more he still has maximum respect
> because his physical or mental state has nothing to do with his
> state of being a father.

The role of father and not the individual acting the role is the
vital factor here because a father actually does very little with
or for his children:

> My father who had a wife and eight children said when he was
> eighty, "It's time for me to die, all my friends and *compari* are
> gone. Why am I left here all alone? I have no one." Now, he had
> his whole family but he had spent his life with his men friends
> and not with us.

The mother is responsible for all decisions affecting young children and unmarried adult daughters while the father is responsible
for adult unmarried sons. The father-daughter tie is formally
broken when the girl reaches puberty. Formal distance should
be maintained because the father's only function in relation to
his daughter is the protection of her purity, and this is felt to
demand distance so that the daughter will not be able to impose

her wishes on the father. Intimacy is impossible between these two; *vergogna* operates even more strongly here than between mother and daughter. But in fact fathers in Sicily love their daughters and outside the house display pride in their accomplishments and beauty. She, on the other hand, usually loves her father and feels secure under his protection. Parsons (1967) has described the deep-rooted, though hidden, relationship between father and daughter which she found so common in Naples. This is impossible among the working-class families in rural Sicily because the concept of honor based on female purity is so much stronger in this area. However, the seeds of this closeness are there even though they may never be allowed to flourish. There exists a deep affection between the father and his daughter, made possible because he is not the actual protector of the girl.

A father and his son are distant with one another. The father's harshness, which he sees as necessary to the taming of young men, prevents any affection between the two. The son inwardly rebels from this display of authority, and although he obeys the father, he does not like or love him. The first man quoted above added that he did not go to his father for help or advice but preferred a brother, a friend, or even a stranger because he could not talk to his father. The son who is being trained by his family and society to take his place as an authoritarian male must at the same time bow down to his father, and this rankles so deeply that terrible fights often break out. Respondents declared this to be the most serious and the most awful of all arguments which occur between close kin. Until very recently sons traditionally followed their father's occupation. The boy was isolated from other people most of the time and until he was quite old he had to acknowledge his father as the expert in matters of work. This actual dependency on the father aided in keeping filial resentment under control, but the situation is today very different. Land is being abandoned and sons follow newer, easier, more lucrative occupations; this can aggravate the tension between father and son. Fathers are delighted to have their sons leave the land because "a man who works with his hands is his own slave." A mechanic or a construction worker not only receives more money and works more steadily but also receives greater prestige. This is not considered working with one's hands. But the young man who works in a position of equality with other older men at his job is not disposed to be treated like a child at home.

This situation is intensified even more when one speaks of the eldest son, because he becomes an official stand-in for the father, gradually assuming many of the parental duties and responsibilities. The eldest son is consulted in all family decisions, and many decisions are left up to him alone. He begins by acting the part of a surrogate father, and even husband. He is responsible for reprimanding younger sons and protecting daughters; he represents the family outside the house because he is stronger and gets around more. The father trains the eldest son for this position, but the father retains the final authority over the son. In the beginning the two cooperate in carrying out the duties of the father, but

> as the father ages and the son matures the son becomes the strongest in a certain sense and here it is really rare that there is not a war between the father and the eldest son, a continuous war in which the father tends to abandon this function of head of the family who directs the work, who organizes, who stabilizes the most important things in the house, but he always wants to retain the authority over these things. The eldest son, however, wants always to intervene more, to have a greater voice in things, to always have more to decide, authority to decide, and thus happen a batch of family dramas. The eldest son is always a problem.

The father, having started a process designed to train his eldest son and to relieve himself of work, may eventually be usurped by the son. Frequently the son marries and leaves the house before matters reach such a critical stage, but even in these cases the relationship is filled with tension and ambivalence for years. Any closeness between the two is impossible once the son becomes a man, which happens early in Sicily.

The affective distance and physical absence of the father turns the children to the mother. She is the one to whom the children go for permission to do anything, if they go to anyone. She usually has the authority to decide matters herself, but even if the father's permission must be asked the children go first to the mother who either asks the father for the child or, knowing her husband's moods, advises the child how and when to put the request. The mother intercedes for the children with her husband. Often the child's request is refused either because the father is in a bad mood and chooses to exercise his authority or because the favor requested is slightly out of line with accepted practice. If the reason is the former, then the mother, when the children are in bed, begins pleading for the child. She begins her plea in bed, when "the man is completely in her power." But frequently she can sit at the table and reason with him, explaining that he was tired, that the son or daughter had been good, and that the request is within reason. Most often the father will relent and give his permission. If he personally approves the request but has denied it as a matter of form to teach the children what is right and what is wrong, the mother then places the matter on a personal level, and using the same tactics described above, secures permission. The next day the child is told that the father has thought the matter over and because of various named reasons has decided to grant the request. The mother is not mentioned as having played any part in the proceedings. However, respondents universally reported that "children know who the real boss is, it is one of the first things they learn." The mother, in her self-appointed role as mediator and sympathizer, almost never refuses a child's request unless it is clearly out of the question. But most Sicilian children know what their limits are and rarely ask for anything that is impossible. In their view of the mother as the source of all favors and goodness, they often do the father a serious injustice because he frequently does not have to be persuaded by the mother. He merely makes a show for the children to teach them a lesson and has no intention of sticking to it. But the children, especially the young ones, do not know this, and since fathers do not explain things, they have no opportunity to learn. The mother of course gives her version of the affair which may not differ substantially from that of the father, but it includes phrases such as, "your father changed his mind," or "I got your father to let you go." The father then is perceived as an impediment to happiness while the mother is the vehicle by which their ends are achieved.

Daughters do not have many requests which must be referred to the father because going out of the house unaccompanied by a family member is impossible. Her desires concern buying a new dress or having a permanent wave, and all such feminine matters are in the mother's domain. The mother and daughter are in constant proximity carrying out the same tasks in the same house. The mother is therefore the "boss" of the daughter. When the young girl wants to sit outside and gossip, the mother says she must come inside to help with the bread baking; when she decides to wash her hair, the mother decides she will clean house. Usually the mother does need assistance with her chores, or she may simply feel that such training is good for her daughter. These conditions are found the world over, but such petty incidents can assume a grossly exaggerated importance in Sicily where they are unrelieved by other factors. The teen-age British or American girl goes to school, plays with her friends, and when her schooling is completed works outside the house. Where contact is reduced, so usually is friction. In Sicily, where from the age of eleven or twelve a girl is never out of her mother's sight and has no friends or activities away from the house, tension builds and friction is almost inevitable. *Vergogna* between mother and daughter serves to increase the possibility of friction because real communication which might encourage affection and understanding on both sides is impossible. Gower notes that "quarrels between mother and daughter are referred to in popular sayings, and form the theme of certain popular songs" (1930, n. p.). In Italian communities in the United States "a girl could always confide in her godmother, who usually stood closer to her than her own mother" (Williams 1938, p. 83). As one respondent stated, "A girl never tells her mother anything because the mother would disapprove or forbid it." Parsons's TAT's revealed that the:

> daughter appears to internalize maternal authority but she does so in an ambivalent way . . . it is the mother who teaches the daughter the routine techniques of daily life . . . the informants themselves often state that "these counsels are not very important." [1967, p. 389]

In rural Sicily the mother-son relationship is the most significant family relationship—more than the father-daughter because there affection is suppressed. Parsons, although referring to the urban family of Naples, describes it accurately:

> The son occupies a subordinate position in the sense that authority stemming from the mother is fully internalized and violations of it are subjectively sensed as inducing guilt, in comparison to the father-son relation, where the son may openly express hostility or rebellion in such a way as to put the father in a negative light . . . in many ways the mother-son relationship is qualitatively different from that of our own society or that of Freud, most notably in the continuation throughout life of what might be referred to as an oral dependent tie, i.e., a continual expectation of maternal solace and giving rather than a gradual or sudden emancipation from it. [1960, unpublished, p. 50]

The mother-son relationship is significant primarily in affective terms; in practical terms the husband-wife relationship is the strongest and the most important, but it is rarely affectionate. The son is, for his mother, the source of her greatest joy (and sorrow) and at the same time the object of her fullest love and devotion. Respondents all said that the mother shows more affection for her sons than she does for her daughters and that "a son is the object of her existence—when he marries it is like a pillar taken out from under, the sole support on which her life rested." The mother is too closely identified with and too much in contact with her daughter, is affectively distant from her husband, is separated from her own parents and siblings by her complete identification with the family of procreation; and so the son, in one sense, takes the place of everyone who is missing from her life and fills the void in her affections. He, on the other hand, is the willing recipient of his mother's love and services which he tries to repay by constant devotion and loyalty. The son—young, handsome, and manly—is the one who goes all over, who participates most fully in the life of the community, and as such is a worthy object of his mother's care. He is considered by others to be the product of his mother's work and sacrifice, and her reward is not only the deference of the son but also the plaudits of the community on the perfect product she produced. The household revolves around the father, but it is the son who receives the real sacrifies, services, and devotion of the mother.

One example of this devotion, which may seem far-fetched, is actually typical of many I witnessed or heard about. The mother of the Mascalco family had sent for me to keep her company in her sorrow. Present were her husband, three of her sons, the wife and child of the eldest son, her daughter, the daughter's fiancé, and his mother. It was a day of tragedy because Turi (the second son) had been taken into the army in spite of mamma's repeated pleas that he needed the summer vacation. She talked about him continually. All the rest kept saying how badly she was taking it. Her usual jovial lively air was gone; she sat in one chair all day staring into space and refused to go to the beach because Turi was not there. Three times during dinner, between long sighs and wistful headshaking, she asked me if I didn't feel the absence of Turi. At one point, embarrassed for the other sons, I said "But you have three other sons in the house with you." She replied, "Yes, I suppose so but they are not Turi." After dinner she said to me "My son is sleeping." I looked around the room to make sure that we were all together and thought I had not understood. She repeated the phrase and went on to tell me every minute of Turi's schedule for the day, which she apparently followed in her thoughts. Turi was released from the army six weeks later, thanks to his mother's machinations with the local draft board.

The mother has no actual authority over an adult son (sixteen and older). If she thinks he should stay home in the evening she will appeal to him on the basis that he will be hurting her if he goes out. Her worry will be so intense that she will suffer, and very few sons can bear to see their mothers suffer on their account. But the mother's main concern is with the son and with pleasing him; so if he expresses a desire to go out she usually acquiesces. The mother is a continual martyr for her son, and his guilt at increasing his mother's suffering prevents him from opposing her too strongly if she has set her heart on something. The wife will cater to a husband if the husband demands it, but most do not; the mother caters to a son whether he likes it or not, though most do. An example is what occurs at the dinner table. When the family sits down to eat the mother remains standing nervously anticipating their pronouncement on the meal she has prepared. She ignores her husband and runs to the son to be sure that the food is to his satisfaction. If he is not wholehearted in his praise or if he expresses the slightest reservation, she takes the food away and goes to the kitchen to prepare something else. I once saw a son refuse three successive courses which his mother had prepared; the first was the family meal, which the others ate, the other two he requested but then did not like them either. Men who were leaving for work in Germany or Switzerland could usually not even discuss their farewells with their mothers though many married men left their wives quite easily. "La mamma è l'angelo della casa" (the mother is the angel of the house) is a phrase which all children learn in school, and for no one is this more meaningful than the son.

Siblings have special relationships with each other depending on their sex and age. Brothers for the most part get along, but little intimacy is possible. Outside the house they present a strong united front, and they cooperate together in activities which advance the family group. But other factors interfere between them to prevent a full relationship, although many respondents reported it is easier for two brothers to be friends after marriage than for two married sisters or for a brother and sister at any time. There are reports of brothers who over the years formed bonds of friendship and affection, usually based on cooperative economic enterprises, and among middle-class respondents, brothers were frequently cited as friends. However, in most families this is not the case. Age can interfere in the relationships: the eldest brother is elected to exercise authority over the younger brothers. The authority is his always by delegation from the father, but sometimes the brother does not choose to take the father's place in reference to his brothers because of the possibly unpleasant results. The younger brothers, who already resent the domination of their father, are in no mood to accept gracefully the same domination from one just a few years older than themselves. Another intervening factor is loyalty to the family. If two brothers are friendly and one confides to the other that he is going to do something which could cause a scandal or reflect badly on the family name, then the recipient of this information is torn between loyalty to his brother-friend and loyalty to the welfare of the family. The family usually wins out and the brothers are bitter. To avoid open friction of this kind, they believe it better to maintain some distance and then the problem never arises. A cousin or an outsider is not tied by the same loyalties and therefore is a better person in whom to confide. However, relations between unmarried brothers, while not intimate, are generally considered to be good because they have little to do with one another and they can cooperate if necessary.

Two unmarried sisters may, if their personalities are compatible, be the best of friends and confide everything to each other. They are in the house together for all of their lives before marriage, and the *vergogna* which is so prevalent between other role pairs is not so frequently found here. The two sisters are near in age, have the same problems and questions, and share the same low place in the family status structure. They can be a source of great consolation to each other. The only problem is that they may be equally ignorant of the things about which they have questions. However, this is usually solved by a friendship with an older *comare* and neighbor who, in one fashion or another, answers some of their questions. These exchanges are not so important to Sicilian girls as the opportunity to confide in another girl about boys and prospective husbands. This is a constant preoccupation of these girls who, after all, have nothing to fill their lives and thoughts except the expectation of marriage, which will one day set them free from the bondage of the family and the heavy hand of father, mother, and brothers. The fact that they have absolutely nothing to do with males outside their immediate family is irrelevant for they see boys at mass and as they pass along the street. This is enough to set in motion those daydreams which will one day materialize in the form of a fiancé. Unmarried girls are thought to be silly, frivolous, and giggly and, indeed, they are; they could hardly be otherwise when they are treated as children and when the "prize" is denied in so absolute a form that they may not even look at boys on the street (though they do of course). They may work like grown women but they are still little girls.

A brother and sister relationship is partially dependent upon relative age, but more importantly it is based on the dominance-submission aspect of the sex factor. If a girl is ten years older than her brother, she becomes a little mother to him while he is young; she carts him around with her wherever she goes and usually cares for him more than the mother. But even with this disparity in age, when the brother reaches maturity he is placed above his sister in authority, obedience, and power. The eldest brother is the official protector of his sisters, although all brothers are charged with this role to some lesser degree. Most brothers, who are straining at the bounds placed on them by the father, and aware of their own importance from the mother, treat their sisters harshly and imperiously. They often take out their resentment of the father on the sister and prove their manhood to the mother by their use of authority over the sister. This is a role which the father delegates almost completely to the son, and unless he abuses it unmercifully the father will not interfere. If the father and daughter have managed to retain some affection for each other, as is often the case, then she may appeal on a purely personal and affective level to her father and this is sometimes successful. But usually father-daughter relations have become so constrained by distance and reserve that it is impossible for the girl to make the appeal, and even if she can, he very frequently cannot grant her request. The brother then becomes the villain in his sister's life and turns any feeling she may have had for him to scorn, hate, and smouldering rebellion because she cannot disobey him. Even if she has no real love for her father, she usually retains some respect and admiration for his work and his sacrifices on behalf of the family. Her quarrels with the mother may dispose her to look more leniently on the father who is, she feels, being manipulated by her mother. The fact that the mother uses the father to gain favors for her son only increases the antagonism of the sister for her brother. He is getting everything in the family, all the power, authority, love, and freedom, while she has nothing and is subject to everyone's authority. It is no wonder then that these two cannot get along since the brother's role as protector even rules out the escape hatch of avoidance. He cannot avoid his sister, he is responsible for her and must watch her constantly. There was no subject on which respondents agreed more fully or more vociferously than on the characteristics of the brother-sister relationship.

This may be changing today because many young men claimed that they were deliberately not playing the brother role to the full. These young men came from all levels of Nicuportu society, and although some may have been trying to impress an American, in many cases they were actually behaving differently with their sisters. This applies foremost to the engagement of the sister, though they let the girl decide other things also. An ex-*contadino*, who is now a plumber said:

> It depends on the brother. I am not like that and I don't think it is a good idea to order the sister to do things she doesn't want to. Take my youngest sister who is engaged to a boy of whom I don't approve. I don't think he is a good steady worker and will cause his wife many problems later. I just tell my sister my opinion and add, "If you want to go ahead and marry him, fine, but don't come to me later when you begin to have problems." What would happen if I said "You cannot marry him, he is no good, and it is finished"? She would say okay because there would be nothing else she could say, but she'd keep seeing him on the sly and then one fine day they would elope, with nothing ready for the wedding—no trousseau, no house, no furniture. They would have to live wherever they could find a place. And then when the troubles began she would hate me for forcing her into this marriage.

This change may result from the ongoing change in the occupational structure. Young men follow different occupations from their father's and the traditional role of the eldest son may be breaking down as a result. The father retains more control, the son less, and the added dimension of the son's contact with different kinds of people may presage real social changes in Sicily. If the brother and sister can remain somewhat close after their marriages, then the extended family will be more closely knit, there will be more cooperation among close kin, and the old sex-based antagonisms of brother-sister and husband-wife may go. There is but skimpy evidence on which to base such far-reaching conclusions, but one senses that change is occurring in rural Sicily, and with an expanding economy and industrialization, this could be the beginning of a new Sicily. However, at present the old order reigns and cross-sex siblings remain locked in eternal battle.

It is important to follow the family members after the marriage of the children because great changes occur. However, they are predictable changes if one thoroughly understands the premarriage household organization. At marriage a person leaves his old home and family to enter a new home and build a new family. It is to the latter that he now owes his fullest loyalties, labors, and love. The ties with members of his old family may be broken or strengthened, but they are always different. The parents are morally bound to acknowledge this change because "if there are four children and one marries, the father must cut him off, like that [here the respondent gestured as if to cut off one of his fingers]; as each marries, he cuts them off, they no longer bring money into his house." The loss of a son and his earnings may bring terrible hardships on the parents, and the loss of a daughter and her ability to work in the house (and often bring in money by embroidering) may be severely felt by the mother, but as long as the parents are not destitute, they must struggle along for themselves; they no longer have claim to the resources of the married child. For this reason it has been customary to marry all the daughters before the sons, because if the sons married first it would leave the parents with daughters who are not major wage earners. This is changing somewhat today but it is still preferred if possible.

The father and his married daughter have little to do with one another aside from the usual Sunday visit. Many people claimed that the father relinquishes all claim to his daughter when she marries and turns his protector role over to her husband. Other people say that the father retains this role, which is activated only when the daughter and her husband are having problems. In practice the latter is more often true because the daughter has no one but her father to go to if the husband is abusive or unattentive to the needs of the family. In Australia, where women seldom had fathers nearby, they always said that if their fathers were in the country the husband could not get away with hitting them or spending money foolishly. The father normally lays down certain conditions when the engagement is made, such as "you must never strike my daughter" or "if I hear that you in any way treat my daughter differently than she has been treated in her father's house I will come for you." These are not idle threats and it is these conditions which the daughter activates when there are serious problems with her husband.

The daughter and her mother see one another frequently in the early years of marriage, before too many babies or the ill-health of the mother keep them apart. The daughter depends on her mother for much advice and counsel, and in her role as an adult married woman the daughter may actually be much closer to her mother than she ever was as a girl. In addition, the daughter is free to accept or reject the mother's advice, and this easing of the authority dimension makes her more willing to accept her mother as a human being with problems of her own. Often, however, the friction between them was too great before marriage ever to allow the relationship to develop into something more meaningful. In these cases the daughter pays visits to her mother and may even seek her advice frequently, but they are not close and are in no sense confidants.

Similarly the son and father may come to respect one another, and the son may often go first to his father for advice. But if they were in serious disagreement before his marriage, then this breach is widened after. The son is apt to turn increasingly to his wife's father as the new nuclear family slowly turns it major attention to the former family of the woman. It is often extremely difficult for hard-pressed parents to stop considering their sons as sources of income even though they recognize that such must be the case. If the parents are not willing to completely sever their economic relationship with their married sons, then it is the duty of the sons to do it for them because nothing can stand in the way of the new family. These demands are rarely made on the daughters because it is their husbands who supply the family income and her parents have never had any claim on his earnings.

Two brothers may become closer after marriage even if they were very antagonistic before. Personalities of the sibs play an important part in defining their relations, especially after their marriages because then the formal restraints are lifted. One married respondent of thirty said:

> I am closest to my brother Ciccio because Tonino is only nine-teen, he's too young; Turiddu is too different from me in his judgments, in his thinking, we are just two different people. But Ciccio and I have been close only from the time when I married because before, as the eldest son, I commanded. He had to do what I said and he often didn't like it. He would try to get out from under me, but of course he couldn't and he knew this too. So he resented me and this caused trouble between us. Now it's very different and we get along just fine.

Most often, however, brothers maintain rather formal distant relationships after marriage. Sicilians almost universally say this is because "the foreign sex enters," that is, the wives of the brothers foment trouble and make it impossible for the sibs to be friends. This, to a certain extent, is true because a wife almost has an obligation to separate her husband from anyone who might take something away from the family. But in most cases the wife is only an excuse for the distance which brothers place between themselves. There is a strong Sicilian ethic that brothers should be close and good to one another; when this is not the case then it is convenient to have a wife, an outsider, who can do for the family what her husband should not do: separate the brothers.

Two sisters may or may not be in close contact with one another after marriage but the reasons for friction are different: personality and social status. The husband may occasionally be mentioned as a fomenter of trouble between sisters but he rarely plays an active role. If two sisters were friendly before marriage and if they remain at the same level in the social scale after marriage, then they will continue to be close. The relationship usually becomes even closer through their mutual dependence on one another in the many crises which beset these families. Their children, first cousins, will be friends and the two families will have a great deal of contact thereby cementing the relationship of the two husbands, the brothers-in-law. This extension of the closeness of sisters to the entire family almost never happens in the case of two brothers; if two brothers are close this is as far as the matter goes because their wives have their own families and do not wish to become friendly with their sisters-in-law.

If two sisters were not on good terms before marriage, or if they were but the husband of one is doing markedly better in his job than the other, relations become strained. Where social mobility comes into play, competition is the important element and its influence does not rest with the sisters; husbands and especially the children are drawn into the fray. The nuclear families are now the important units and personal considerations are put aside. The advancement of one family is not only positive for that family, it is by association negative for related families. People do not say only that one sister has done well, they also extend this to say that the other sister has not done well. Here again the advancement of one nuclear family is accomplished at the expense of another, whether expense is calculated in terms of money or prestige. Since among these working-class families prestige can be gained by minor changes in family life, there are very few instances of two married sisters who are on exactly the same social level, at least in their terms. A minute raise in pay, a slightly better piece of land, or the addition of one customer can advance one family and consequently devalue another.

It is apparent by now that brothers and sisters will be extremely fortunate indeed if they have a smooth relationship after their marriages; they are far more likely to have no relationship at all. Contact is kept at a minimum and it is considered quite enough to see one's brother or sister at the parents' home on Sunday afternoon. There is a Sicilian proverb which is used constantly to describe this relationship—"la sora a la batia, lu frate a lu cunventu" (the sister in the convent, the brother in the monastery). This vague proverb is interpreted by the Nicuportese to mean that the sister can stay in her house and the brother can stay in his and they can get along very nicely without one another. If their relationship is relatively good before marriage then they may continue this afterward. The general rule and the general expectation is that sisters and brothers will maintain a cool relationship based on *rispetto* (respect), which is defined by the respondents as "keeping up the appearances." There is a general feeling that brothers and sisters try to remain cool since friction, if it does occur, will almost invariably be crushing and bitter.

The basic fragility of sibling ties, economic rivalry between families in the extended kin group, and the ever-present loyalty to family all militate against closeness among siblings and sometimes cause slights and petty incidents to grow into pitched battles. The most frequent source of these "wars" is the division of property belonging to the family of orientation. A sister who received five acres with a stream is furious because her brother or sister received five acres with a hill or a road; the other complains that he didn't get the stream.

> And so each one thinks he got the worst part and so he is angry at his father and he is angry at his sisters and brothers and so it is no longer a group. From that time on there is this terrible envy and jealousy of the others, and when one gets something that the others don't have, the envy gets worse.

Another respondent who insisted that brothers and sisters are the best of friends after marriage finally ended by saying:

> No, you're not right, brothers and sisters always have a certain respect for each other, even after they are married. Of course, when *interesse* enter then there are problems. And of course there are almost always interests, whether they are about thousands of hectares of land or about a tiny piece too small to be farmed. . . . This splits up the family because each one is concerned with advancing his own new family, and then trouble comes in. They almost never are in agreement, the brothers and sisters.

The Sicilian nuclear family, composed of mother, father, and unmarried children, is the center and the core of the social organization. Each individual's loyalty, devotion, labors, money, and sacrifices are freely and willingly given to further the interests of the family. The individual in return derives his status, prestige, and position in the community from his status, prestige, and position in the family. No one exists without a family, and the socialization techniques employed make it impossible for individuals to exist alone. The unmarried child learns that the world outside the family is dangerous and that outsiders are untrustworthy persons who will harm one if the family is not there for protection. All decisions are made by the parents, and the child is trained to depend upon the group to make his decisions for him: he is too inexperienced, too ignorant of the world, and too fallible to shoulder responsibility alone. This fear is heightened by the value which places responsibility for his acts not on the individual but on the family. It is therefore imperative that the group that will suffer if a mistake is made be the group which makes the decisions.

The outward unity of the family and the dependence of its members on one another does not indicate that relations between them are harmonious. Other factors intervene which set up a series of barriers to an affectively based intimacy. Some of these factors are: male dominance and female submission, age grading, distance between husband and wife, *vergogna*, and the omnipresent loyalty to the family. Many of the disruptive forces are kept under control while the children remain unmarried, but at their marriages relations with parents and siblings usually begin to disintegrate. This process is accelerated by competition between siblings, their wives, and their children.

Married siblings and their parents form the extended family and it can now be seen how and why the tension and division in the larger group came to be. They are not simply the result of marriage or Sicilian inability to form groups. They are instead the logical results of life-long relationships which are formed by the values of the community and intensified by the precarious nature of life in this underdeveloped island. Sicilians have faith only in the family—not in themselves, not in other people, not in the community, not in the nation, and not even in God most of the time.

PART TWO
The Sicilians: Australia

7
AUSTRALIA

Australia is a lucky country run mainly by second-rate people who share its luck. It lives on other people's ideas, and, although its ordinary people are adaptable, most of its leaders (in all fields) so lack curiosity about the events that surround them that they are often taken by surprise. . . . A nation more concerned with styles of life than with achievement has managed to achieve what may be the most evenly prosperous society in the world. It has done this in a social climate largely inimical to originality and ambition (except in sport) and in which there is less and less acclamation of hard work. According to the rules Australia has not deserved its good fortune.

Donald Horne

THE DISCOVERY of Australia is credited to Captain James Cook who in 1770 landed on the coast of the present New South Wales near the city of Sydney. Britain acquired possession of the continent because it was in need of new lands following the loss of the American colonies in 1776. After 1787 these new lands were required to accommodate criminals sentenced to deportation or transportation. New South Wales was declared a British crown colony in 1824, and 1821 marked the beginning of assisted immigrant passage schemes which were later to play a large part in the populating of the continent.

In 1840 transportation of convicts was abolished. Eleven years later gold was discovered in New South Wales and Victoria, which became a crown colony the same year. Responsible government was granted to the colonies of New South Wales, Victoria, South Australia, and Tasmania; in 1859 Queensland was established as a separate colony, and in 1890 Western Australia was granted responsible government. The Commonwealth of Australia was proclaimed in 1901 as a federal republic consisting of six states and a federally controlled territory in the north. This form of government has continued to the present.

Australia is an island continent about the same size as the United States (excluding Alaska) and more than three times the size of India. The climate is generally mild on the northern coast, tropical in the part which lies north of the Tropic of Capricorn (almost two-fifths of the total land area), and torrid and uninhabitable on the great inland deserts. The country, its history, and its people have been and still are affected by a severe scarcity of water. Australia is the driest land mass in the world. This shortage of easily cultivable land has kept people near the coast and is responsible for making Australia "one of the most highly urbanized and industrialized countries in the world. Almost four-fifths of our population live in urban areas" (Borrie 1957, p. 17). According to the 1961 census, 56 percent of the population live in the five capital cities of the mainland. Only 17 percent of all Australians live in rural areas. Australia which in 1960 ranked fortieth in population size in the world (10,508,191) has two of the world's forty largest cities, Sydney (2,215,970) and Melbourne (1,956,400).

In 1914 Australia was a primary producer of wool and to a lesser extent of cereals, dairy products, meat, and fruit; manufactures accounted for 27 percent of net worth (Barnard 1962, p. 496). By 1920 one man in five was employed in manufacturing and there were 16,291 factories. The 1950 census revealed that 30 percent of the total work force was employed in manufacturing whereas only 13 percent were engaged in agriculture. The number of factory employees doubled between 1939 and 1959, and unemployment has averaged 1 percent, far less than the average in the United States.

Australia today ranks tenth in total world exports, eighth in per capita exports. "Australians eat more meat, fruit, cereals, and sugar than either Americans or Britons. There are twenty-four motor cars and sixty radios for every one hundred people. . . . Australia follows the United States and Canada on the list of countries with the highest level of individual prosperity" (Younger 1963, p. 6).

THE LITERATURE

Although there are few scholarly studies of Australian society, there are any number of books on the subject, mainly collections of articles by observers. Australia is urban, homeowning (60 percent of the population own their own homes), and middle-class (over one-fourth of the population is engaged in white-collar occupations) and "over half the population feels it belongs to the middle class, which is higher than in either America (42%) or Britain (35%)" (McGregor 1966, p. 21). Sports are the main recreational outlet for much of the population and Australians have long excelled in world competition swimming and tennis, a not inconsiderable achievement considering the size of the population.

Australians are characterized as egalitarian, easygoing, and "second-rate" because they are willing to leave the management of business and government in the hands of experienced professionals so that they may enjoy their leisure time:

His values are unique. He does not want to be a capitalist. He is satisfied with a reasonable standard of living, with leisure to do what he likes. He does not often attend union meetings. If his vote is required, a stop-work meeting will be called because it seems a pity to waste his evenings. [Eggleston 1953, pp. 12–14]

Australians in general are content to live the good life with an undemanding job, a house in the suburbs, a family, and enough money to enjoy the limited amusements which appeal to them. There is no urgency to excel or to get ahead.

Advancement in business is not highly valued and neither is education: A boy with a father in a higher administrative job has fifteen times the chance of going to a university . . . than one whose father is a semiskilled or unskilled worker. And Commonwealth university scholarships, so far from getting rid of these inequalities, tend to go to children from wealthier families . . . in a single year . . . 33 per cent of the young men leaving school came from unskilled or semiskilled backgrounds, [of these] only 1.5 per cent entered university. In contrast, though only 2 per cent of the male school leavers came from a university background, 35.9 per cent went on to university. . . . A 1964 survey of the proportion of students educated to senior secondary and tertiary level in twenty European countries, the United States, Canada and Australia, showed that Australia was only twelfth on the list. The United States educated 66.2 per cent of those in the 15–19 age group, the Soviet Union 48.6 per cent, and Australia only 20.3 per cent. [McGregor 1966, pp. 356–58]

Although important, it would be difficult to give a detailed account of the Australian family, because

the Australian family is a subject which until now has escaped the serious attention of scholars in this country. The explanation undoubtedly lies in part in the fact that there have been few departments in our universities concerned with training in disciplines appropriate to this field of research. . . . Such observations as have been made upon the family—as upon many other of our social institutions—have too often been at levels of generalization that have not probed below the rather obvious surface. [Borrie 1957, p. 1]

While this statement by Borrie, the most eminent of the senior social scientists in Australia, is still true today, there are a few studies of the Australian family which present quite surprising findings (Davies and Encel 1965; Elkin 1957). In general it would be correct to say that the Australian family is very similar to the British family and the American family in its general kinship system, terminology, role relationships, power structure, values, and norms; however, there are differences which are only today becoming somewhat clear. It is of course an oversimplification to speak of the "Australian family," since there are many kinds of Australian families based on such factors as residence, occupation, and class—working class, middle class, country aristocracy, and "squattocracy"—but it is still not possible to distinguish between the kinds of families or even to ascertain how many there are. Australian social scientists have not devoted themselves to this kind of research: anthropologists work with aborigines or New Guinea natives, and sociologists have concentrated on immigrants, which is a real loss because a comparison of working-class families in England, the United States, and Australia, for instance, would be extremely enlightening both for the similarities and for the differences. One can say now that the Australian working-class family is somewhat like the British working-class family (see Young and Wilmott 1962) and the American working-class family (see Rainwater 1959; Komarovsky 1967), with some features which are peculiarly Australian. However, this does not tell us what the family is like and there are very few studies of working-class families in Australia to date. Those researches which do exist have been carried out almost entirely with middle-class families and even here the sample size is usually so small and the scope of the study so restricted that it is misleading and even dangerous to extend the conclusions to a wider portion of the population.

Fallding (1957) surveyed thirty-eight Sydney families: twenty professional and eighteen in the trades. He found that all these families retain close contact and intimacy with spouses' parents, but other relatives were not seen often, nor was intimacy great. Neither were these families involved with neighbors and neighborhood activities: "Most people preferred to 'keep to themselves' rather than have their neighbors 'tell them what to do'" (p. 57). Husband-wife relations were much more egalitarian in the professional families; one-half of them reported a partnership in the management of family affairs while only three of the eighteen working-class families reported the same.

Several Australian researchers have used the Day at Home questionnaire designed by Herbst and first used by him in Melbourne in 1952 (Adler 1965, p. 149). This interview schedule, which is administered to school children, explores the interaction of family members in their everyday pursuits and is aimed at the various facets of the husband-wife relationship as seen through the eyes of children. Since that time the same questionnaire has been used by Taft in Perth, Bollman in Brisbane, and by Adler and Cooper in two California communities; it was translated into Spanish and administered by Cooper in Guadalajara, Mexico (Adler 1965, pp. 150–51). The most striking observation from the Australian studies is the importance of the mother in actions and in decision making; this is so marked that it has been termed "matriduxy" by Adler. A comparison of the Australian, Mexican, and American families reveals that matriduxy does not occur in the Mexican family, characterizes the American pattern to some extent, and is most marked in the Australian family. However, Adler adds,

> the differences between Australian and American culture are placed into sharp focus by the preponderance of *co-operative* interactions in the American group and their negligible occurrence among the Australians. Further, if we compare (in our samples) the *participation* of American and Australian fathers in their respective family regions we find that 90 per cent of the Americans, but none of the Australians, take part in all or all but one of these regions. . . . Thus in the Australian family, the mother plays a strong leadership role in the absence of full father participation. In the American family, where co-operative patterns predominate, the mother-leadership role is less strong. . . . [pp. 153–54]

This is fascinating material which was most surprising to Australians who pride themselves on male-oriented homes. Although little detail is given, one is reminded of the Young and Wilmott study in London with the mother-centered and directed homes. Anyone who has spent time in Australia will naturally tie this entire configuration into the mateship syndrome (also unstudied) which prevails not only in the working class but extends to the middle and even the professional class. Australians themselves refer to "weekday professionals" who, like their working-class counterparts, gather in the pubs after work and enjoy sporting activities on the weekends. The entire question of the Australian family and the Australian way of life needs serious attention from social scientists.

Australian Immigration

Australia, like the United States, Canada, and Israel, is an immigrant country, that is, it has been formed and its structure has been influenced by a continual flow of immigrants from Europe and Asia. Although no other country equals the United States in number of immigrants received, the ratio of immigrants to total population is high in the three mentioned above as well as in countries such as New Zealand, Argentina, and Brazil. The first major immigration to Australia occurred in 1788 when Captain Phillip landed at Botany Bay with 1,500 persons, nearly 800 of whom were convicts. Colonization by free and imprisoned people continued, and by 1850 the population had increased to 405,800. The great immigration waves occurred in the 1850s, 1880s, and 1950s thereby increasing the population to almost 11 million in the 1960s. Immigrants were drawn mainly from Great Britain as a result of a government policy to restrict immigration to those English-speaking peoples who would, it was felt, fit in best and assimilate most quickly and easily. Native tribesmen who could not be physically excluded are symbolically excluded, even now: "the population of each of the states and of the federally-controlled territories at the census of June 30, 1961 (excluding full-blood aborigines) . . . ."

In 1891 the total Australian population was a little over 3 million; 68 percent were born in Australia mainly of British stock, 26 percent were born in Great Britain, and 6 percent were of other foreign origin—the six main groups being French, German, Norwegian-Swedish, Danish, Italian, and Chinese. By 1961 the Australian population had grown to 10,508,186: according to the census in that year 83 percent were Australian born, 12 percent were British born, and the most numerous other foreign-born were Italian (154,026), Dutch (75,762), Greek (60,883), German (60,477), Yugoslav (27,396), Polish (22,417), Hungarian (14,-000), and Ukranian (5,029). The change in the pattern of immigration is apparent as southern and eastern Europeans replaced northern Europeans, and immigrants from Britain occupy a much diminished place. It is not possible to state with accuracy how many Sicilians have entered Australia nor how many today reside in that country, but on the basis of prior sociological estimates, approximately one-fifth of the total Italian population would be Sicilian. Using the 1961 census figure given above for Italian-born residents, that would mean there are about 31,000 Sicilians living in Australia.

Australia has from its earliest years pursued a policy of directed immigration beginning with the famous, or infamous, White Australia policy which restricts the entry of permanent residents on the basis of race or skin color. There has never been a written law regarding this exclusion but its presence is well known and well thought of by the majority of Australians. For example, thousands of Chinese were admitted in the country to serve as laborers during the gold rush period, resulting in a Chinese population of 40,000 in Melbourne alone in 1857; however

> by pursuing a rigid, racialist and exclusivist White Australia policy they have managed to reduce the permanent Asian minority in their midst from 3.5 per cent in 1861 to 0.348 per cent a century later—and the figure would be smaller still were it not swollen by the presence of Asian students studying in Australian universities. . . . [McGregor 1966, p. 301]

Although the Australian government has never set up a system of quotas by statute as has the United States, it has always had an administrative quota system, which is

> fixed under some general statutory power enabling the executive to control immigration by whatever administrative devices it thinks best. The statutory quota has the advantage of publicity and the disadvantage of rigidity: the administrative quotas are much more flexible but they sometimes lack much publicity. Quotas imposed by Australia have always been administrative, and their existence has not always been realized. [Price 1963, p. 87]

As thinking about immigration and immigrants changed so have the quotas which restricted or permitted the entrance of southern Europeans. At times there was virtually no restriction; at others, sponsors or sums of money or both were required. There have even been periods when Greeks, Maltese, or Italians were forbidden to enter under any conditions. Thus from 1890 to 1940 only 25,680 Italians, including 3,915 Sicilians, entered Australia (Price 1963, pp. 18–20), whereas in the year 1952 over thirty thousand Italians immigrated to Australia (yearly bulletin, Commonwealth Bureau of Census and Statistics). The difference between the prewar and the postwar figures are of course not entirely the effect of government policies; Price notes that government control was relatively unimportant and that the personal desires of the immigrants played a much more important role in influencing a desire to emigrate to Australia (1963, p. 100).

The Australian government has since its earliest days assisted migrants to Australia since the long voyage is so costly. This assistance is usually in the form of free passage to Australia and return after two years if requested, plus help with finding jobs, homes, and so forth in the early period of arrival. Less than one-third of the southern Europeans have received any assistance from the Australian government; between 1945 and 1962 approximately 115,000 were assisted and 270,000 were not (Price 1963, p. 99). Price does not discuss government policy in this matter; however, not one of the several thousand Sicilians that I encountered or heard of during my research had been assisted, and a confidential Italian government source stated that Italians south of Rome have systematically been denied assistance by the Australian government. This statement may or may not be true, but Price and others note that the government has always given preferential treatment to northern Italians in the belief that they are more like Australians and will therefore fit in better.

Also relevant to the treatment of immigrants is the internment policy that was followed by the Australian government during World War II. The subject has remained veiled under the Official War Secrets Act, and the sole mention of the subject among numerous histories of Australia is the following:

> Whilst enemy aliens were interned, neutral aliens were for the most part drafted into the Civil Construction Corps. . . . [Barnard 1962, p. 570]

Price, an Australian sociologist, also mentions it:

> During World War II ultra-patriotic feelings again boiled to the surface, and led to large-scale internment of Italians in most states of the Commonwealth. While wholesale incarceration was quite understandable in the early days of the Japanese invasion threat, continued internment later on arose very largely from suspicion of unassimilated alien groups and failure to understand the process of immigration. . . . [1963, p. 214]

The internment was carried out hastily and in a panicky state which led government officials to round up members of all clubs which were suspected of treasonous activities and to pick up individuals who were reported, often anonymously, as enemy agents. Many thousands of Italians were taken out to the middle of the Queensland desert and left there in shabby camps for the duration of the war; others were allowed to return after their names had been cleared. Many Italian men had been forced to join the Overseas Fascist party in order to bring their wives and children later. After the arrival of their families, though often no longer members, these men were picked up. Several people reported that this scare was used by some persons to get rid of people they did not like and did not want around. Usually only husbands were taken, which left wives with small children to support themselves as best they could. Many second-generation adults remarked that they remembered no parents or home life when they were growing up because the father had been interned and the mother was running the shop. In one case the husband and one son were interned while the other son was drafted into the Australian army. The wife died during the war and at her funeral in Sydney the husband and son were on one side of the coffin surrounded by armed guards while the other son was on the other side of the body in an Australian uniform. The old man has never recovered from this experience and many immigrants remain deeply bitter about such callous treatment of men who were citizens of Australia at the time of the war. Others are cynically humorous and one very old man, when asked if he belonged to any clubs or organizations, replied, "Not me! I did it once and landed in jail for five years. I don't join anything."

The "New Australians," a government-coined term, are today welcomed by the government but merely tolerated by the old Australians because:

> Trade union pride and prejudice apart, most Australians have always tended to patronize, perhaps even to be contemptuous of non-British peoples, their institutions and ways. They have been proud that the Australian community is "98 per cent British," convinced that their own country is the "best in the world," and are apt especially to be conscious of their superiority over eastern and southern Europeans. [Partridge 1955, p. 408]

Since the early sixties Australia, which is so isolated from the rest of the world that Sydney receives fewer visitors from abroad in a year than Paris does in a week (Younger 1963, p. 6), has been committed to a vigorous policy of recruitment of peoples from southern Europe. There is no doubt that the postwar influx of immigrants has started alterations in Australian thought and custom which should continue in the future.

The prewar immigrants arrived in an Australia which bears little resemblance to the country today. Australia was a primary producer of meat and wool, and industry throughout the entire country employed only 28 percent of the male work force. Sydney was small and its customs were those of "home"—England. There was work for everyone but a somewhat stagnant economy limited the number of construction and unskilled factory jobs suitable for unskilled, non-English-speaking immigrants. Australians had not developed any kind of response in dealing with non-Anglo-Saxon peoples, and the southern European immigrants were pushed into their own ethnic worlds. That it was possible for them to associate with Australians is shown by the experiences of one respondent, but it was not easy. Lack of work, continued feelings of strangeness, and a severe government internment policy during the war made the lot of the early immigrants a hard one, though there were some compensations.

The immediate postwar immigrants arrived in the midst of the most ambitious government campaign to attract non-British immigrants ever known in Australia. A booming economy, rapidly growing industry, and a need for manpower in a seriously underpopulated country all made the Australia of 1950 or 1952 an almost ideal period in which to enter. In addition, the vast numbers of immigrants and displaced persons made the personal climate more welcoming to the immigrant who for once was surrounded by other foreigners.

The past ten years have seen a continued growth in the Australian economy; there are jobs for everyone, wages are high, and social services are good. The attitude of Australians has undergone another change. There is an acknowledged need for manpower, accompanied by a related questioning of which peoples are best for Australia. Southern Europeans rank low on national prestige scales, and Italians rank lowest of all. Australians feel they do not fit in or are not becoming Australian-like. They have their own way of life, and even though the New Australians are good workers and loyal citizens, they are "different" and in Australia, more than in most immigrant countries, this is not a good thing. One English migrant noted that in order to get along well in Australia one must assume a real or artificial attitude that "the worst thing in your whole life is the fact that you were not born an Australian."

Very few people are openly nasty or hostile to immigrants, but there is little tolerance for differences. The skills that Americans over the course of almost two hundred years have picked up quite unknown to themselves are nonexistent in Australia; people who do not speak Australian-English talk "funny" or "ugly" (as my own accent was once characterized), and Australians are not able to understand persons who speak with accents different from their own. A Scottish immigrant with a very strong accent who had spent several years in the United States remarked:

> Do you know that Americans can always understand me but Australians never can? And the reason is because Americans know how to listen to foreigners and they feel an obligation to understand while the Aussies don't know how to listen past the accent, and

132

they always feel that it's the obligation of the foreigner to change his way of talking, not the obligation of the Australians to help him be understood.

New Australians are, with this label, permanently branded as different from old Australians. One very old Sicilian talked in a derogatory way about Sicilian New Australians and when asked if he too was not one, replied with vehemence, "I was a dago and now I'm an Australian because you can learn not to be a dago but you never can do anything to learn not to be a New Australian." The immigrants feel this exclusion very strongly and almost universally prefer pejoratives such as "wop" or "oil-eater" to the more neutral, but much more damaging, term endorsed by the government. One educated immigrant related that on a trip to the United States he was in a taxi in Buffalo, New York, and the driver told him about the thousands of Poles, Italians, and Germans in the city. The respondent then asked, "But where are all the Americans?" The driver stopped the cab, turned around and said, "Why, we're all Americans, man, all of us." This Sydney Sicilian, who had earlier changed his name from Giuseppe to Joseph, returned to Australia with a new sense of his own worth and changed his name back to Giuseppe. Acceptance is possible if the foreigner is willing to divest himself of anything and everything which marks him as different from the "mob."

The Australian Study

Forty-eight respondents, forty-five men and three women, were asked identical questions in two separate interviewing sessions. The two interview schedules (see Appendix A) were used only in Australia; the first was designed to elicit information on the emigration experience and on socioeconomic variables such as education and occupation; the second was drawn up to secure information regarding family, friends, and satisfaction with life in Australia. The responses to each question were coded and percentage distributions were made for group totals. Distributions for thirteen important socioeconomic characteristics are shown on table 3. The sample of first-generation Sicilian immigrants reveals a great deal of diversity on all the variables. This was the purpose in accordance with the social change hypotheses which were to be tested in the field. This is not the usual "group" of immigrants who live in an ethnic ghetto and are for the most part in working-class jobs necessitated by the peasant uneducated background. Although the sample is small, so much is known about

TABLE 3
SOCIOECONOMIC CHARACTERISTICS OF THE SAMPLE
(In Percent)

Birthplace		Years in Australia and period of immigration	
Western Sicily	40	1–11 (later postwar, 1954–64)	27
Eastern coastal Sicily	37	13–17 (immediate postwar, 1948–52)	38
Lipari Islands	23	26–57 (pre–World War II, 1908–39)	35
Number of children in family of orientation		**Number of children in family of procreation**	
One or two	10	None (unmarried respondents)	8
Three to five	46	One or two	52
Six to eight	44	Three or four	31
		Five or six	8
Education		**Marital status, 1965**	
Five years or less	67	Unmarried	8
High school graduate	21	Married	84
University graduate	12	Widowed	8
Travel before emigration		**Ethnicity of spouse**	
None	64	Sicilian-born	63
Residence in Italy, 2–10 yrs.	17	Australian-born Sicilian	23
Extensive travel (Europe, Africa)	19	Australian	6
		(Unmarried)	8
Own and father's occupation in Sicily		**Occupation in Australia**	
Professional-managerial	12	Professional-managerial	15
White collar	21	White collar	23
Blue collar	67	Blue collar	62
Age at emigration		**Age at interview, 1965**	
13–20	33	21–36	30
21–25	33	37–50	35
26–56	33	51–77	35
		Household composition, 1965	
		Nuclear family	66
		Nuclear family plus relatives	19
		Other (alone, with boarder, etc.)	15

the individuals in it that the relevance of particular variables to change can be tested with some degree of accuracy and precision, and in addition other, heretofore unknown, findings might emerge.

Bivariate frequency distributions of each of the dependent

variables were obtained against the four independent variables—age at emigration, time in Australia, education, and occupational mobility—and the chi-square significance test was applied. The probabilities of these distributions were determined. Distributions with a p value greater than .05 are omitted from the following analysis. For over fifty questions, or dependent variables, it is possible to give the distribution of answers within the total group and to note which, if any, of the four independent variables were significantly associated with dependent variables and to indicate the direction of change. Chi-square results are given in Appendix B. By utilizing a diversified sample of forty-eight immigrants it is possible to indicate with some degree of precision who within the total group is changing, what the direction of the change is, and with the help of a full understanding of Sicilian social structure, the reasons for group and subgroup patterns as they emerge.

AGE AT EMIGRATION

There are psychological and sociological hypotheses which claim that ideas and habits which are learned early in life are the most resistant to change. Speech patterns and food habits are two examples of such integrated idea-habit patterns although there are many others. It follows then that changes which are introduced early in the life of an individual will receive a more open acceptance than changes which come after the individual has matured or reached old age. This is borne out in studies of language learning and while all the possible consequences of early relearning have not been detailed, it is still fair to assume that the principle holds in most of the major areas of life. It was therefore hypothesized that the younger the individual at emigration the easier it would be to make changes in values and behavior and, conversely, the older the emigrant the more difficult such changes would become. If there were no other intruding factors we would expect persons who emigrated young to be more changed than those who were older; there would be a high correlation between age at emigration and change. To be sure, there are other intrusive factors in the life situation of every individual and a one-to-one correlation which is theoretically possible was not postulated, but there was a chance that the younger emigrants might show a tendency to accept new ideas and new habits, and if the tendency was strong enough to influence the life of the individual, then the results should be apparent.

The age at emigration of subjects in the sample was 13 years to 56 years, but the forty-eight respondents fell into a natural three-part division: 13 to 20 years of age, sixteen respondents; 21 to 25 years, sixteen respondents; and 26 to 56 years, sixteen respondents (only one in this last group was over 39). This means that the middle group spans fewer years than the other two but this is a reflection of the fact that approximately one-third of the emigrants were in their early twenties. However, this distribution does give us a group of adolescents, a group of young adults, and a group of older and middle-age adults which should permit differences in age groups to be revealed.

TIME IN AUSTRALIA

Time is often mentioned, though seldom tested, as a factor in the rate and depth of change, that is, the longer the individual has been exposed to new factors the more factors he will incorporate into his own life. This hypothesis is applicable to any situation in which an individual is exposed to a new and different social structure, such as a university, the army, or a religious order and is not reserved solely for instances of change by immigration. Therefore, ignoring all other possible influences (age, sex, education) we concentrate on the number of years that the immigrant has lived in the new country and anticipate that those who have been in Australia longer will be more changed whereas new arrivals will show few signs of change. This is a variable readily tested because it is only necessary to have a set of individuals who emigrated between x number of years ago and y number of years ago and the differences between the individuals at the two extremes will give us the amount of change. Other factors, such as age at emigration, are tested separately, but if there is a very high correlation between any or all of these four variables, then the patterns they reveal should be very similar.

The sample has not been divided evenly according to number of years; instead there are three groups: 1 to 11 years in Australia, thirteen respondents; 13 to 17 years, eighteen respondents; and 26 to 57 years, seventeen respondents. It would have been preferable to have had four groups with fewer respondents in the 13–17 year group and to make two groups of the 26–57 year category. However, the division used is a reflection of the rate and period of immigration for Italians in Australia because there was no immigration between 1939 and 1947, the period of World War II, and the rate of emigration from Italy soared in the immediate post-war period. However, the actual distribution is not so skewed as to hide or disturb any major trends caused by time as an independent variable.

Many immigrants in Australia have little or no schooling, but Sicilians in Australia often have a fair amount of education. Education for these immigrants is correlated very highly with social class in Sicily, as we would expect in a static and near-feudal, agriculturally based society. This variable therefore is really two combined variables—education in Sicily and social class in Sicily. Educated men and women can understand, ask why, and think through for themselves new customs and new ideas. The illiterate peasant on the other hand is mystified, confused, and can become belligerent when confronted with new ideas and customs, as so much of the sociological literature on disorganization in immigrant communities shows (see, for instance, Thomas and Znaniecki 1918). My own experience in Sicily led me to believe that uneducated people frequently cannot understand new ideas and take refuge in defensive stands which glorify the known and degrade the unknown. Educated individuals often do not like new things they hear about, they may be passionate defenders of their own ways, but they do understand what they hear and see. Their defense is based on intelligent comparison, whereas the uneducated defense is based on ignorance, a sense of inferiority, and fear of the unknown. It is my contention that if a person rejects a new idea because he does not like it for a particular reason he is more apt to finally test the idea and then begin to use it until it becomes a part of him. However, if the idea is rejected because it is not understood, then it is unlikely that a test will ever be attempted and the idea will remain unknown and unused.

One topic under constant discussion in Sicily furnishes a perfect example of the difference between the educated and the uneducated, and convinced me that there would be major differences in the change patterns of these two groups. Divorce was against the law in Italy at that time and the American divorce rate was the subject of almost daily discussion among the Sicilians in Nicuportu. The uneducated claimed that it is a mortal sin to secure a divorce. I explained at length that the civil law and the religious law are separate in the United States while they are joined in Italy, and that a civil divorce has no effect on the religious standing of a person unless a remarriage takes place. No one understood the fundamental difference. The educated, however, while most did not approve of divorce, did listen and did understand and never used this particular argument again. They had been trained at school as well as in their middle-class homes to listen, to discuss, and to think and this they do in their daily lives. It seemed most unlikely that these differences would not carry over into a new social environment.

The sample of forty-eight immigrants in Sydney included six university graduates and ten graduates of either the classical *liceo* or very specialized highly regarded high schools such as the Merchant Marine Academy. The two groups were combined because there were so few university graduates that no meaningful statistical tests could be run and also because a careful examination of their responses revealed no significant differences. The university graduates might be somewhat better read though not necessarily because the broad liberal arts training in Italy is received in high school and the university is reserved for a specialization. All six graduates specialized in law or philosophy. The thirty-two "uneducated" immigrants have five years of school or less. Most can read but only with difficulty (except for a few who read a great deal). Elementary education ends at the fifth grade in Italy and although most respondents left school to work, many had to stop because their small *paesi* had elementary school only and there was no opportunity to go away to high school.

OCCUPATIONAL MOBILITY

This is a variable which I did not anticipate in Sicily. It was not until I had administered about twenty interviews in Australia that I began to see that these individuals were different. I did not even realize for a long time what the uniting feature was because in many respects the socioeconomic characteristics of individuals in the group of the occupationally mobile are very different. Occupational mobility is not usually a one-dimensional variable because most people do not advance in their jobs simply for the sake of the job. Rather there are social, economic, and personal motives which drive some individuals to succeed and to improve their standard of living. Some men may wish to advance occupationally because they desire more money, others may want power or social prestige, but there are certain traits common to the majority who can be classed "occupationally mobile." First, these individuals are not content with their given or present lot in life: they wish to maximize their access to the "good things of life," however these are defined. Second, they are individuals who do not look down and accept; they look around them, they see other people and other ways of living and for whatever reason they too wish to have what they see. Third, they are people who become expert at seeing opportunity when it presents itself, even in its most vague form. In sum, they want more out of life, but they do not necessarily wish to change their personal or private lives in order to get more: in many cases they want life to be better, not different.

Occupational mobility means that an individual has moved from a job which is considered by the general public to be lower in status than others to a position which is higher than that held previously. The man who begins his working life as a department store clerk and ends as president of that store has been occupationally mobile. If this mobility has been accompanied by changes in his life style, residence, friends, and associations, then we can say that he has been socially mobile as well. The situation with immigrants, at least with this sample of immigrants, is somewhat complicated by the fact that all of the respondents began their life in Australia at common laboring jobs and therefore all have been occupationally mobile since none are still in this lowest of working-class categories. Using this as a measure of mobility would defeat the purpose of such a category. But if an estimate could be made concerning how much mobility had occurred from the last job in Sicily to present position in Australia, then there were some very definite signs of occupational mobility both in the middle-class and in the working-class groups.

In Sicily the immigrants were either working class—peasants, artisans, or fishermen—or they were white collar—such as bank clerks, journalists, steel salesmen, drug detailers, and owners of small factories. The social classes in Sicily are fairly well defined, especially when interclass differences are considered, and there is no argument about the fact that some jobs are middle class while others are below this. The restricted range of jobs in Sicily makes this task much simpler than it would be in an industrialized area such as Turin or Milan.

To ascertain the relative order of prestige of occupations, I first used a survey by Congalton (1962) in Sydney in which people were asked to rate the prestige of a selected sample of occupations. However, since this survey dealt with a restricted number of occupations and did not contain many jobs which are represented in the present sample, I used the NORC occupational prestige scale (Reiss 1961) and made a list of both the Australian and the American ratings for the eleven jobs which appeared in both samples. With this list the Pearson product moment correlation and the rank-order correlation were applied, and correlations of .92 for the former and .97 for the latter were obtained. The high correlations between the relative prestige of a selected list of occupations in the two countries showed that the American prestige scale, which is much more comprehensive and which includes all the occupations represented in the sample of immigrants, could be used alone.

Last occupation in Sicily was then correlated with present occupation in Sydney to find those individuals who have advanced occupationally above the Sicilian level. This meant of course that all individuals so designated had gone through an interim period on arrival in Australia in which they held laboring jobs of the grimiest sort—the first job of one university graduate, for instance, was cleaning up in a slaughter house. Using this method, it was determined that fourteen immigrants had advanced occupationally in Australia, thirty-two remained at their pre-emigration level, and two dropped below it. Table 4 lists the fourteen occupationally mobile with their Sicilian and Australian occupations,

TABLE 4

SOCIOECONOMIC CHARACTERISTICS OF OCCUPATIONALLY MOBILE
IMMIGRANTS

Sicilian Occupation	Australian Occupation[1]	Education[2]	Years in Australia
Journalist	Psychiatrist	U	14
Steel sales	Owner, large const. company	U	15
Owner, fish processing plant	Officer, Italian government	U	16
Bank clerk	Executive, advertising	U	15
Drug detailer	Officer, Italian government	U	15
Shoemaker	C.P.A.	UE	28
Domestic	Medical assistant	HS	12
Peasant	University student	University	5
Clerk	Executive, industrial corp.	HS	37
Mechanic	Owner, garages, motorsales	HS	29
Barber	Owner, real estate	3 yrs.	27
Carpenter	Owner, small factory	5 yrs.	30
Contadino	Draftsman	1 yr.	8
Contadino	Real estate sales	5 yrs.	13

[1] Australian occupations have been altered to preserve the anonymity of individuals, but substitutions have been carefully chosen to retain socioeconomic characteristics.
[2] U = university graduate   UE = university equivalent   HS = high school

140

education, and years in Australia. The job pattern of these individuals is very unlike that of the nonmobile immigrants: it is characterized by frequent job changing in the early years in Australia and by a tendency to look, observe, and then act, even against sound advice, when the opportunity seemed right.

8

THE EMIGRATION
EXPERIENCE

*Away from Sicily they have the same life as here, but there the
husband works all the time and nothing will change because they
emigrate for economic reasons only and not to have a new life—
only a better one.*

Nicuportu respondent

WITH the exception of Eisenstadt (1954) very few writers have
explored the significance of the emigration experience itself. There
is instead an assumption that the periods immediately before and
immediately after emigration are eventful but meaningless to
later ideas, attitudes, or changes. Emigrating is not the same as
taking a trip. It is not even the same as going to live in a foreign
country for a year or two; it is, rather, a wrenching traumatic
experience touching every facet of an individual's thoughts and
feelings, whether that person is a sophisticated cosmopolite or an
illiterate peasant. One knows or expects that the move is permanent: friends, family, familiar surroundings, and a comfortable—
if disliked—way of life are being put behind one for an unknown
world peopled by strangers who have different ideas and customs.
No matter how much one dislikes one's life, no matter how terrible
life may be, it is still a blow to undergo the emigration experience.
To discover if pre-emigration preparation and immediate postimmigration impressions had any relation to later changes, the
immigrants were asked a series of questions about these two inter-
locking periods.

Four questions were asked concerning preparations for leaving
Sicily: (1) Why did you emigrate? (2) Was Australia your first
choice as country of emigration? (3) Why did you emigrate *x*
years ago? Why not before? Why at that point? (4) Did you plan
to stay permanently in Australia?

Most studies of immigrants assume that the ordinary immigrant

142

(as opposed to special types such as political refugees) emigrated to have a better life. Social historians, such as Handlin, have stated that most European immigrants to the United States came as a direct result of famines, droughts, and waves of pestilence; life in the small rural European villages was so terrible that anything was preferable to the thought of an early and miserable death. This point of view is no doubt true for many immigrants, but it is not valid for all—or even for the majority. In this study, 50 percent said they emigrated to advance themselves or their children; 37 percent to have a better life through the acquisition of material possessions such as a house, car, television set, and refrigerator; and 13 percent emigrated for idiosyncratic reasons, such as loss of business, disgust with government, chance to join children, or desire to learn English. Educated individuals emigrated to satisfy some personal desire or whim; the occupationally mobile emigrated to advance themselves and their children socially, occupationally, and educationally; uneducated, low mobility individuals emigrated to Australia to gain possessions, such as cars and houses, that make life more comfortable.

The first set of reasons cannot be argued with because they are so personal, the second fit well with middle-class American ideas about advancing oneself and getting ahead, but the third category which relies so heavily on money and material satisfactions, often dismays educated middle-class individuals. They feel that the better and more enduring intangibles such as freedom, personal liberty, education, culture, and understanding are the true valuables of our world today, and they cannot understand the extraordinary emphasis placed upon "things" by these and many other immigrants. But this emphasis is easier to understand in the light of their previous hardships and agonizing struggles for which there were no rewards, tangible or intangible, at the end of the day or in old age. I quote in full the statement made by one of the uneducated immigrants who came to Australia for these reasons:

> Usually I was a coffee bar man in a cafe in Palermo, and in my little home town. And then because there was never enough money in my family I had to find some heavier work which paid more because my father was dead early and that is the very worst thing which can ever happen there. So I went to work in the grain storage bins carrying sacks of grain, loading, things like that. It was brutal work but it paid $1.50 a day. It was hard but necessary. That money, it seems like nothing here, but it was pretty good there. In the bar they paid $22.00 a month with board and room and you worked

trom 6 A.M. to 1 A.M. In the grain bins I worked seven days a
week. Then I worked at the threshing with a hand flail in the
season; that work was even worse under that scalding sun. But it
was all necessary to better our situation. We had nothing, understand? Nothing! My mother opened a little store which sold everything, and we had a very little restaurant, but those only brought
in a few lire a day—and there were six of us kids. We never had
garbage, we ate it. And most of the time the noon dinner was a
little pasta with a lot of water and then at night some dry bread.
But often I would give my piece of bread to my little sister who
had to have it. No one who has not seen it can know what that
kind of life is like. You work to the death, every day is so long
with hard work and suffering and then when you are finished you
have a few lire in your hand and you know it's not enough. The
Australians can never understand us until they understand this.

This not untypical statement epitomizes the entire economic way
of life of working-class Sicilians; it may not always be so desperate,
but even when there is enough pasta their plight is not much
relieved, because of the almost universal drudgery, physical
exhaustion, uncertainty, and above all the knowledge that the
pittance paid at the end of the day is just not enough for more
than survival.

The largest group consists of those who emigrated to advance
themselves and have a better future, which for most includes
education, a professional occupation, and a certain sense of refinement. The latter is extremely important to Sicilians, who use the
term "illiterate" (analfabeta) to refer not to a man who cannot
read and write, but rather to a person who is "uncouth, rough,
ignorant, and who does not know how to present himself
[presentarsi]." Many of the immigrants in the contadino and
artigiano category left Sicily not because they did not have work
(most did), but because the work they had did not satisfy them:

I had a pretty steady job in Sicily on a construction gang after I
left farm work but it wasn't interesting and it was making me
mentally an old man. So I decided to leave and have the opportunity
to do something special which would open my mind and at the
same time give me enough money to allow my children to go to the
university so that they will be able to choose work which is
interesting to them and not be forced to take the only thing which
is open to them.

The data do not specify which individuals did not have enough
work and which, as above, had work but found it unsatisfying.
I believe now that this is very important to later changes in
values and attitudes because for those persons on whom I do have
such specific information, a real difference between the two types

appears in their goals and in their perceptions of how to attain them. The immigrant literature assumes that working-class immigrants left because they were lacking something quantitative—bread, work, etc.—whereas these data suggest that many individuals left because their lives were not qualitatively satisfactory. It may well be that those who left because there was not enough work are those who will be fully satisfied with "things" in the new country and with a low level job by which to attain them. On the other hand, there are those persons who left because their life, though sufficient in material goods, was not fulfilling. If the present study has any value as an exploratory effort which will raise questions based on field data, then the problem of motivation for emigration is one of those questions.

Twenty-seven percent of the Sicilians nominated Australia as their first choice of country of emigration, mainly because they had relatives and friends there. Seventy-three percent of the sample said that America was their first choice, but that Australia was the only place open to them. America was preferred by so many because wages are better, opportunities are greater, and their knowledge of the United States is, in many cases, better than their knowledge of Australia, even after many years in the latter. The United States repeatedly turned up in the interviews as *the* haven for immigrants, often in what appeared to be an irrelevant context. For example, one man stated that he preferred his children to marry Australians because hybrids are stronger and more vigorous as proved by experience in America (for Italians, "America" always means the United States). America is for some a mythical land with streets paved of gold, but for most it is a real place exhibiting positive and negative characteristics. They know in detail about racial problems, crime in the streets, and the current unemployment rate, but they also know hourly wage and salary scales for a variety of industrial and professional occupations. Other countries such as Brazil, Venezuela, and Argentina were mentioned as having been briefly considered; most respondents have one or more relatives living there, but the unstable political situation all over South America dissuaded them from giving serious consideration to that area of the world. Canada, which is a real possibility even today for Italian immigrants, was curiously absent in these discussions. When asked directly about Canada they always hedged somewhat and finally came through with the notion that it is a bare, frigid, tenth-rate United States and that Australia is better by comparison.

Fifty-four percent of the total group left Sicily immediately when they decided to emigrate while 46 percent had to wait from two to ten years. Because of the Fascist government, which prohibited emigration, and the war, they postponed their hopes for many years but they did not give up. Others had to wait for a sponsor (the law on this has fluctuated over the years ranging from no sponsor required to a member of the nuclear family required as sponsor). A few others waited until they were old enough for their families to allow them to leave, and a few others had special problems, such as illness, which had to be worked out through official channels. This question was asked on the speculation that a person who must wait to emigrate and who is willing to wait and live in this suspended state is a person who is more negatively oriented toward his homeland and at the same time more positive in his attitudes toward the host country. This may have some effect on later attitudes and patterns of change.

The educated left immediately upon deciding to emigrate whereas the uneducated had a long wait. It is likely that the educated individuals, who were not desperate to leave Italy, would not have waited to emigrate; they had enough skills and talents to enable them to find places somewhat satisfactory to them in Italy. For most of this group, emigration was a spur-of-the-moment decision, and probably they would have reconsidered had it been necessary to wait for a year or more. The uneducated individuals had no such options open to them; they could remain in their present state or they could leave, and in those days before numerous employment opportunities opened up in the Common Market countries, leaving meant overseas immigration. They would apply to leave Italy, live their unsatisfying lives as best they could, and hope for the day when the necessary permission would come through.

Fifty percent of the sample did not plan to stay permanently in Australia when they emigrated; 17 percent were undecided; 33 percent did plan to remain permanently. In terms of the independent variables, the three groups cited above are very mixed. The latter group which did arrive with plans to remain had a strongly negative orientation toward Sicily and felt that anything would be better; typical was one respondent's comment: "I always knew I would like it, it wasn't Sicily." The undecided group were open to whatever came and usually commented that "I had decided if I liked it I'd stay, but I didn't know what to expect so I wanted to wait and see." The largest group, who did not plan to remain in Australia, will be taken up later.

In summary, the majority of respondents were somewhat negatively oriented toward Australia; it was not their first choice as country of emigration, they left shortly after their decision to emigrate, and they did not intend to remain in Australia permanently. In addition, uneducated and low mobility persons emigrated to find the jobs which would enable them to buy material possessions; educated individuals left Sicily for idiosyncratic reasons; highly mobile men emigrated in order to advance themselves and their children.

IMMEDIATE POSTIMMIGRATION EXPERIENCE

The other side of the emigration experience is the immigrant's early impressions and experiences in the new country. If an individual emigrates with a somewhat negative or even a neutral orientation, what effect, if any, does this have on his first day or his first year in his new home? How do the two sides of the immigration experience fit together, and how do these mesh with later adjustment, satisfaction, and changes? Four questions were asked on the immediate postimmigration experience: (1) What were your very first impressions of Australia? (2) How was your first year in Australia? (3) What was your one greatest difficulty in settling down in Australia? (4) Why did you decide to remain permanently in Australia?

Fifty-four percent of the respondents had a negative first impression of Australia, 10 percent were neutral and self-oriented, and 36 percent had a positive orientation. Most people spoke of their first day or two in Australia when answering the first question, but the points they chose to emphasize varied. Some concentrated on the physical appearance of the city while others remembered most vividly their personal feelings of loss and isolation. Almost everyone spoke at length in response to this question and their experiences years before were still fresh and vivid in their minds. Many of the stories are sad, a few are funny, but all are filled with eminently believable detail. Those who were favorably impressed by Australia on arrival fell into one of two categories: those whose impressions pertain to external factors and those whose memories revolve around themselves. The majority of the favorably impressed fell into the first group who found everything to their satisfaction:

Of course I remember. It was in the morning and Sydney was beautiful. I hadn't known what to expect, I had never been anywhere, I was young.

It was beautiful—there was work and going out with girls.

. . . it [Sydney] was so wild and bush-like but as we approached the city it got better and better and the city was good. I loved it straight-away.

Those immigrants who remember Australia in terms of themselves speak in this way:

I was very happy, always I have been as happy as a lark here and this even when I got a letter a few days after landing saying that my wife and baby were ill and dying. But I'm not the type to say that Australia is no good, it depends on you yourself—everywhere. With confidence you can do everything, no one cares anywhere, so it is up to you, no matter where you are.

The immigrants who arrived with a neutral outlook had actually prepared themselves to accept, but not necessarily to like, almost anything they found:

As things come along we take them in our stride. We didn't expect a paradise, so we had no real thoughts about it and so we weren't disappointed.

The largest number of immigrants had an unfavorable impression of Sydney and these, as with the first group, fall into two classes: those whose impressions are of external factors and those whose impressions pertain to self. Many individuals had very good reasons for their unfavorable impressions, but it was not so much Sydney and its physical setting as much as the way they were treated and the way of life they found there which are still remembered with horror:

The major impression was that I did not know how to speak English. I felt terrible. I couldn't even buy a pack of cigarettes. Once I lost my way between my house and work and I wandered around for more than an hour trying to find my way; I couldn't even stop someone and ask. I found the way finally because I met a *paesano*.

It was too different. It was all strange, too dark, too much sadness. I had thought it would be better, more life, more transport and things at night. But it's not like that. Here the trams don't even run at night. We come with a dream instead of the truth.

I had very bad impressions. You know, as a child you have very impractical ideas. I landed at Wooloomooloo at thirteen and I was expecting the promised land and then they took me to my brothers' shop, which is not in the best area of Sydney, and there were all those old dilapidated houses with wooden sides and tin roofs, all unpainted. My brothers were bachelors and the house was not very comfortable or fixed up very nicely. I mentioned how messy it was and they told me to get the broom and sweep it. I was horrified: in Sicily I had never had to do anything, you always had your mother and sisters around for all that.

I'll never forget when I landed here. I waited and waited on the dock for my sponsor and he never showed up. So finally hours after landing I saw an old man sitting on a bench. I eyed him and knew he was Italian so I went over and asked him what I could do. Well, of course, it was the man I wanted. I was wild with him that he had not searched me out. There I was all alone, with no one here, no relatives, no one. He took me to his fruit shop and let me stand there all by myself for hours until the rush was over and he could leave. He had gotten me a room in another house with an old Australian woman who didn't speak a word of Italian. And so there I was all alone in that miserable little room. That first night I sat down and cried.

There are three reasons why some respondents reacted negatively: age, isolation, and status loss. Some were very young and had led sheltered lives until they found themselves in a new world with new demands. Others felt an overwhelming sense of isolation and unimportance:

The first day was quite traumatic. I was really lonely. No one met me and I thought that if I dropped dead no one would care. It was a feeling of not being important to anyone else and so you are not important even to yourself.

Those who suffered from status loss spoke of "having taken a step down" and of "having been better off in Sicily." The most highly educated had the most negative first impressions. Their reactions were almost all concerned with loneliness, isolation, and status loss—perhaps educated persons could handle the problems and confusions of a new environment, new language, and new way of life, but they could not adjust so well to loss of individuality, personality, and position. Uneducated working-class immigrants had no status to lose, but their provincialism and lack of experience of the world made adjusting to a new language and a new environment very difficult indeed. The only individuals among the low education group who managed this initial period rather well are those who had had military service outside their *paesi* and therefore had previously faced problems similar to those of a foreigner in a new country. The very young were most divided on this variable; some took the whole experience as a lark and seemed to feel that new experiences were adventurous, others were shocked and horrified by the newness and difficulty of it all. The main impression is that those who were positive were very happy, while those who were negative were miserable.

Fifty percent of the respondents reported that their first year in Australia was bad; 27 percent said it was composed of both good and bad elements; 23 percent said it was good. Negative responses came from individuals who emigrated in all three time periods, but their reasons for finding Australia bad are very different. Those old timers who came before World War II entered a Sydney that was not highly industrialized; the factories and construction jobs which are now the main source of employment for working-class immigrants were not to be found, and those few which did exist were reserved exclusively for Australians. The immigrants did not know the language nor did they have the capital necessary to launch enterprises of their own, and so they were driven into some kind of small-scale commercial enterprise. This is a pattern common to Greeks in Australia and to both Italians and Greeks in the United States:

> From door-to-door vending, to push cart peddling, to the establishment of a store and perhaps branches, business steadily expanded. In city after city the pattern repeated itself . . . until the role of Italians as suppliers of fruit and vegetables became an accepted fact. [Pisani 1959 p. 72]

Italians in both countries gravitated toward fruit and vegetable selling while Greeks in Australia and in America mainly started small restaurants and fish shops. The fruit and vegetable shops in Sydney are small dingy places where a few counters have been built as the single improvement. The fruit shop business is, even today, a hard way to earn money, but in the years before the war it was a brutal, exhausting way of life which took the combined resources of an entire family working full-time. A fruit shop owner and his son or cousin or nephew left the house at 4 A.M. to buy the day's supplies at the central wholesale produce market and would return in time for the wife and daughters to open the shop at 6 and so catch early shoppers on their way to work. The shops remained open until 11 or 12 P.M. to attract people on their way home from parties and visits. Seven days a week was the rule, and Christmas and Easter were the only holidays in the year. Returns were small and although such a shop could support a family it was not a good living. This way of life then is what the prewar immigrants objected to when they spoke of their first year in Sydney:

> I went to work in a fruit shop, and was glad to get it, because that's all there was for us then. I got 10 shillings a week working from 3 A.M. to 10 P.M.

That first year was really black, I cried all the time. I had lost everything and I came into a really hard life. I wasn't used to standing all day, working those terrible fruit shop hours.

Those immigrants who came after the war found a very different situation—abundant employment opportunities in factories and construction as well as in the shops. There were almost no complaints about work, although some say that the money was not nearly so much as they had expected. Some of the dissatisfactions of the educated group are evident in these examples:

They were the most awful days of my life, everything was awful. I had lived in the city all my life and then I went to Millerville which is ninety-three miles from Perth and is all bush, cows, goats, and chickens. I had been working as an accountant in a publicity firm in Sicily and here I worked in a cheese factory.

It was shocking, terrible. There was my pride. I lived in a good place and all that, but I think it was harder for me than for most because I couldn't express myself. As a university graduate in Italy you always take great pride in speaking well and elegantly and here I was with the same ideas and I sounded like a child. All those beautiful thoughts and they came out sounding as if I was retarded.

I had been an officer in the navy and I was accustomed to a different life. The majority of people I lived and worked with were illiterates, semi-illiterates—crude. You can't assimilate yourself with them. It was very hard but you've got to kiss a hand that should be cut off.

The uneducated had such complaints as:

That first year, I didn't like it—for work in the factory because I had never worked under another person, for eating, for being alone, for everything. Like stupid things we were, less than nothing. It's always the language.

I didn't really find myself that first year, the environment was different, the language was so hard and I was so far from my mamma I was like one with a handerkerchief in front of his eyes—blind. I worked, went home, cooked, and then tomorrow back to work. I spent one year like that because I had debts for the trip and clothes.

Those immigrants who found both good and bad in their first year have this to say:

It was very good for living, work, for the hygiene in the houses, different from Sicily. It was very hard for the language.

It was a little strange for the language and for going out to work every day, but now I love going to work and it's fun learning this language [female respondent].

Finally, we come to those respondents who found their first year in Australia very, very good:

> I began to work, I was happy, I enjoyed myself, I went dancing. I'll tell you that after three months I forgot Italy and I've never thought of it again.

> I did what I wanted, I was able to do what I wanted finally, and it was a good life.

The answers to this question reveal a surprising mixture which shows the importance of the individual. Of those who came before the war and met really difficult situations, some reacted very negatively while others, admitting that life was hard, were still positive in their feelings. Among the educated there are those who felt their loss of status very keenly and those who saw it as a natural consequence of emigration and were prepared to cope with it.

In the answers to the third question, concerning the one greatest difficulty, these individual or personality factors become more impressive still. The answers fell into three categories: 17 percent said that everything was very difficult; 27 percent said that nothing was really difficult; and 56 percent cited one of three specific things as a difficulty: the language (cited the most times), status loss, or economic deprivation (too much work for too little money). Two individuals who reacted negatively to their first year answered that they had no single difficulty that was greatest. On an individual level even members of the same nuclear family who share precisely the same background reacted very differently: one brother finds problems in everything, while for the other, life was beautiful. In this case, age alone was different, the first brother was thirty when he emigrated, the other was only eighteen. That people react differently to the same experience is a fact often overlooked in immigrant studies.

We have now seen a broad picture of why and under what conditions these Sicilians emigrated to Australia and how they reacted to their initial period in that country. The actual conditions the immigrants found when they arrived in Australia have been sketched. The four independent variables are significant in the following ways:

Education. Educated immigrants left Sicily for idiosyncratic reasons; they left immediately upon making the decision to emigrate; their first impressions of Australia were negative, primarily for reasons concerning loss of individuality and status. Uneducated immigrants left Sicily to make money to buy material possessions; they had to wait for long periods in order to leave.

Occupational mobility. The occupationally mobile left Sicily to advance themselves and their children. The nonmobile left Sicily for money to buy material possessions.

Age at emigration. Those who left Sicily at a young age had a period to wait before leaving and after arrival in Australia found no great difficulty in settling down. Those immigrants who left Sicily when they were much older found everything to be very difficult.

Time in Australia. The prewar emigrants left Sicily immediately upon deciding that they wished to go. The recent emigrants had a very long wait before they were able to actualize their dream of emigrating.

In hypothesizing rate and breadth of change on the basis of these facts, I would state the following:

Educated immigrants would change fairly rapidly and completely because they were anxious to leave Sicily, and their negative first impressions were based on reasons which are remediable. In addition, their greater sophistication and ease in handling the complexities of everyday life would make it simpler for them to adjust to the differences between the Australian and the Sicilian ways of life.

Uneducated immigrants would change rapidly and completely because they left Sicily to find work and this was available in Australia. There may be a difference in the prewar group, which though it found work, discovered it to be demoralizingly difficult. Uneducated immigrants held on to their hope of emigrating for long periods of time, perhaps signifying a greater future satisfaction with their new home.

If people left Sicily to advance themselves socially and occupationally and they are now in the group of occupationally mobile, we should expect a very high rate of complete change because they found what they came to find. The nonmobile would change rapidly and completely, as the uneducated immigrants, because there has been steady work and pay in Australia.

The young immigrants had a very positive outlook on Australia after their arrival and this may predispose them to satisfaction with Australia and with subsequent change. Older persons who emigrate find everything to be very difficult, and since it is rather unlikely that they will adjust and overcome all of these difficulties, their change would be incomplete and their satisfaction low.

Time in Australia is not a good indicator of probable change and satisfaction because only one question is significant—whether they had to wait to emigrate or could leave immediately—and this fact is open to various interpretations.

Two additional points are important here. First, there is no correlation between individual answers on the pre-emigration indices and the postimmigration attitudes (as measured by Pearson product moment correlation). For instance, those who were very positively oriented toward emigration and Australia did not follow through with these orientations after arrival in Australia. Individuals in both pre-emigration groups are found in all three post-immigration groups. Therefore one individual may have planned and dreamed for years to emigrate to Australia, but this cherished desire has no effect on his subsequent reaction to Australia. (It may prove to have an influence on his later change pattern however.) The second point is that some individuals who reacted very negatively in their initial period in Australia (placed at one year in this study) overcame many objections to the new country. People said they got used to differences or they grew to see that there were good things; so it cannot be assumed that if the earliest period in one immigrant's life is shocking or traumatic, his entire outlook will be negative and he will be permanently alienated.

9

THE PUBLIC SECTOR
OF LIFE

MOST immigrant or culture change studies divide variables into
(a) acculturative, those indices such as food habits, naturalization,
occupation, and language ability that describe changes in culture
and (b) assimilative, those indices such as friends, associations,
primary relations, intermarriage, and identification that describe
changes in social structure, values, and ideals. I propose a fourfold
division based on a public versus private distinction: (1) public
sector of life—ability in the new language, residence, and occupation; (2) private sector of life—food, home language, friends,
associations, and family (extended family, husband-wife dyad, and
nuclear family); (3) public satisfaction—with job, house, the
Australian government, and Australia as a place to live; and
(4) private satisfaction or identification—with Australian people
and the Australian way of life. Such a division will reveal if
change occurs only in those aspects which are necessary to living
in a new country, that is, in the public sector, or if it also occurs
in those areas which are private and personal to each individual
and which no democratic government or structure (social, occupational, etc.) will insist be changed—the private sector (see chapters
10 and 11). Satisfaction and dissatisfaction with the country, its
people, and its way of life will be examined separately (chapter
12) so that one may judge how much the immigrants become like
the Australian natives and how the immigrants themselves evaluate
such change or lack of change.

LANGUAGE ABILITY
Fifty-four percent of the immigrants display a very high English
language ability while 46 percent are low on this index. High
ability means the capacity to carry on sustained conversations in
English without reverting to Italian. The twenty-six individuals in
this group are somewhat divided in their style of speaking: only
one speaks perfect English, some speak with slight or heavy accents
but use grammar and vocabulary perfectly, others display no
Italian accent but have a poorer command of grammar and vo-

cabulary. All are more at home in English than in Italian and when they speak Italian frequently revert to English (except for those who are educated) when encountering difficult grammatical constructions or complicated thoughts. Individuals of low language ability cannot carry on sustained conversations in English, have poor command of grammar and vocabulary, and are much more at home in Italian or Sicilian dialect than in English. In fact, about one-third of these Sicilians (15 percent of the sample) speak practically no English at all, and the English used by another third is almost incomprehensible when attempted. Some are on the borderline between the high and low ability groups but frequently lapse into Italian when meeting some difficulty in English and so were placed in the low ability group.

Most educated immigrants and prewar immigrants and all occupationally mobile immigrants speak English well. Educated Sicilians either knew English well before emigrating or knew French and because of their generally superior learning ability were able to learn English easily. The second group, the old-timers, learned English in their shops where they were forced to speak daily and constantly to Australians. This service industry, which exacted such a physical and emotional toll in its demands, did reward its workers by enabling them to quickly and rather painlessly learn English. Many of these high ability men deprecate their English, calling it "fruit shop English," but they speak good Australian-accented English which, though not elegant, is still the standard speech of the country.

The correlation between spoken and written second language is low. Many other variables such as education and method of learning the new tongue are crucial factors. No matter how well immigrants speak English they cannot read or write it if they have not been taught those skills. Others who are competent in Italian just picked up English and therefore do not have the ability to read, much less write, in English. The lag between speaking and writing has its most important consequences in the job sphere where men are forever doomed to factory operative jobs without hope of advancement because skilled or managerial positions demand the ability to keep records and write reports.

On the other hand, uneducated, new, or occupationally nonmobile immigrants are in the low ability group. Length of time in the country would seem to be a relevant independent variable in language learning because most of the prewar immigrants are uneducated and nonmobile; however, two important factors enter at this point—how and why the immigrants learned to speak English. In the prewar group three knew English before emigrating (all high school graduates), two studied English in school after immigrating, and the remaining twelve just "picked it up" (a phrase used by everyone, and always in English). This means that through a combination of work, recreation, and general living they learned informally to speak the new language. Those who studied, of course, practiced in work and recreational settings, and even those who knew English before migration mentioned that they very quickly improved their English through constant use.

In learning a new language three factors are operative: knowledge, time, and practice. The prewar immigrants were all employed in service industries which brought them into constant contact with Australians. During the period in which these people emigrated to Australia there were few Italian immigrants in Sydney and no concessions were made by government or the average Australian for the fact that the newcomers were still feeling their way in a strange environment. There were no Italian speakers in banks or government offices, no Italian professionals, office workers, or shop clerks, and therefore it was a necessity to learn some English, at least enough to take care of the ordinary business of living. The smallness of the Italian community also meant that there were fewer English-speaking Italians available to run errands or talk for one. A bus ride to the dentist (an Australian dentist), was a formidable journey, which required more than minimal English; landlords were Australians; priests were Australians; everyone except fruit and shoe shop workers were Australians. These long-time immigrants speak of the new Sicilian immigrants with scorn:

> The New Australians who come here now don't bother. They are spoiled, they get a good job with short hours in a factory and then they want to play, they don't want to work and study—spoiled they are. They say they can't learn English, they are too tired after working, but they're not too tired to go out and dance all night. No, there are schools here for them, night schools, and they just don't care. We had nothing and we all learned English.

The prewar immigrants were not spoiled, they never had the opportunity to be, but neither did they go out and study English. Only two of the prewar immigrants today display low English language ability. They are the two oldest men in the sample and have been in Australia the longest time. Both men have forgotten much of the English they once knew as attested to by their own

chagrin and by the testimony of relatives and friends. It is probable that their ability was once relatively high but their age and
withdrawal from active life have combined to diminish their
English ability. All of the prewar immigrants speak or at one time
spoke very good English, but not because they were dying to speak
English. Their work and the lack of Italian-speaking persons in
Sydney forced them to learn the new language well. Their wives,
although not included in the sample, also speak very good English
because they too worked in the shops.

The postwar group of thirty-one individuals contains eleven
high language ability and twenty low ability immigrants. For the
total group, five had studied English in Italy, ten studied English in
Sydney either in night school or on their own because they were
dissatisfied with the free government night school classes, and sixteen again "picked it up." A surprisingly large number have
applied themselves to the formal study of language which disproves
the claim of the prewar immigrants that the later arrivals are
spoiled. Language study pays off because all but three of the high
ability Sicilians studied English in Italy or in Australia whereas the
majority of the low ability persons made no special effort to learn
the new language. Most of the low ability immigrants feel that it
is not really necessary to acquire a speaking knowledge of English.
Since the end of World War II and the arrival of large numbers of
immigrants, both government and business began to realize the
importance of employing foreign-language speakers in their offices
and shops to serve the rapidly increasing number of immigrants
from all over Europe. More than this, the postwar migration
brought a sizeable number of educated Italian immigrants to
Sydney who then opened professional offices and ethnic stores. It
was becoming easier to get around Sydney without a knowledge of
English if one remained in the areas where other ethnics con-
gregated. These immigrants, for the most part, worked in factories
with many other southern Europeans although the majority of
workers were usually Australian. For the newer immigrant there
were shops, offices, and work places where employees and even
employers spoke his language, or if not there was a *paesano* available who spoke English and could interpret for him.

If time in Australia alone were responsible for the difference
between the early and the later immigrants, then after five or ten
years in Australia, every immigrant should be speaking much better
English. However, many in the postwar group have been in Australia for eight or fifteen years and their English is minimal, to

say the least. It is the presence or absence of like-foreign-language speakers, not just numbers of years in Australia, that is responsible for the difference between the two groups. Most of the later group will probably never speak more than a few sentences of English because there is no real need, and they are not motivated to learn the new language.

The ability to speak English is, from an objective point of view, extremely important because, as the immigrants themselves so often said, "without that nothing else is possible." One cannot get a skilled factory job or a white-collar position without the ability to write and read reports; one cannot participate in the national communication system of radio, television, and newspapers; one cannot have Australian friends or even talk to Australians in stores or at work. In other words, one is isolated in an Italian-speaking world from which there is no escape until English is learned. All of the immigrants are keenly aware of these facts but very few of the low ability individuals have done anything to break out of this vicious circle which keeps them tied to low-paying jobs and denies them forever the opportunity to participate in the Australian community.

RESIDENTIAL AREA

Residence or residential area is always mentioned in immigrant studies because most such researches are set in ethnic ghettos. When an immigrant lives in a nonethnic area he is not included in immigrant studies. In the present study an effort was made to include residential diversity as one of the bases of the sample. Respondents live in thirty-one different suburbs. The term suburb is used here in the British way to mean neighborhood area in the city proper and not outlying regions as the term is used in the United States; in Chicago, Old Town, Hyde Park, and Rogers Park would each be a suburb. There are two ways of ranking suburbs in which immigrants live: by social status and by ethnicity. The two indices in Sydney are not perfectly correlated although the very high status suburbs are the lowest in ethnic residents and the lowest status suburbs are the highest in ethnic concentration. It was hypothesized on the basis of other immigrant studies that if an immigrant lived in a middle or high status suburb he would be more changed and, conversely, if he lived in a low status, or working-class, suburb he would be less changed, that is, less Australian. Ethnicity of suburb would follow the same pattern but with a negative correlation: the people living in the low ethnic areas would be more changed, those in the high ethnic areas less changed, or unchanged.

Suburb status is taken from a study by Congalton (1961) in which he interviewed over three hundred Australian-born Sydneysiders and asked them to rank the hundred or more suburbs of the city. He then broke their rankings down into eight categories running from high status to low status. I then arranged the suburbs of the Sicilian respondents on this scale. For ethnicity the 1960 Australian census figures of suburb ethnicity in Sydney were used, and the percentage of Italians (not Sicilians because the figures are not broken down this finely) in each suburb was calculated.

Twenty-three percent of the respondents live in very high status suburbs, 63 percent live in middle status suburbs, and 14 percent live in low status ones. The first fact of importance is that long-time immigrants live in high status suburbs while new immigrants live in low status suburbs. This is not a simple correlation of time in Australia and suburban status because the immediate postwar group (fifteen to twenty years in Australia) is very divided among the eight ranks of the scale. It is noteworthy that neither the educated immigrants, who have middle-class occupations, nor the occupationally mobile live exclusively in better suburbs. Nor do the working-class families live only in low status areas; the primary reason lies with the fruit shops. The prewar immigrants who had shops lived behind their shops for many years and when they bought their own homes they lived near their shops. The shops are scattered all over the city and the better suburbs are better sites for the shops because produce prices are higher and wealthier people buy more fresh fruit and vegetables. Therefore the immigrants either tried to find shops in the better suburbs or often just happened to find shops for sale in these areas. Their work brought them into the upper status suburbs and kept them there when they bought their own homes. It also gave them a taste for living in the better areas which are prettier and, as they say, "nicer." Many of the prewar immigrants scorn the working-class western suburbs and constantly berated the newer immigrants who cluster there for being ignorant and without ambition.

Turning from suburb status to suburb ethnicity, it quickly became apparent in the field that census figures for the latter factor were misleading; suburbs are territorially large and a percentage of Italian-born residents in some cases represented widely scattered immigrant households and in others represented small concentrations of like-nationality ethnics. This is an important difference because in the first case the immigrants might or might not have any contact with other Italians while in the second instance there would be at least a strong suspicion that the immigrant preferred to live with fellow immigrants and thereby limit potential relationships with native-born Australians. Therefore, using census tract maps, I calculated the percentage of Italian-born individuals for a four-block radius from the home of each respondent. This gave the concentration of Italians near the home of each respondent and showed the great disparity between the figures for ethnicity of suburb and ethnicity of ethnic enclave.

The totals for suburb ethnicity show that 25 percent of the respondents live in high ethnic suburbs, 52 percent live in medium ethnic suburbs, and 23 percent live in low ethnic suburbs. While these figures may appear high, it is important to note that the actual percentage of Italians in the most Italian suburb is only 11.1 percent and that the majority of the respondents live in suburbs containing several thousand people where between less than 1 percent and 4 percent are Italians. A glance at the figures for ethnic enclaves within suburbs shows even better how few respondents live closely with fellow Italians; 18 percent live in high ethnic enclaves, 38 percent live in medium ethnic enclaves, and 44 percent live in low ethnic enclaves. This means that even though the immigrant may live in a suburb which as a whole is relatively high in ethnicity the immigrants are scattered and have not formed ethnic clusters. The inescapable conclusion is that in choosing where to live, at least for this sample and for all Italian immigrants in Sydney, there are other factors much more important than common residence with fellow Italians. The nature of these other factors will be examined in chapter 10.

Considering the four independent variables, it is only the occupationally mobile that tend to live in nonethnic suburbs. This is a very important finding because while most Sydney suburbs contain both good and poor areas, some suburbs, such as Leichardt, are definitely considered Italian in the minds of Sydneysiders. Therefore, the occupationally mobile person who can buy a home in one of the better sections of almost any suburb must be more careful in his selection of suburb by ethnicity. Occupational mobility is closely tied to social mobility and is a normal measure for it, whether the mobility is considered to be within the ethnic group or out of it, and as such the socially mobile individual must be very careful not to be tagged too ethnic. He may, as some studies have shown (for example, Whyte 1943), be selective and pick a few Italian customs to follow but he should avoid being labeled "Sicilian." Social mobility implies a change in life style for adults as well as children in the family and it is important that the physical setting be one which will enhance opportunities for consolidating present social position and for advancing further in the future.

Why do immigrants live where they live? Table 5 details their reasons for choosing the house in which they currently reside.

TABLE 5
REASONS FOR HOUSE CHOICE

	Number of Respondents
House and neighborhood.....................	14
Near work................................	9
House price...............................	9
Near relatives............................	5
Lived here always.........................	5
Near relatives and work....................	2
Near friends.............................	2
Miscellaneous (lives with sister, received house as wedding present)..........	2
	48

OWNERSHIP OF RESIDENCE

Eighty-three percent of the immigrants own their own homes; eight who rent houses are divided between six new immigrants who have not yet raised enough money to make a down payment on a house, which is very high in Sydney, and two men who rent because their extra income goes to keep their children at the university. During the first years in Australia a small modest house in a working-class neighborhood is quite enough because no one can expect more, but this soon changes. Forty-six percent of the Sicilians have moved four to six times, 52 percent have moved one to three times, and 2 percent have moved seven to nine times. About half of these changes of residence occur when buying and selling houses. Most of the immigrants are shrewd thinkers:

> Do I believe in luck and destiny you ask? Yes, of course, I do—but luck is all up here [pointing to his forehead], it all depends on you. I'll give you an example of luck. When I came to this country I bought a little house, a very modest house for about $4,500 [U.S.]

and a few years later I sold it for about $9,000. Is that luck? Because you see I studied where to buy the house, I studied the area and its prospects and so I made a good gain and could buy this house which is in a good area too and I will be able to sell it for more in a few years. This is luck, but luck depends on me.

Among Sicilians in Sydney, especially but not exclusively working-class Sicilians, one of the highest forms of praise, and one of the most frequent, is "they bought a house two years after they came." Even among Australians this is a source of praise and wonder. They marvel that immigrants can arrive with nothing tangible, not even skills or the language, and save enough money to make a large down payment on a house one, two, or three years after arriving. Wages are not very high in Australia: the average semiskilled workman earns about $50 or $60 a week but this is higher with overtime (and none will take a job which does not include frequent or constant overtime). Houses, on the other hand, are by American standards expensive. An old fibro house of three-bedrooms in a working-class neighborhood goes for about $17,000. The rents they pay while waiting to buy a house are high—$25 a week for a very old and run-down two-bedroom fibro house. Life is not as difficult economically for them as it was for immigrants to the United States at the turn of the century, yet those in Australia still earn wages which are far from commensurate with house and land prices, and it is a terrible struggle to accumulate the down payment.

OCCUPATION

The Sicilian immigrants who have been occupationally mobile have already been discussed (in chapter 7). The job status of all the immigrants has not been touched. Sixty-two percent are employed in blue-collar jobs, 23 percent are working in white-collar occupations, and 15 percent are in professional or managerial positions. The blue-collar workers are unskilled and semiskilled factory operatives, owners of fruit shops or corner grocery shops, and construction workers. All but two of these thirty individuals are drawn from the peasant or artisan class in Sicily. The two exceptions are high school graduates who emigrated before the war and found no outlet for their skills. But this is not to say that the blue-collar workers have made no occupational advances, because all have. Many have moved from unskilled to semiskilled and even, in a few cases, to skilled positions while others have increased their skills within the same level. Two representative comments are:

> I've only had the one job here in Australia and I'm very happy at that plywood factory. I began just as a laborer there but now I've learned many machines and do many different kinds of complicated work. I would like more money of course but I like the place so much that I wouldn't leave it for more money at another factory.

> I work in a plastics factory. I do all kinds of work there because I'm unskilled on the line, the cutting machine, boxing, carrying, everything now. It's a deluxe job.

Some of the immigrants, like the man who works in the plastics factory, came to Australia with no skills and a job history of subsistence farming only; others, represented by the man in the plywood plant, had skills such as tailoring which they have now abandoned for jobs they consider more stable and promising.

The eleven white-collar occupations are held by five educated men, four uneducated but mobile individuals, and two who are both educated and mobile. The seven immigrants in professional and managerial positions include one mobile man and six educated and mobile persons. It it clear that if one wishes to make great advances occupationally it is advantageous, or perhaps necessary, to be educated or socially mobile, or both.

The three most important variables in the public sector—language ability, residence, and occupation—are extremely complex indices of immigrant experience. English-language ability is importantly affected by education, occupation, and by conditions in the country in the period in which the emigrants entered. Therefore these variables are extremely important in assessing the changes which the immigrants made or wished to make in the lives of their family, but these changes are direct carry-overs from ideas formed in Sicily and very often were the reason for emigrating. Immigrants may see and talk to Australians and certainly they are aware of the Australian way of life and all it implies, but we must not assume that all mobility aspirations were acquired in Australia. The values of prestige, mobility, education, and property are more viable and real in southern Italy than they are in Australia where mobility is frowned upon and only the upper strata send their children to the university. In the case of these Sicilian immigrants, "acculturation" is change based on Sicilian ideals and values. These variables are therefore not reliable measures of change if one assumes that the immigrant is changing because he has learned new values which are substituted for his native values. The basic assumption in most studies of social change is that all changes, especially among relatively uneducated working-class immigrants, are the result of learning new ideals and ends. It is true that the immigrants have changed their jobs, houses, and in some cases their language, but these alterations have occurred in response to the public demands of a new environment or to the social conditions which prevailed when the immigrant arrived. They are, at this point, only habit changes and we may not infer that value changes have occurred.

10

THE PRIVATE SECTOR
OF LIFE

THE PRIVATE sector is defined as that part of one's life which is lived away from the scrutiny and direct control of society and its members. In the public sector, a man who does not work will become a charge of the community and suffer, in the case of an immigrant, deportation. Or if he takes up an occupation which the laws of the country declare illegal, he will be punished by imprisonment or deportation. Certain jobs demand a command of the native language and the person who cannot successfully meet this demand will lose his job. If a house is not kept in good condition and becomes a fire or health menace to the community, legal and law enforcement agencies will step in to remedy the problem. But in the private sector of life a person is free to live as he chooses provided he does not become a public menace. A fruit shop employee is forced to speak English to his Australian customers and thereby becomes proficient in the language, but in his home he is free to speak any language he wishes. If a father decides that his family needs to be ruled with an iron hand, he may do so, and no one in the community will feel it his duty or right to step in and make official complaint. It is, in fact, impossible to do such a thing in a free democracy such as Australia (always assuming that firm control of family does not include beating, clubbing, or other brutal and illegal treatment).

The immigrants themselves recognize this distinction between the public and private sectors of life. Many respondents spoke with pride of being good Australian citizens and obeying the laws of the country to the letter but of being free to do as they wish in the home:

> From door to door in my house we are in Italy. In the way of eating, comportment, thinking, talking, and even shouting. Outside I'm a good Australian.

> I put together the best of both and made my own way of life. But my family is typically Italian. Twenty-nine Butterworth Street is a little piece of Italy, when you step in you land in Sicily, that's for sure, you are in Catania. Outside, it's Australian, the democratic

way of life socially. I play their Australian game, I smile and when I am corrected I stand thus but inside I know how superior I am to them and how I could put them to flight with a few words if I chose to. But they never know. I play the fool with a mask and so they are happy.

Several attitudes are apparent. There are immigrants who truly feel loyalty to Australia and are thankful they are free to continue their Sicilian way of life at home; others are bitter and condescending and play a game of being Australian outside the house while inside they have re-created Italy.

There are five general categories in the private sector: (1) food and housekeeping habits, (2) number of children, (3) patterns of language usage, (4) friends and associates, and (5) membership in clubs and associations. A sixth category, kinship, divided into three parts—extended family, husband-wife relationship, and nuclear family—will be discussed in chapter 11.

FOOD AND HOUSEKEEPING HABITS

The dependent variable which changed in the most instances but to the least degree is food habits. Everyone changed their eating habits somewhat, but no one changed completely. Sixty percent revealed only slight change, 32 percent eat both Italian and Australian food, while 8 percent eat Australian food only. The literature on immigrants draws the same conclusion that food is one of the last ethnic customs to change. If the sociopsychological hypothesis put forward by, among others, Spiro (1955) and Bruner (1954) is true—that those things learned first are the slowest to change—then the eating habits of the Sicilians in this sample will go toward validating the theory. Food habits in Sicily follow a pattern with only minor class differences: breakfast is coffee with heated milk; lunch is usually the main meal of the day (although for peasants out in the fields all day it is not) and consists of three courses—*primo,* pasta with sauce, *secondo,* meat or fish and salad, and *terzo,* fruit or sweet. Evening supper is light and includes soup and salad or leftovers with fruit. This basic menu of course varies from day to day and especially from season to season, but by and large the only big difference is the presence or absence of meat. Australians, on the other hand, eat as do English or Americans with minor modifications: breakfast of bacon and eggs, lunch of sandwich or meat pie, and dinner of roasted meat, vegetables, potatoes, and a heavy dessert.

For many respondents the only admitted changes in food habits are (1) the inclusion of much more meat in their diet and (2) taking the main meal in the evening instead of at noon. However, the inclusion of meat has other consequences noted only as a complaint and not as a fact by many immigrants. If one eats meat twice a day, at lunch and dinner, then there is no need for the heavy, filling pasta which serves this function in the Italian diet. In Italy, even when meat is served the amount is small and no one, not even a child, could fill up on it alone; therefore, pasta is taken first in surprising quantities and the individual is satisfied at the end of the meal. But the immigrants who begin eating meat in Australia also wish to eat pasta and they simply cannot. Rather than give up meat, which remains a luxury, they cut down on pasta and bread, sometimes substituting lighter rice or potatoes, which changes their diet considerably. Very few immigrants in this group were able to see the connection between meat and pasta, even when it was pointed out to them, and they blamed their inability to eat both on the Australian "air"—a frequent Sicilian scapegoat for minor ailments of all kinds.

Other Sicilians in Sydney have begun to eat Australian food; it was not unusual for a meal composed of both Italian and Australian dishes to be served, especially if a guest is present. A small bowl of pasta is served with a special sauce for the first course, and then a plate of boiled beef, vegetables, and potatoes for the second, while dessert consisted of *cannoli* (a very rich Sicilian sweet) and a bowl of jello and ice cream. Ordinarily, however, families which have begun eating Australian dishes have either all Australian food or Italian food at any one meal. The families in this group have also acquired a taste for potatoes, which most Italians do not like.

The third group are those families which eat Australian food almost all the time, occasionally serving spaghetti or lasagna as is common in many American and, increasingly, Australian families. However, the wives continue to use Italian spices, herbs, and oil. Although almost everything in the diet has changed, Italian flavoring is retained.

Two independent variables, education and time in Australia, are significantly associated with food habits. Individuals with high education reveal high change in food habits while low education persons reveal low change; long time immigrants are very changed in food habits and new immigrants have hardly changed at all. In other words, if a man is educated, or has been in Australia a long time he now most likely eats Australian food, with Italian spices, while uneducated people and those who are new to the country are still eating Sicilian food (with more meat and less *pasta*).

Southern Italians in general tend to be very conservative in food habits preferring that which is known and loved and usually refusing even to try anything new. They eat at specified times and no others, and they associate certain foods so rigorously that on several occasions in Sicily men refused to eat at all because there was no bread, which must be present if meat or fish are served. It is, therefore, surprising that so many Sicilians did make major changes in their dietary habits and that so many Sicilian women were willing and eager to try new foods. The women who had been in Sidney since before the war were pleased and proud of their ability to prepare Australian food and many had acquired American cookbooks which they laboriously worked through in an effort to understand the recipes. Others religiously watched cooking programs on television, and one woman even went to cooking classes sponsored by the gas company. Ordinarily anything which is not traditional is rejected immediately. For instance, the meat which is usually eaten in Sicily is veal. Beef is hard to find, more expensive, tasteless, and tough. This habit carries over with a vengeance in Australia. In Sicily meat is eaten no more than once a week at most and for many, many families once a month is normal. However, one family (new and uneducated) served veal almost every day for eight months. Sometimes there was chicken on Sunday or a fish but these were extremely rare occurrences and so veal it was—and veal prepared in precisely the same way every time. Any attempts to introduce other kinds of meat or even to prepare the veal differently met with failure because the husband claimed that any other meat or preparation would make them sick because of the "air."

It is still hard to tell why the older immigrants were different, or to phrase it more accurately, why, with time, Sicilian women are willing and eager to change their cooking habits and Sicilian men willing to try new foods. But there seemed to be a feeling of "see, I too can cook as well as the Australians"—a feeling of pride in having mastered a new accomplishment. In some cases the old time immigrant women mentioned that children were instrumental in bringing Australian food into the home, but most picked up the knack and the interest by themselves over the years.

One other difference which separated the educated and older

residents from the rest was the use of the kitchen, kitchen appliances, and all household appliances. Women in the first two groups would be indistinguishable from Australian or American women in the quantity of appliances such as vacuum cleaners and washing machines that they possess and in the frequency of their use. But the newer immigrant women simply did not know what to do with refrigerators, for example. All of the homes, even the most humble, had a large new shiny refrigerator in the kitchen, but even a casual glance inside showed that it contained only fruit, vegetables, and uncooked meat; everything else was kept in little kitchen cupboards. Cooked food, butter, and cheese were stored in cabinets and consequently gave off odors and spoiled rapidly. The housewives were not in the habit of using a refrigerator and claimed that cooked food would get "too cold" and thus not be reusable if stored in the cold.

Another example of this outlook concerns washing clothes. Almost no one in Sicily has a washing machine and since women do not work they are free to spend an hour or two each day washing the family linen by hand. But in Australia the women in the group referred to here worked in factories from 6 A.M. to 5 P.M. At home they had dinner to prepare, dishes to wash (usually without hot water), children to be put to bed, and lunches to be prepared for the next day. On top of all this they had the washing, a staggering load if it is to be done by hand. One women had an enormous tub of clothes soaking on the back porch at all times, and she spent two evening and much of Saturday doing this laundry—spanking it, scrubbing it, soaking again, and finally hanging it out. It was an endless task which is not only never finished but is very punishing physically. This family owned a refrigerator, car, television, jewelry, watches, and good clothing, and they went out dancing every Saturday evening, but they never even thought of buying a washing machine. The wife said that it would be a waste of money for the present because she could do it by hand, and when it was suggested that she take the laundry to the laundromat two blocks away on Saturday, she just stared and shrugged her shoulders. She is still doing the laundry by hand. There is an outlook here which does change—none of the older immigrants did laundry by hand—and it would be extremely interesting to know when and how. The newer women are attempting to continue their household way of life as they knew it in Sicily while at the same time they have taken on an entirely new set of chores since they now work fulltime and are away from their homes for ten or eleven hours a day. Their lives would be far easier and more enjoyable if they used the appliances which they can afford and if other adults in the family, husband and children, gave a hand with the work. But such is not the case—at least until they have been in Australia for more than fifteen years.

NUMBER OF CHILDREN

Table 6 reveals an unexpected correlation between education and number of children; educated immigrants have more children. This finding is most striking at the extremes since only one of the uneducated has more than four children—most have only one or two. The university graduates, on the other hand, are represented only in the upper ranges.

TABLE 6
ASSOCIATION BETWEEN EDUCATION AND NUMBER OF CHILDREN
(In Percent of N)

Number of Children	Uneducated N = 31	Educated N = 13
One or two	77	23
Three or four	20	54
Five or six	3	23

NOTE: Total sample equals forty-four. Unmarried respondents not included.

The size of families of working-class immigrants has been severely cut in Australia. Most of the wives in this group are employed during their child-bearing years and the usual pattern is to have one child immediately after marriage, as if to prove oneself, and then wait ten or even fifteen years while both husband and wife earn money for a down payment on a house and for other things which they desire to buy. This is one instance, but not the only one, in which something is sacrificed to gain an economic end.

Although it cannot be documented, there also seems to be a significant change in attitude toward numbers of children after emigration. Most working-class and many middle-class Sicilians in Sicily believe that three and preferably four children is the least which a good, proper family will produce and that more than this, within limits, is good. This attitude is changing today in Sicily, to be sure, but an even more rapid change and a more drastic revision of attitudes are notable in Australia. This was first evident in the hesitation of respondents to do genealogies. After some head shaking and hemming and hawing, they stated, "This is

going to shock you—the number of children in these families."
They were embarrassed and ashamed that their relatives had so
many children. Their feelings were compounded of two ideas:
first, that to have many children implies ignorance of birth control
methods, and second, that laziness or lust overwhelms the couple
who cannot think beyond immediate pleasure to thoughts of providing properly for their children. The key here is the changed
concept of "providing properly" because in Sicily it is enough to
provide a good, though humble, home which is honorable and
respected, whereas in Sydney it is as important, though not more
so, to provide opportunities for the children to "advance" and to
"have a future." The peasant immigrants are socially and occupationally ambitious for the sake of their children, if not also for
themselves, and are at last in a position where it is possible to
realize their dreams of saying "this is my son, the doctor." In Sicily,
such is impossible for peasants and therefore one may as well
have a horde of children who will add to the family prestige by
their mere presence, but in Australia more children will reduce
the opportunities open to each.

Birth control methods were almost never asked about because
it is not a subject which is openly spoken of. However, some
women did discuss it and it appears that many Sicilian women
still resort to abortion, as they do in Sicily, but that birth control
is much more prevalent in Australia and that the most common
form is coitus interruptus. Although abortion is illegal in Australia,
there are many excellent private clinics where abortions can be
obtained from qualified physicians in a hospital setting for a
nominal charge. Several couples who were still struggling financially spoke openly about their fears of having another child,
which would force the mother to stop work, at least for some
months. Those women who have young children and infants go
to work regardless, leaving the children with Italian or, more
usually, Australian neighbors to care for them during the day.
This is such a common practice that it is not even mentioned as
something special. Most young couples with one child want to
have another after ten years or so, but they believe that two
is quite enough.

PATTERNS OF LANGUAGE USAGE

English language ability has already been discussed but it is also
important to look at patterns of language usage—where each
language is used and by whom. These two aspects of language

must be separated because, as demonstrated in chapter 9, learning a new language is often conditioned by socioeconomic background, occupation, and historical period in which the emigrant entered the new country. However, using the new and the old language is much more up to the personal preference of each individual, and it is here that one sees some real changes which are based on choice and not on force or accident. Three languages are utilized by the immigrants—Sicilian dialect, standard Italian, and English—but the Sicilian-Italian difference can be dispensed with by stating that only educated individuals use Italian while all the others, if they are not speaking English, use Sicilian dialect. They are able to speak imperfect Italian, but they are more comfortable in dialect; it is the language used in the majority of immigrant homes when English is not being spoken.

Possible combinations of languages used in the home are: Sicilian/Italian only, both Sicilian and English, and English alone. There are of course variations in the proportion of English or Sicilian spoken in the homes which use both. However, respondents were asked to specify who uses which languages when both are found in the same home, because most immigrant studies, especially those concerning Italians, assume that the children speak English while the parents use the native language. Prewar immigrants use English in the home, immediate postwar immigrants use both Sicilian and English, and the most recent postwar group uses Sicilian; most mobile individuals speak English only in the home. Percentages for the group as a whole (44 families) show that 32 percent use only Sicilian at home, 45 percent use both Sicilian and English, and 23 percent use English only.

Among the occupationally mobile, the prewar immigrants, and the educated—the three groups which have enough ability to use English constantly—only the first two actually speak English at home. There was no significant association between amount of education and English as the home language. In twenty-six homes the immigrant's capacity to speak English is high and in twenty-two homes it is low. It should not be assumed, however, that those who do or do not speak English make a choice only on the basis of emotional or ethnic preferences; table 7 shows some of the other practical considerations which influence choice of language.

Beginning with the fourteen families who speak only Sicilian/Italian at home, it is apparent that foreign language ability of both husband and wife is the single most important factor, although nationality, time in Australia, and occupation are signifi-

TABLE 7

HOME LANGUAGE AND RELATED SOCIOECONOMIC CHARACTERISTICS

(In Percent of N)

	Sicilian Italian N = 14	Sicilian and English N = 20	English N = 10
Respondent's English capacity			
High	30	55	100
Medium	40	30	
Low	30	15	
Spouse's English capacity			
High	7	45	100
Medium		30	
Low	93	25	
Spouse's nationality			
Australian			30
Sicilian-Australian	7	25	50
Sicilian	93	75	20
Time in Australia			
Old	7	45	70
Intermediate	30	55	30
New	63		
Occupation			
Office	7	25	50
Shop	7	55	30
Factory	86	20	20
Occupational mobility			
High	22	20	50
Low	78	80	50

NOTE: Total sample equals forty-four. Unmarried respondents not included.

cant. All the wives in this group except one are Sicilian-born and due to their recent entry into Australia their English language ability is low. In addition, most of the husbands work in factories which appears to retard language learning. These families speak Sicilian at home not because it is the preferred language but because they have little choice: only in one family do both husband and wife have the ability to speak English. Most said they expect to become bilingual families when they have been in the country longer and when their children are older. The couple which has high English capacity is very different: they are both well-educated, the wife is fluent in English although Sicilian born, the husband is a professional, and they are in the group of the occupationally mobile. These two speak Italian (not dialect) at home out of preference but insist that all members of the family maintain high fluency in English as well so that they will appear as educated Australians outside and educated Italians at home. It is therefore obvious that language ability of both husband and wife must be considered instead of assuming that a man, the usual sociological focus, who knows English but speaks Italian at home is unchanged.

The largest and most complex group is the twenty families who use both Italian and English at home. One factor, occupation, can explain why bilingualism is the rule, but the number of patterns concerning who uses which language with whom and when are far too complex to be detailed here. However, some common use patterns can be mentioned. The majority of the husbands are in office or shop employment and the same number speak excellent English. Almost all of their wives speak equally good English either because they were born in Australia or because they too worked in the shop. Half of the couples, all in shops, came before the war while the remainder arrived immediately after the war; none are recent immigrants.

The most common pattern is for the husband and wife to speak to each other and to the children in a mixture of English and Italian, but the children speak only English. Another frequent pattern is for husband and wife to use Italian with each other most of the time but to use English with the children. Occasionally, with educated, occupationally mobile husbands, the man alone uses Italian while everyone else speaks English.

The reason for using two languages is usually that "it's easier." But one frequent result is that the children complain of not being understood by the parents. Many almost stop talking to their mothers and fathers, bringing about a generation gap which is never bridged. In some cases the parents really do not comprehend English well enough and the children can no longer communicate in dialect. But in most families where this pattern has developed, it seems that actually the two generations do not understand one another's ideas and language has become the scapegoat. Bilingual immigrant families reveal clearly many of the tensions and gaps between the generations, and a detailed study of this area would analyze much more than language patterns.

The English-speaking homes reveal an expectedly different pattern. All of the ten respondents are high ability English speakers. Eighty percent of their spouses cannot speak Italian or dialect because they are either non-Italian Australians or second-generation Sicilians who never learned to speak in their parents' language. The Sicilian-born wives either worked in the shops or were highly educated. Most of the men do not work in factories and those who do, plus many of the others, are occupationally mobile and therefore insist that everyone speak English. Although it is possible for the husbands and the children to talk in Italian and leave the wife out, this is a very difficult pattern to put into practice. Mothers simply spend too much time with children and when the mother's use of English is reinforced by Australian playmates and teachers, the husband must be a very determined man to continue using Italian at home. Several tried it and failed.

One of the most intriguing findings to emerge from this analysis is the high number of couples who allow or encourage their children to speak English at home. One reason for permissiveness in the home is the fact that all of the uneducated immigrants speak Sicilian dialect and not Italian as their first language. There is a general feeling, in Sicily as well as Australia, that dialect marks a man as inferior and that it is a "beautiful" thing to speak standard Italian. An additional factor is the strong feeling that dialect is not good for anything—"What kind of a job can you get with dialect?" Most Sicilians commented that if they spoke Italian at home they would insist that the children speak it too, but dialect is useless in the business world and therefore there is no sense in fighting with the children to make them speak Sicilian.

The children learn English quickly and use it constantly. Even before they begin school they learn many words of English because in play groups with cousins and friends the little ones are told to "speak English" if they want to play. Even three-year-olds use some English and when they start school they switch permanently; within a few years their ability to speak dialect is severely curtailed. One reason that so many parents allow English in the home is that many people who cannot speak English do understand quite well. This is as true for wives who stay home all day as it is for the husbands who go out to work.

One other index of language is the interview itself. The individual was allowed to select the language in which the interview was to be conducted; there is a perfect correlation between ability and the interview language. Low ability immigrants all chose Italian, and while they interlaced some of their conversation with English words they were consistent in using Italian. High ability people all used English although some tried Italian. Many persons in this group eagerly selected Italian when they discovered that the interviewer spoke the language, but they could not keep it up. A question would be asked in Italian; they would begin to answer in Italian but when a complex thought was encountered they would switch to English and then complete the answer using English. After much shifting some finally said sheepishly, "I guess we better use English." Others never admitted the discrepancy between their desire and their ability, and the interviews ended with the American researcher speaking Italian and the Italian respondent replying in English.

FRIENDS AND ASSOCIATES

The fourth dependent variable in the private sector is personal interaction with friends and acquaintances. Who are the people, other than relatives, with whom the immigrants spend their free time? Do they have many Australian friends? Do they want Australian friends? Do they have any Italian friends who are not Sicilians? What do they think about Australians as friends?

Forty-four percent of the immigrants have Australian friends while 56 percent do not now nor have they ever had an Australian friend. Many of the people in the first group interpreted the word "friend" very loosely: five of the twenty-one answered this question "yes" because they have friends from work with whom they occasionally go to a pub after work, but none bring Australian friends to their homes or invite them to parties. The remaining sixteen immigrants do associate socially with Australians. Sicilian and Australian couples go out together for an evening of dinner and dancing, and they ask one another to parties. Fourteen of the sixteen are educated and all are high in their ability to speak English. The remaining two are a very independent widow who lives alone, speaks perfect English, emigrated before the war, and goes all over the city visiting friends, and a widower of many years who lives on income from rental property and spends his time in a round of civic and service activities maintained almost exclusively by Australians. The only significant association is between education and Australian friends: highly educated persons have Australian friends whereas low educated immigrants do not. Time in Australia, age at emigration, and occupational mobility are not associated with having Australian friends.

MEMBERSHIP IN CLUBS AND ASSOCIATIONS

The fifth dependent variable in this sector is membership in Australian associations: 23 percent are active and 77 percent are not active in such groups. These associations include professional societies, sports clubs, Rotary, Kiwanis, Chamber of Commerce, Returned Servicemen's Leagues (equivalent to the American Legion), and the YMCA. Two independent variables are associated with membership in Australian associations: education and occupational mobility. Highly educated people are active in associations and low educated persons are not; highly mobile immigrants are active in associations while nonmobile persons are not.

Respondents were also asked if they were members of any Italian organizations in order to ascertain the general rate of participation in such activities. Italians in Italy and abroad have always been noted as "nonjoiners" who prefer to stay with their families (Barzini 1964; Glazer and Moynihan 1963). Forty-two percent belong to at least one organization while 58 percent are not connected with any outside group. Of the eleven respondents who do belong to some Australian club or organization, eight also belong to at least one Italian organization. There are not many Italian clubs in Sidney, reflecting the general tendency not to form groups, but there is a cultural Dante Alighieri Society connected with the University of Sidney. There was a semiwelfare association, staffed entirely by immigrants, which helped new immigrants learn the ways of Australia, but it is no longer functioning. A social club for Italians and Australians called the APIA provides, for a very low entrance fee, dances with orchestras three nights a week, a bar, and slot machines; their facilities are located in a new building donated by Alitalia Airlines and the Flotta Lauro shipping company. There is also an APIA sports club which sponsors a soccer team. Of the nine immigrants who belong to both Italian and Australian organizations, one is a member of the APIA social club, two are members of the sports club, and five belong to both the Dante Alighieri and the immigrant welfare league. Of the thirty-seven immigrants who do not belong to Australian associations, twenty-eight are not associated with any Italian organization either, seven are members of the APIA social club, and two belong to the APIA sports and the Dante Alighieri. It is clear then that the largest number of joiners belong to the APIA social club, which is not really a group; it merely provides a relatively inexpensive evening in pleasant surroundings and there is no mixing of groups or visiting at other tables unless the people are known from other contexts. Therefore, discounting the APIA, very few immigrants belong to viable organizations in which they must or can mix socially with Australians. The only men who do participate in such activity are those with education or those who have been occupationally mobile.

A summary of the associations among the four independent variables considered throughout the Australian study suggests some of the deeper implications of the figures and also reveals some of the relationships between private and public sector variables.

Age at emigration. This independent variable is associated with food habits—those individuals who were young at emigration are more prone to change their traditional foods and begin eating Australian food, while those persons who were over thirty at emigration are much more resistant to change, and in fact have not changed except to substitute more meat for pasta, which they themselves do not perceive as change. This finding fits in with the social-psychological hypothesis that those things which are learned first are the most resistant to change and therefore those individuals who have maintained a practice for a longer period of time would be the less willing to give it up. Young people are more willing to experiment and to try something new, particularly in the area of eating and food where no permanent change or damage will result if a foreign food is eaten once. Age at emigration is not an important variable when assessing changes in language usage, friends, or organizational membership.

Time in Australia. This variable is associated with two of the five dependent variables discussed in this section—food and home language. People who have been in the new country for more than twenty-seven years eat a lot of Australian food at home and speak English in the home, whereas the new immigrants (in Australia less than eleven years) still retain their Sicilian food patterns and speak dialect at home. Increasing time in a new country does appear to be a relevant factor toward change in these two areas of private life. However, as pointed out the matter is not so simple. Those immigrants who speak English at home have been in Australia a long time, but they arrived during a period in Australian history when there were very few Italian speakers in the community so that newcomers were forced to acquire a fairly good speaking knowledge of the language. The scarcity of industrial jobs drove these immigrants into a service industry where they had to speak English all day to their customers. These two related facts forced, or allowed, immigrants to gain a basic understanding of the English language, and with additional pressure from their

English-speaking children in following years, today all the prewar immigrants speak excellent English and have difficulty carrying on conversations in Italian or dialect. The newcomers will never learn English well because they are employed in factories in which there are many other Italian speakers, and Sydney offices and shops deliberately employ foreign-language speakers to help and to attract the business of the mass of immigrants who came after World War II. These are uneducated people who speak Italian poorly and who have a fear of attempting to learn a foreign language that they consider extremely difficult. The only two men in the most recent group of immigrants who speak English well are both occupationally mobile.

Food habits are much more open to the influence of time and without doubt the new immigrants will, in years to come, eat much more Australian food and cook a more Australian way. Since learning to prepare new Australian dishes appears to be a source of pride, and since children often ask to have Australian food they have eaten outside, the wives and mothers will try new dishes to increase their own prestige and to please their children in this area of life which is so very important to mothers and children.

However, time in Australia is not a relevant variable when assessing changes in primary relationships—either friends or organizations. Some long-time immigrants have Australian friends though most do not, and some new immigrants have Australian friends though most do not. Almost none of the immigrants belong to associations or clubs of any kind except a few who joined the local social club so that they would have a place to go in the evening with their friends. Friends are family and *paesani* and most declare that they have no need for other friends or groups because "I have my family."

Education. This independent variable is significantly associated with three of the four private sector dependent variables: food habits, friends, and organizational membership. In all cases the highly educated immigrants have changed while the uneducated have not. More of the educated respondents are married to Australian or Australian-born women and this may account for some of the change in food habits, but educated people the world over are more sophisticated and are less resistant to change. All of the educated, excepting the two men who emigrated before the war, are in middle-class occupations and have more opportunities to meet Australians through their work. The opportunity, of course, without the inclination may go unused, as is the case among the uneducated immigrants employed in factories—very few ever get to know their Australian co-workers. On the other hand, immigrants who never meet Australians will rarely have Australian friends.

Educated middle-class people in any country are usually more like middle-class individuals in other countries than they are like peasants in their own country. Sicilian middle-class persons have ideas which are very different from those of Australian middle-class people in many areas of life; however, when the two meet, their approximately equivalent education and use of similar mass media allow them to talk and converse about world events, national politics, or a local election issue. Working-class people tend to live much more in small personal worlds bounded by family, friends, work, and neighborhood; and when working-class Australians and working-class immigrant Sicilians meet in a social or other non-work context they have little to say to one another. Their lives at home are filled with discussion of the daily experiences of family members and local gossip, rather than current events and ideas. Therefore, although both educated and uneducated immigrants have approximately equal opportunity to meet Australians, only the educated take advantage of this opportunity. In addition, middle-class people with their greater knowledge of the world are much more likely to ignore or overlook differences in others while working-class people are more apt to perceive differences in speech, dress, or ideas as indicative of insurmountable barriers to intimacy. Nowhere is this more true than in Australia where people have not been exposed to a variety of peoples and customs as have Europeans with their proximity to other foreign countries or Americans who have successfully integrated millions of foreign-born nationals.

While this study concurs with the results of other studies in the assertion that southern Italians in general do not join organizations, it also demonstrates that educated people are much more likely to be members of civic, religious, professional, or social groups. Their education, experience, and occupations, especially in the professions, make them invaluable members of formal groups, whether Australian or Italian in nature. The middle class in Australia, as in England and the United States, is responsible for most of the community organizing that is often necessary in a modern urban society, and though this tendency to come together in groups is less active in Australia than in the United States, there is still a wide variety of organizations active today.

Occupational Mobility. Immigrants who have been highly mobile speak English at home and belong to Australian associations; those who have not been mobile speak Italian at home. This makes sense when one realizes that (1) people who are moving up from the working class should appear Australian to Australians and (2) this mobility is not only for the immigrant but also his children, who should eventually improve upon the position gained by the father. The occupationally mobile speak excellent English, and to retain this ability and ensure that their children are not hampered by an inadequate knowledge of the language it is spoken in the home.

This group does not necessarily bring Australian food into the home, nor do they have Australian friends. The only two dependent variables in this section which are significant for the occupationally mobile are those two factors which will enhance their mobility. Consider home language in more detail for a moment. First, children raised in Italian-speaking homes are handicapped in school and very often never have the command of English which children in English-speaking homes have years before they begin school; second, the children in the occupationally mobile group are sent to the better Catholic schools in the city where they meet children of middle-class Australians. If the children of the immigrants are to compete equally with natives and be accepted as social equals, then it is important that their homes be like the homes of the other children: they should not be ashamed of their homes or their parents and the home atmosphere should never make Australian children feel odd or ill-at-ease. It is not necessary that food habits be changed because Italian food (modified by the addition of meat) is just not that different from Australian food, and in Sydney Italian food now has a certain prestige value of its own. Many of the respondents commented that their children's friends like Italian food and enjoy eating at their home. But they also noted that they serve only those dishes, such as lasagna or spaghetti with meat sauce, which are acceptable to Australians, while "odd" Sicilian foods such as squid, lentils, and bitter greens and oil are reserved for the family.

It is also important for middle-class people or those who hope to be, to belong to organizations—civic, professional, and service. In this way, men meet other people in the community, and since so many middle-class jobs (insurance, real estate, law) are service connected, it is important that they meet and know a vast number of people: contacts are good business. A factory worker has no need of the contact offered by the Rotary Club or its services, nor does he have much to offer such an organization; but the man who has his own business or who is an executive of a large corporation would be an asset to an association. The educated belong to these organizations too, but they also have many Australian friends whereas the occupationally mobile frequently do not.

Those immigrants who have been mobile through their occupations display a tendency to adopt those elements in the Australian social structure which will further their occupational and social aims in the public sector and to leave untouched those factors which are strictly personal and which will have no bearing on their mobility.

11
THE FAMILY SYSTEM

WHAT happens to the Sicilian family system in a new country, especially in a country such as Australia which, like the United States, rests on a principle of personal freedom and independence? It is, of course, perfectly possible for a Sicilian family to remain quite unchanged in Australia. There are no glaring oddities in the system, such as plural marriage, which the laws of the new land would prohibit. On the other hand, the family may change completely. The decision is up to the members of the family and nothing in the institutional structure of the host society will actively aid or impede change. Therefore, changes in family values, patterns, and relationships are to be considered along with other dependent variables in the private sector of life.

Most changes begin in very minor ways and progress slowly over a period of time, usually culminating in a change of custom or idea. If the teen-age daughter in a Sicilian family asks permission to go out at night with girl friends, the parents may forbid it because Sicilian girls do not go out without their parents, or they may allow it because they are "in Australia now" and this is the custom or because they do not want their daughter to be different from the other girls—there are many such reasons. The point is that no difficult skill need be mastered before the change can be effected, and it is precisely for this reason that family and kinship variables are so valuable in assessing how much the immigrants change.

Because the fieldwork data in Sicily revealed such a complex and multilayered family system, it was difficult to hypothesize about change in Australia. The main source of the difficulty was the "real-ideal" duality that is fundamental to the functioning of this social system. For instance, relatives should be kind and helpful to one another, but they rarely are. Many of the factors which seem to foster divisiveness among the relatives are family prestige, honor, lack of financial resources, and community sanctions. If a number of Sicilians move to a city or country where there are jobs and money for all, where the Sicilian community, as such, does not exist in a physical sense, and where the individuals are exposed to new and different ideas, then what effect will these changes have on kin relationships? Seemingly, change could go in either of two directions. Since the ideal says that relatives should help one another, perhaps in the kinder, more generous environment they would act on that level and realize the tendency to form united extended family groups. On the other hand, the availability of money and new sources of prestige might force members of the extended family further apart as they use these resources to consolidate their position and thereby get ahead of the others. Both tendencies are present in Sicily and the ideas which lie behind each are taken to the new country with the individuals. The husband-wife relationship exhibits the same duality and so, similarly, two possible kinds of change could be imagined: the husband and wife, in egalitarian Australia where the wife will gain more freedom, could develop a truly equal relationship—that is, they would allow the equality which existed privately in the home to show in public—or the husband as a successful wage earner might become the authoritarian husband in fact.

Ignoring the findings of the American studies, which by and large depend on faulty background information and are areally based, I predicted: (1) there would be some diversity among the immigrants based on the four independent variables with, for example, the educated immigrants changing more; (2) relatives would not be able to overcome the centuries of hostility, jealousy, and competition and therefore in Australia would have little to do with one another; (3) husband and wife would become more openly equal, and the husband, because of more free time, would play a more active role in the household than he did in Sicily; (4) children would continue to be subservient to the dictates of the parents and the needs of the family. Some of the predictions were generally correct, but others were very wrong. Certain factors which should have been considered were not because I was looking at the Sicilian family system in Australia as a social science researcher and not as a Sicilian immigrant. The reason for emigrating and the emotional impact of the immigration experience are two of the most important variables which have shaped changes in this family system, and socioeconomic factors in the Sicilian background such as education and family traditions play a much more important role in subsequent changes than envisioned.

THE EXTENDED FAMILY

Over thirty questions were asked about the extended family and relatives; some questions were factual and required the respondent to use his own experiences as a referent while other questions were hypothetical and explored values. (See Appendix A, Interview 2).

CONTACT WITH RELATIVES

At the time of arrival in Australia 15 percent of the immigrants had many relatives in Sydney, 64 percent had a few relatives, and 21 percent had none. "Many" indicates several siblings, aunts, uncles, and cousins; most of the people in this group counted fifteen or twenty relatives at arrival. "Few" indicates that the immigrant had one or two relatives in Sydney. Therefore 79 percent of the immigrants had at least one relative to whom they could turn if help and advice were necessary. Of the thirty-eight immigrants who had someone present on arrival, thirty-two had own blood relatives while six had a wife's brother. The ten respondents who had no one are scattered among all groups, prewar and postwar, educated and uneducated, etc. The high percentage of immigrants who followed other relatives to Australia reflects the chain migration phenomenon described and analyzed for southern Europeans in Australia by Price (1963). This hypothesis posits that certain demographic patterns noted among immigrants in Australia, as well as in the United States and Canada, are the result of relatives following each other to new countries. The main pattern noted is that immigrants from one large area, such as Sicily or Calabria, are not drawn from all sections of the area equally, but instead tend to come in great numbers from specific towns; in Sydney, for instance, there are over a thousand immigrants from the small town of Poggioreale and virtually none from others near it. Almost no one in Nicuportu had ever heard of Australia; yet Poggioreale is only a short distance away. Price's book details this process extremely well for immigrants from Italy, Greece, Malta, and Yugoslavia. Most of the immigrants in the present sample had heard of Australia first from relatives and received most of the scanty information they had before emigrating from them. Often other people in their home town had been in Australia or had relatives who were there and these people talked about the country too, but as one man said, "Who can believe what other people say? When my brothers went out and said the same thing, then I believed it."

Australian law on sponsors has changed many times over the years, but for most of the time since 1900 it has been necessary to have a sponsor who would guarantee the conduct of the emigrant and who was a close relative, such as mother, father, sibling, child, spouse, aunt, uncle, or cousin, or sometimes under special agreements an employer. At the beginning of 1965 the law read that only members of the immediate family could sponsor an immigrant, but about six months later the law was changed to include other blood relatives. Sixty percent of the respondents had own relative as sponsor, 15 percent has wife's relative, and 25 percent had a friend or employer. Three did not need sponsors, one came out as an Italian government employee, and four others did not provide this information. Of the twenty-four with own relative as sponsor the breakdown is as follows: twelve siblings; eight uncles, cousins, or nephews; two fathers; one child; and one husband. This detail reflects the youth of the immigrants and the small number of elderly people who emigrate. Many respondents who had friends or *paesani* as sponsors noted that they had asked a relative to sponsor them but were refused because the relative did not wish to assume the responsibility. They perceived this refusal as just another treacherous but expectable act on the part of relatives: "They're too concerned with themselves and their own families to think of anyone else."

When they first arrived in Sydney, 52 percent of the immigrants lived with relatives, 25 percent with friends, and 23 percent alone. There is a rather large discrepancy between the number of immigrants who had relatives in Australia and those who lived with those relatives, showing again the Sicilian hesitancy to live with relatives even if, as in this case, it often meant living alone in squalid rooms. Most of those who did move in with relatives left as soon as they possibly could, although several lived happily with a sister or an uncle for several years—usually until the respondent's marriage. There were many unsolicited comments from the respondents about the perils of living with relatives, the general thought being:

> It was a terrible mistake. I lived with my aunt and my cousin for three years but you should never live with relatives, there are always arguments; about using too much electricity, my aunt always asking me where I was going, with whom, etc. I'd say "Look, I pay my rent so let me do as I please." But that doesn't work with relatives, you have to be part of them, they have to know everything.

Forty-one percent of the respondents found their first job through a relative, 44 percent through a friend, and 15 percent through the newspaper or an employment agency. Friends, mainly *paesani*, figure surprisingly large in this category considering that most of the immigrants had been sponsored by relatives who were legally responsible for finding them jobs. Immigrants who came to relatives who owned fruit shops often found jobs through friends because a fruit shop can employ only a few people or because sometimes immigrants did not want to work in the shops; then it was necessary to ask a friend who worked in a factory to find a job for the newcomer.

It is usually assumed that southern Italian immigrants, because of their extended family orientation, often live together in one house or in several apartments in the same building. The pattern in Sicily is not, nor has it ever been, one of joint family residence. There is a very strong feeling that married couples should live by themselves and this feeling is carried over to Australia. Sixty-six percent of the immigrants live with their nuclear families alone. Of these thirty-two families, one has no children, four have all their married children living away from the parental home, and twenty-seven are composed of husband, wife, and unmarried children. Nineteen percent of the respondents live in homes in which one or more relatives of both husband and wife live with the nuclear family. In two of these cases the relatives are recent arrivals in Australia and their stay in the home is temporary until they can find their own homes. In all the rest of the cases the relative is one parent or sibling; in no cases do two nuclear families share a household. In 15 percent of the cases there are other arrangements, mainly concerning widows, widowers, or boarders. It is noteworthy that none of the widows or widowers live with married children or other relatives, even though all have a close relative available with whom they could live. Therefore, in only seven families out of forty-eight are relatives living permanently in the house. In this matter the Sicilians very closely approximate the Australians but not because they have changed after emigration; the pattern of household composition reflects the preferred living arrangement in Sicily. It is not indicative of change, acculturation, or assimilation.

Fifty-eight percent of the immigrants today have "many" relatives in Sydney as opposed to 15 percent on arrival; 29 percent have few relatives as contrasted with 64 percent; 12 percent have none as compared to 21 percent on arrival. Many relatives in a fair number of cases means more than one hundred as the genealogies revealed. The genealogies were especially helpful in ascertaining quantity of relatives because most of the respondents in the interviews refused to count and merely estimated the number of "close relatives" in the city. This shows again the Sicilian preference for nuclear family and their utter disregard, in most cases, for relatives.

Very few respondents, eight only, have parents in Sydney but all of these either have the parent living with them or see him at least three times a week. Some of the other respondents had had parents in Australia but the parents died some time before. Most, however, are reluctant to bring aged mothers and fathers to a new country because they realize how terribly difficult and lonely it is for these old people who will never learn the language and do not understand many of the customs. Only seven respondents have married children, all of whom live away from the parental home. These respondents see their children at least once a week, usually on Sunday, although it is not uncommon for them to drop in on one another during the week. It is unfortunate that the age of respondents in this sample is so young because contact with married children is an important factor in understanding the pattern of contact with relatives.

Of the thirty respondents with living siblings in Sydney, 50 percent see them about once a week, 20 percent see them about every three weeks, and 30 percent see them about once a year or on occasions such as weddings and funerals. Of the fifteen respondents who see their relatives very often, four are educated and eleven are in the newest group of immigrants; of the nine respondents who see these relatives rarely, eight are prewar immigrants and one came just after the war. Six of the long-time immigrants, who are older in age as well, are the six respondents who see their married children at least once a week. Therefore, while the number of these respondents is not large enough to make completely sound conclusions, there is nonetheless a real trend for either age or time in Australia to be correlated with kin contact; younger and more recent immigrants maintain much more frequent contact with close relatives such as siblings, seeing them about once a week, than do older (time and age) immigrants, who see relatives very rarely but who maintain very close and intimate contact with their married children.

Figures on contact with other relatives, cousins, aunts, and uncles, are: 26 percent see these relatives about once a week, 26 percent see them about once every three weeks, and 48 percent see them never, once a year, or on special occasions such as weddings. These proportions are what one would expect from Sicilians who regard relatives as superfluous under the best of conditions and from whom there is no expectation of closeness, aid, or help.

These are "wakes and weddings relatives," the most frequent description of persons who are placed in the outer ring of all relatives and who, after all, "have their own families to care for." The exclusion of distant relatives from the on-going part of one's life is consistent with the Sicilian pattern and does not change in Australia. Those persons who maintain close contact with these relatives are in every case those who see their own siblings very frequently as well.

The interesting point is the differences in contact between the newer immigrants and the older immigrants. Specific questions about contact in the early years in Sydney were not asked because I did not realize how important this point would be; I now believe that it is one of the most fundamental factors in understanding changes in the Sicilian family system. It becomes even more important when one contrasts this pattern with the one usually described in the American literature on southern Italian immigrants where the big united extended family is the rule. Only one case of a real extended family which maintained close and constant contact with each other was found. In all other cases of persons who had high contact with siblings, only one or at most two siblings were involved. The feeling is best expressed by one of the prewar immigrants who has seven brothers and sisters in Sydney, sees them at weddings and funerals, but visits his married son and daughter at least three times a week each:

> It's all the family together, just the two children and their families, not the brothers and cousins, they have their own. Friends and relatives we used to see a lot, visiting, but you grow away from them. Now when we visit we go to my son or daughter, not to relatives and of course the same thing is happening to them [the relatives].

The hypothesis suggested by the data but which must be verified by further fieldwork is that kinsmen, who in Sicily are important only for maintaining the honor of the group, become important and necessary at the point of emigration because of the emotional shock of transplanting oneself in a foreign society. The only people to whom one can turn at arrival are the relatives, because friends, who will help to a limited extent, have their own families and relatives. Relatives live together or near one another, they find jobs for the newcomers and generally act as the agents through which the rules and customs of the new society will become intelligible. The principle that relatives should help one another becomes a reality at this time, and those who came first do spend vast amounts of time and energy helping the new arrivals to find themselves in Australian society. The help is freely given but complaints of abuse and ingratitude are frequent on the part of the helper and accusations of not helping enough or supplying false information come from the helpless new arrival. Although the newcomer cannot do other than accept aid and the relatives can hardly refuse that help, the old ingrained feelings of distrust about relatives cannot be completely overcome.

For a time, usually five to ten years, the immigrants crowd to-gether, seeking in the family group that security and confidence which they cannot find in the outside world. But after some years most of the immigrants begin to take their place in Australian society and become more confident of their own abilities to "get along" in this no longer new world. They have occupations, home, families, friends and, having made great or small changes in their ideas of how life should be lived, have come to terms with their new lives. There is no longer an urgent, practical need for trans-lators. These middle years are busy and tiring though rewarding and most men are intensely occupied with their jobs and their immediate family. So contacts with relatives are cut down and the kin now meet only on social occasions.

As the immigrants grow older and enter the late fifties and sixties their children marry and form their own households thus rewarding the mother and father by their success in life and happiness in their new families. The old people, who by now have often retired, turn toward the children and grandchildren for their social life and now see their own sisters and brothers only on rare special days such as weddings and funerals. Even holidays, which in the middle period they spent with the close relatives, are now passed with their children. No one feels guilty about the loss of contact and intimacy with relatives because "they are doing the same thing."

History has also brought changes which have affected the social life of the older immigrants. In the days before World War II there were few Italians in Sydney and those who were there knew each other. Amusements were few and money was always scarce so they went out together for big picnics and the men went to the clubs such as the Aeolian Island Club which flourished for many years and then faded away at the time of the war. Many respon-dents noted that they have telephones today and so it is not neces-sary to see relatives; one can maintain some contact by phone and this is sufficient.

The commonly described pattern in the United States of Italian immigrants forming large extended family units that remain solid over a series of generations is not the case in Australia, and it is doubtful if it was ever true for the majority of those in America either. Some immigrants are trapped in the initial period of intense kin contact, the kind of kin relationship one would expect in an ethnic ghetto where working-class people are in close physical proximity. The most intense and deeply felt Sicilian values revolve about the nuclear family, not the extended kin group, and while shock and inexperience may bring the relatives together for a time after immigration, there is no reason to assume that the condition is permanent.

NAMING PRACTICES

There are two aspects of naming practices that are relevant in the examination of change: the names given to children at birth and the names which the immigrants use in Australia. Each respondent was asked whom he and his siblings were named after. Eight older prewar respondents did not know, nor did they seem to care. Of the remaining forty immigrants, 65 percent came from families in which the naming rule (described in chapter 6) was followed exactly and 35 percent were from families in which the first two sons or the first four children were named after the grandparents while remaining children were named after assorted kin or after nonkin. In only one family were the children not named after any relatives. No particular section of the island or social class is represented by the minority of families which did not follow the rule completely. The respondent was then asked how he named his own children. Sixty-seven percent followed the rule; 27 percent named the first two or four children following the rule and gave other children names of assorted relatives or of nonkin; 6 percent named none of their children after relatives. There is therefore remarkably little alteration of the traditional pattern on this index.

Very few Italian names are used by Australians. Maria is the main exception, but most Italian names can be changed into English. Salvatore becomes Sam, Giuseppe is Joe, Calogera is Carol, and Antonio is Tony. Only a few short names, such as Mario, which are not common in Sicily, remain unchanged. Since a foreign name marks a person as having some kind of ethnic association it is reasonable that those people who were changing more or faster might alter their names to the English version. Thirty-eight percent of the immigrants have retained their Italian names, 31 percent use their Italian name at home and their anglicized name with Australians, 31 percent have anglicized their names completely. Almost all of their children were baptized with Italian names but sometime during childhood the name was changed and has remained so. In many cases it was the child himself who initiated the change, but in many cases the parents, realizing that with Italian names their children would be "too different" from their friends and schoolmates, initiated the change. Several immigrant couples gave the children anglicized names at birth but claim that they are Italian names in honor of certain relatives. For instance, Lucia becomes Lucille, a modification that satisfies everyone. Twenty-one percent gave their children Italian names, 25 percent used Italian names in baptizing which were later changed, and 54 percent gave English names at birth. A considerable change in naming is evident. In addition, 79 percent of the immigrants with very young children stated that the child's name would be changed when he began mixing with Australian children.

When asked what they thought of the Sicilian naming rule, 63 percent of all respondents stated that the rule is good and should be followed because it is the traditional Sicilian way and shows respect for one's ancestors or gives pleasure to living relatives; 12 percent showed some conflict, stating that the rule has been followed but that they do not like it or that it is used only if they like the name assigned; 25 percent completely rejected the rule, stating that it is not used any longer or that the custom is dying out in Australia. There is a significant association between changes in naming patterns and education; the association between these changes and time in Australia approaches significance.

RELATIVES AND GODPARENTS

The godparents loom large in almost all studies of Mediterranean or Latin American societies and since data from Sicily indicated that this society is rather different from others, a series of questions about baptismal godparenthood was included. Godparenthood in most Roman Catholic countries appears to be used as a means of solidifying social relations, either between kin, or more usually, between unrelated persons. But in Sicily it appears to be mere conformity to a rule of the church. I therefore wondered if relatives in a new and strange country assume more importance at least in this honored but formerly neglected area of kin relationships.

Respondents were first asked about their own godparents in order to establish a basis for comparison; 46 percent have relatives as their godparents, 4 percent have both a relative and a non-kinsman, and 50 percent have nonkin. The proportion of kin to nonkin godparents for the immigrant's own children is almost the same: 33 percent were given relatives as godparents, 31 percent were given one relative and one nonkin, and 36 percent were given nonkin. Although a slightly higher percentage of nonkin were asked to be godparents in Australia, this may simply reflect the smaller number of kin available to stand as godparents. Several older immigrants noted that they would have asked a relative to be a godparent but that since this person had already been a god-parent so many times, it was not fair to ask him to assume obligations and expenses one more time.

The institution of San Giovanni, friends as godparents, is activated by most of the immigrants if a *compare* or *comare* made in Sicily is also in Australia, but none reported having made a new *compare* through the bond of San Giovanni in Australia. All respondents added that this custom is never used by their second-generation children even though it is known to them. It therefore appears that changes in the life style of most of the immigrants and important alterations within the nuclear family eliminate the need for this means of validating friendships.

Many people in Nicuportu claimed that a godparent—of baptism, marriage, or San Giovanni—becomes a relative and has all the rights and obligations of a relative. To test whether this is a regional value, respondents were asked if friends become relatives when they are *compari:* 29 percent said yes, 50 percent said "no, but they become closer friends," and 21 percent said no or "no, they think so but I don't." So godparenthood does not for the majority of first-generation Sicilians in Sydney give a nonkin god-parent the status of relative. Most of the comments indicated that "relatives" is a special category and includes only those connected by blood or by marriage, not by godparenthood. Answers to this question revealed no correlations with regional or class differences within the sample; however, those who replied yes are, for the most part, those who maintain close contact with their own relatives. The value placed on relatives is important in determining one's feeling about godparents because many respondents prefer friends to relatives.

EXTENDED FAMILY VERSUS NUCLEAR FAMILY

In the detailed description of the relatives and the nuclear family in Sicily (chapter 4) it was stated that the latter always takes preference over the former except in circumstances involving honor. To determine the attitudes of immigrants in Sydney on this issue, I again used the proverb "the real relatives are those inside the house" (all but four men from the east coast of Sicily had heard it before) : 81 percent said they agreed with the proverb and felt it meant that the nuclear family alone gives the "support, affection, trust, understanding, strength, and protection" which result from one's "own blood" and "pure motives"; 6 percent said that they did not agree with the proverb because "all relatives are my blood" or "some relatives are special"; 13 percent stated that they did not agree with the proverb because everyone, both kin and nonkin, are important in this world and "you must think of everyone." A few of these added that this kind of thinking is "used as an excuse when something is going on, when there is some trouble," and one educated man said that Sicilians "don't trust anyone. Others, the outsiders, are wrong a priori. You and yours are right and the others are wrong. I think it depends on who is right, look at the facts of the case."

There is very little, if any, change from the responses in Sicily. Those few who included relatives in the family qualified their disagreement by stating that only "some relatives" are different; the remainder still act in such a way as to buttress most Sicilians' negative feelings about relatives in general. Respondents were also asked to specify who is "inside the house." Nobody included relatives, not even a few favored ones.

Although the Sicilian position on relatives is extreme, it still follows a general pattern found in Great Britain, the United States, and Australia. In Sicily, the one unusual feature was the almost universal insistence that married children are out of the "house," meaning family, and on their own. Most English-speakers would not take this position but would assert that children, married or single, living at home or away, are still part of the family and remain so until their old family of orientation is dissolved by death. Fifty-six percent of the respondents replied that married children are no longer in the house, but 44 percent stated that they are in the house and the family until they die. This distribution for the immigrants is indicative of a real change in values brought about primarily as a result of the enormously improved economic situation of the Sicilians in Australia. The only way in which a new family in Sicily can survive and enrich itself is to make clear its freedom from any and all obligations to the two parental homes. In Sydney, on the other hand, where all of the Sicilians have at least adequate incomes and many have made considerable sums of money, this attitude is no longer necessary.

There is work and income for everyone, first and second generation alike; families are not so large; the father has the resources to help his married children if necessary even though this help is not normally needed. The improved occupational and economic picture in Australia has helped to remove those fetters which forced parents and children to maintain a distance if anyone was to advance. In addition, many parents noted they had changed their ideas on this subject after seeing how Australians manage and, of course, their own Australian-bred children aided in this process. These immigrants were delighted with the Australian ability to maintain both distance and intimacy at the same time and have endeavored to emulate them. They claim that the new way is the better way because in Sicily no matter what you do you lose your children. These men and women are very active in promoting this new idea among other immigrants and I have participated in a number of very long, often acrimonious, but always heartfelt discussions on this topic.

In Australia, Sicilian children are much more likely to remain an integral part of their natal family after marriage, but what about the disposition of parents after the children marry and set up homes of their own? In Sicily, even though married couples do not want other relatives living in the home, an unmarried sister or an aged parent has every right to expect that he or she will be cared for by one of the children. There are many elderly people who prefer to stay by themselves but most do move in with a married child, usually a daughter because it is so difficult for a mother and a son's wife to get along. I asked, "Do you think the children of a widowed mother have the right to leave her to live alone, assuming she has enough money?" Fifty-six percent said that the mother must be cared for; 25 percent said that it is up to the mother; and 19 percent said that there is no obligation to care for the mother in the home. So there is little change among the immigrants. The group which puts the decision up to the mother were mainly elderly people who, putting themselves in the place of the mother, said there is too much noise and confusion in the homes of children and grandchildren. Their own comments are, as always, most illustrative and the three groups are presented in the order listed above.

1. *Care for mother*
   No, this is not permitted. If the mother is good they won't lose respect for her, one of them must take her.

No, they stay together, take her of course, it is the children's duty. We are doing the same thing for my mother in Italy. It would be unfair and a disgrace to the name, dignity, and reputation of the family. I firmly believe this.

2. *Mother's decision*
   It's not right in a way, but the mother would have to leave her home and she might not like that. Most want to stay where they are, children are noisy, and she would have no independence, especially with the daughter-in-law; there is more freedom with the daughter, but still it's better for her to be on her own.

3. *Leave mother*
   If they are married they could leave her alone because they have their own families.

   I don't think it's ever a good idea and I wouldn't have wanted to do it. I think the best solution is to fix up an apartment or a place for the mother nearby so she can visit and be in on things and still not be permanently in the house.

Two factual and three hypothetical questions concerning help and advice to and from relatives were asked. This set of questions was designed to test real behavior as opposed to ideal values or feelings, since people could state that they did not see relatives and that only their immediate family counted and yet rely upon relatives for help when a problem or emergency arose. The first question was "Who do you go to for help and advice?" Sixty-five percent stated that they go only to wife, adult children, or no one; 21 percent go to a friend or an expert such as an attorney; while 14 percent go to a relative. The general trend toward staying within the limits of the nuclear family does not change in Australia.

The next question was "Who do others [other Sicilians] go to for help and advice?" Forty-four percent stated that others stayed within the confines of the immediate family; 37 percent said they go to a friend or an expert; and 19 percent stated they go to a relative. The number who declared that the others would go to another relative for assistance remained low, but a great number said that they would leave their homes and seek some kind of outside nonkin based help.

To the question "Do relatives help each other as much as they should?" 37 percent said no; 26 percent said some do, some don't;

and 37 percent said yes they do. However, when the last group was asked what they expected of relatives, about half said, "Virtually nothing; they do that little bit and we're O.K." Most said that the only help expected of a relative would be in case of an extreme emergency, but many added, "It is what you would expect of anyone, not just a relative." Therefore, expectations of help from relatives are low for about one-third of the respondents and the rest, who expect more, are that much more disillusioned.

Then the following hypothetical situation was described: "If one sister or brother is well-established here in Australia and the others are struggling along, does that one have an obligation to help the others?" Sixty-nine percent said no while 31 percent answered yes. The majority of those answering no were definite and emphatic in their replies, usually restricting their comments to short phrases such as "no, not at all," "no one does," or "no, mine don't." Others seized on the word "obligation" as being the key to the question (the Italian word *dovere* has much greater meaning than our own word obligation and is taken more seriously). They said that it is definitely not an obligation though the sib should try to help "if the others merit it." There was a very real sense of having to earn help from a sibling and a feeling that a brother or sister who does not get along well is loafing or wasting his money—"I worked for it and so can he. I might lend him a bit but don't give it because you have your own family to think of." Sicilians frequently discussed Jews, a new phenomenon to them. Some of the conversation was about religion because Sicilians in Sicily are taught by the church that "the Jews killed Christ" and in Australia, meeting Jews for the first time, they begin to question this and ask educated people what really happened. But most of the time the conversations were about the real or imagined Jewish quality of helping relatives. Everyone seemed to be hearing the same stories about Jews in Australia and they were all very impressed with the kinship solidarity they believe Jews exhibit. Often, when two relatives got into an argument, others would say, "Now look at that. If we were Jews we would be helping each other instead of trying to do everybody in. Sicilians are *tintu* [wicked]." They were forever telling each other that they could all advance economically if they could combine their resources, as do the Jews. This was the first time that most of the uneducated immigrants had come into contact with or heard in detail about a people who were different from themselves (other than Americans) and whom they admired and respected for their business acumen and family helpfulness. There is, therefore, a real feeling that it is a good thing, if only in a practical money-making sense, for relatives to stick together and help one another, but this is overshadowed by the even deeper feeling that it is an impossible task for Sicilians.

The final question was taken from a questionnaire used by Florence Kluckholn in her work on values, but for these immigrants it proved to be a poor question because it depicts a circumstance which is too extreme. The question is "If a man lost everything in a fire and he must have help to get started again would it be best if he: (a) depended on his brother and sister or other relatives to help him as much as each one could, or, (b) would it be better for him to try to raise money on his own, without depending on anybody?" Sixty-nine percent stated that it would be better to go to an outside source while 31 percent said they would go to the relatives first. However, many people added qualifying statements such as "in such an extreme case," or "for this the relatives would have to help but normally I would go to the bank." Therefore, while the distribution of answers follows the general trend observed throughout this section, rather more respondents indicated they would approach relatives. Those who indicated that they would approach relatives only in such an emergency were coded no since the concern was in over-all trends and normal happenings—not in the effects of a catastrophe. Those who would go to the relatives generally contented themselves with observing, "this is the rule, that's what relatives are for," while those who would not seek the help of relatives were verbal in their replies:

> Go to the bank, then you don't say thanks to anyone.

> Oh, you can go to the relatives but you'll get a no, so not to mortify yourself and not to have an obligation to anyone go to the bank or even a friend.

Time in Australia is the only independent variable which is significantly associated with questions about the extended family on a combined index. Immigrants who have been in Australia the longest time are the least changed, that is, they are the most negative in their feelings about relatives, whereas the newest, most recent arrivals are more moderate in their feelings and display some change. This association is extremely important because it buttresses the argument that recent immigrants need and get more help from relatives than those who have been in the country a longer time. The middle group, which was not significantly associated, are mixed in their feelings about relatives, and this again is expected since they are moving out of the need category and many are now able to stand on their own and do not need or want the help of relatives while others either still need this assistance but will later shake it off or will remain in the position of new immigrants forever in a need for and appreciation of relatives.

The next four questions do not form a unit but since they are informative they are placed together here. First, "Can a person trust a friend as much as a relative?" Thirty-eight percent replied "yes, more"; 33 percent said "they are the same," and 29 percent stated no. Almost no one in the group who replied yes let the answer go at that; almost all added that friends are "better than relatives because they are more sincere and less jealous." Those who trust relatives more than friends usually qualified their answers to read "some relatives are better than friends." Again, of the one-third who rather consistently exhibit positive feelings toward relatives there is always a qualifier to exclude some kin. The personality of the relatives and ego's own experience with various kin make a difference; it is not simply a matter of all related individuals against all those who are not related. Selectivity is important, not in designating kin because Sicilians do not deny that individuals are related to them nor do they confuse kin categories, but because they select kin on the basis of personal feelings and differences. Many respondents who feel that friends are more trustworthy than relatives noted the fact that they can choose their friends according to their own requirements and needs while relatives are assigned and therefore may or may not be compatible.

Two questions related to physical proximity of kin. In answering "Do you think it is important to have relatives living nearby?" 69 percent said no and 31 percent said yes. Those in the no category added, "the farther the better because there are always fights and problems because they don't mind their own business." Many who wanted relatives nearby stated that it was for their wives' sake and not their own because then the wife has a relative nearby in case of need. The second question was "Are any of your relatives living nearby?" Forty-eight percent replied yes and 52 percent answered no. Knowing where their relatives lived, in most cases, I was able to ascertain that "nearby" means from one block to one mile but no farther. Several individuals who would like to have relatives living near do not have kin close at hand and they noted that with cars and telephones it is not so very important.

One question was asked which touched on their own perceptions of change in kin relationships since immigration. "Do you think relatives change when they come to Australia?" Eighty-three percent said yes, 13 percent said "some relatives do and some don't" and 4 percent said no. Change, when it occurs, as it appears to in the majority of cases, is always for the worse: "They think only of themselves. They have work and money and so they're independent"; "Yes, it's the freedom to do as they please. They are less united, less close, there is more jealousy and envy."

The over-all picture which emerges from this section on extended family relations among Sicilian immigrants in Australia reveals that the generally negative or hostile view of the relatives which existed in Sicily remains virtually unchanged in the new country. If anything, feelings of hostility toward the relatives are intensified since there is more money available and there are more opportunities to "do them in" or "show them up." There was an incredible number of comments and long statements about relatives which express far more vividly than percentages the dislike, hostility, and rivalry which most of these people feel toward their own kinsmen, especially sisters and brothers:

> A friend loves you and if you want to do something he won't give bad advice. Instead a cousin will always discourage you, "it's too difficult," etc. Friends will help you plan to get what you want while a relative will try his best to see that you don't get it because that will make you look better and it will make him look worse.

> They are jealous. Out of envy my sister said "You're too big for yourself," because I wanted to buy a house and send my boy to the university. My brother is rich and could have helped all of us but he never gave us a penny and is jealous when we get ahead anyway. And then I did so much for my cousin and her daughter when they came here and once they got set up they never even came to visit.

> With the relatives there is always . . . well, if an uncle has a good piece of meat, the others all say it smells. Such jealousy!

> I needed money desperately to buy this shop and went to my brothers and sisters and they refused—and they had the money. So then I went to some Italians I hardly knew and they gave it to me. All the relatives, all of them, are untrustworthy.

> The relatives are so catty and jealous, not like friends. They came to see my wedding gifts—"Ummm, very nice but my daughter got. . . ."

The fact that there were few significant associations is a reflection of the very high number of respondents who answered in a similar fashion on most of these questions. The few significant associations, as noted above, referred entirely to the hypothesis that immigration, for a time, encourages kin contact. Most relatives, who in Sicily have little to do with one another, clump for a time at the point of immigration and then return to the old pattern of having contact and positive feelings only toward members of the nuclear family; a few do remain in the pattern of seeing and feeling well-disposed toward relatives. Therefore it can be stated that only a small amount of permanent change in attitudes toward relatives takes place; the change which does occur is, for most individuals, only temporary.

THE HUSBAND-WIFE RELATIONSHIP

The Sicilian husband-wife relationship in Australia could remain the same, become more egalitarian, or become more male-dominated. This relationship as it is acted out in Sicily contains the germs of both egalitarianism and authoritarianism and it was a question which of the two would predominate. I felt that the probable outcome would be a trend toward more openly democratic relations between the married couple. The change in life style which permits the husband to be a full-time breadwinner who also has more free time to spend at home with his family might dispose him to assume some of the duties and responsibilities which the wife carried in Sicily. There was also the related problem of female and male role expectations in a changed environment. Women, who in Sicily are governed by public opinion and traditional forms of protection, might in Australia, where women are the theoretical equals of men, begin to publicly assert their own personality and their own worth. Men, though they play a very commanding role in public in Sicily, cannot for the most part, adequately support their families. Does their own sense of self-esteem increase with an increase in wages and opportunities for the family? And if both men and women begin to feel a new and greater sense of their own worth, then how, as marriage partners do the two work out a mutually compatible relationship?

Forty-four of the forty-eight immigrant respondents are now or have at some time been married; this section is therefore concerned only with the married couples in the sample. Sixty-three percent of these immigrants were unmarried at emigration; 37 percent were already married to Sicilian spouses. Of the twenty-eight who married after emigration, 50 percent married spouses who had emigrated from Sicily after the age of sixteen, 40 percent married second-generation Sicilian-Australians, and 10 percent married Australians. A surprisingly high proportion (32 percent) of the married men in this sample married women who were not Sicilian-born and reared.

In Sicily courtship, engagement, and marriage are family centered, family arranged, and carried out following rigidly traditional procedures. The respondents were asked a series of questions regarding their own courtship and engagement to determine any differences between those who were married in Sicily and those who married in Australia. First each respondent was asked how he met his spouse. This question was answered in two general ways: (1) the traditional Sicilian methods of seeing a girl and following her home, proxy marriage, meeting through a friend or relative at their home or at a family party, or acquaintance since birth; (2) encounters at outside places such as a dance, party, wedding, or work. Table 8 shows the distribution between

TABLE 8

Courtship Customs

(In Percent)

Country Where Married	Meeting		Engagement	
	Traditional	Nontraditional	Traditional	Nontraditional
Sicily	69	31	94	6
Australia	68	32	82	18

the two patterns of meeting (first two columns) for those married in Sicily before emigration and those married in Australia after immigration—irrespective of whether those married in Australia have Australian, immigrant Sicilian, or second-generation Sicilian spouses. The distribution reveals that the pattern is the same for both groups.

Table 8 also shows the distribution of answers to the question: "How did you become engaged?" There are two main categories: (1) the traditional methods of going with a relative or a *ruffiana* (go-between) to ask permission of the parents without speaking to the girl first, by elopement, or by proxy; (2) the nontraditional way of asking only the girl herself and later telling the parents of the decision. This pattern of responses reveals quite clearly that there is a difference between the two groups: those engaged and married in Sicily almost all followed the very traditional way, whereas almost one-fifth of those engaged and married in Australia followed the nontraditional way.

These figures show that how one meets one's spouse is not changed by place and it may well be that these figures represent a pattern common among Australians as well. The second question, however, does show some considerable changes. This implies a change in outlook and in values which is perhaps not immediately apparent. If the decision is first made by the two young people without any assistance from adults then one of the most prized of Sicilian values, that of service and deference to the family, is violated. Such choice does not mean that parents play no part in the decision because they can and do make their ideas known, but rather it shows that the young people consider themselves capable of making such an important decision. Young people in Sicily, even when they rage against the "system" still feel incapable of taking the full responsibility for such a decision and need the security and protection offered by the group when the group has had a voice in the negotiations. The immigrants who chose the Australian way are, of course, deviant since they were socialized in Sicily and all of them married girls who had relatives in Australia who should have insisted upon the traditional custom.

Considering only those married in Australia (twenty-eight immigrants), there is a difference in type of engagement according to nationality of the spouse. Of those marrying Sicilian-born spouses, 93 percent became engaged the traditional way. But of those marrying Australian-born spouses (the majority with immigrant Sicilian parents), only 71 percent followed the traditional pattern. Time in Australia is mainly responsible for this difference. Women who emigrated to Australia in young adulthood with parents or older siblings are more protected since less time has elapsed in which the fiancée or her Sicilian guardians might have absorbed some Australian ideas on the subject of engagement and marriage. In addition the more traditional, or less changed, respondents may have deliberately chosen to marry more traditional rather than less traditional spouses, preferring to keep their own cultural traditions, after marriage as before, intact. From a few comments made by respondents this might well be the case in many seemingly random choices of marriage partner. People who continue to hold very traditional Sicilian ideals and ideas feel that women who are allowed any measure of freedom are, at best, suspect and, at worst, "loose women." They do not wish to marry such women and therefore would be drawn to a girl who lives in a home that has maintained Sicilian cultural traditions in respect to the behavior of its women. A few of the immigrant respondents commented on the fact that they refused to marry or even consider a girl who was "too Sicilian" because they felt that Australia is a new country and calls for a new outlook and, to some extent, a new way of life.

The principles concerning division of authority and responsibility in the house affect all behavior and set the tone of the husband-wife relationship. In Sydney, as in Nicuportu, respondents were asked who has the ultimate authority: 65 percent replied that the husband commands while 35 percent said that no one commands, that instead there is an equal sharing of authority between husband and wife. They were then asked "Who is responsible for decision making?" Forty percent stated that the husband alone makes the decisions while 60 percent stated that both share this task equally. In answer to the question "Does the wife have any authority?" fifty-six percent said that the wife does have the power of authority but that it is always limited by or given to her by the husband, 19 percent said that the wife is the one with the authority, and 25 percent declared that no one person has authority and therefore the authority of the wife is equal to that of the husband.

Here again is the Sicilian pattern in which the husband reserves the formal authority or command to himself in the majority of cases, but the daily decisions which run the house and the family are made jointly by the husband and the wife. In Australia, it appears that the husband alone commands less often but that decisions are made by the husband alone more often. The data indicate that, as a group, the immigrant perceives the formal attributes of the marital relationship less traditionally and allows a more egalitarian pattern to emerge while decisions are more often in the hands of the husband whose role has changed in a new country. It was noted before that one of the changes which could occur would be that the husband would assume a greater share in the actual operation of the house and family because of his increased prestige as a full-time wage earner and also because he would have more free-time to spend with his family in Sydney.

The Sicilian pattern of work and rest hours changes drastically in Australia; husbands work from 9 A.M to 5 P.M. five days a week and then, without the piazza as a meeting place, spend more available hours at home. However, at the same time, the wife, who may or may not go out to work (most of the women from working-class families do or have done so in the past), at least is free to go out of the house for purposes of visiting, shopping, and running other errands. She thereby becomes more openly capable and efficient and her roles as wife and as female are accorded, by most respondents, more prestige and respect. The men then become more home centered while the women are less housebound, and this set of changes helps forge new patterns of authority and responsibility. Both command together or no one commands because a command is no longer necessary, and the husband assumes more responsibility for decisions.

To the question "Do you think women have more freedom and independence in Australia and do you think this is a good thing?" 21 percent said no, that their freedom or lack of it is the same, while 79 percent said that women had more freedom in Australia. Sixty-two percent said that this increase, real or hypothetical, in freedom is a good thing while 38 percent stated emphatically that it is not good. The comments of the respondents show clearly how differently the two groups perceive this change.

1. *Pro freedom for women*

It's beautiful, they should have it, this is 1966. Once she is grown up she is old enough to look after herself and she will do everything she wants to do even if she is in a locked room. You need to give an education to your children and they must know the world, it's part of that education.

Yes, they are free to find a place in the house and in society for themselves. She shares responsibility with the husband. They both start a new life. In Sicily she stays home and wastes time. Here she has freedom of thought and action and can reveal her own identity and personality more clearly.

2. *Against the change*

Yes, it changes because it's another environment. They work, go out alone. I don't like it because if they are free they can commit sins.

It changes here but it can be an ugly thing. I let my wife go to work and I don't know what she does. I can't control her. In Sicily I can and so do the others. Here the women can do bad things easier; in Sicily they can do them too but not like here. Yes, I prefer the Sicilian system where there are always neighbors, friends, and relatives about and you must think about it first before you go to do something bad.

If men view this change negatively it is usually on sexual grounds with the assumption that any freedom or liberty will automatically lead a woman into the bed of another man. Women (and men too in other contexts) must be controlled; there is no idea of self-control which is so important in the English-speaking world. Control is an extremely important concept for Sicilians, and the change from being controlled to controlling oneself is great and its effects are widespread. In this context it is the husband aided by neighbors and relatives who controls the actions of the wife or daughters and when this control is lifted it is expected that women will run wild. In fact, very few married women and only a few unmarried girls did take advantage of this freedom to form alliances with men. I did not even hear much gossip about such cases, but for some Sicilian men the possibility is always there. If, on the other hand, the men saw this change as a good thing which liberated the woman in her actions and in her personality, they did not so much as mention control. There was an implicit assumption that women are quite capable of taking care of themselves, and with their greater freedom in Australia they are in a position to become real people and realize all their potential which is controlled out of existence in Sicily.

Although few women were interviewed, many did talk informally about their new lives. Some did not approve of increased freedom for other, especially younger, women. But most were delighted with the freedom available to them and most took full advantage of it:

The woman is freer here. What I want to do I can do because I have my own money and I know my way around. It's kind of funny that in my own country I was ignorant and knew nothing but here, with the freedom to go out and see things, I know a lot. In Italy I couldn't do anything, or I could do some things but always having to ask my husband for the money and the permission. I like this here, yes, I like the Australian life.

I like Australia very much and would never want to go back to Italy to live, because after visiting there, and we were very glad to get back here, I realized that I've become very Australian in many ways. I really get around here and you know that in my *paese* I couldn't even leave my house. Here, I go way out to the other side of the city every week to visit my mother and because I don't work now I don't like being in the house all the time so I just get dressed up and go downtown.

Sicilian women who, in their homeland, were virtual prisoners as far as allowed freedom is concerned (as opposed to that taken by married women because of necessity) blossom in Australia: they work, have their own money, learn their way around the city, meet new people, and when they are tired and bored in the house they just go out. No one who has not seen these same women in Sicily can appreciate what a startling thing it is to hear them talking airily about "getting dressed up and going downtown." This is simply impossible in Sicily.

Their husbands may for a time be bewildered by and dislike the new woman they see emerging and may attempt to curtail her activities, but in the majority of cases this is not successful. Most husbands are quite pleased about the freedom of women in Sidney although they may not have been when it began in their own homes; the women are not the timid violets known from the literature and not only speak up but give advice on speaking-up to younger women:

> My husband and I are equals now but during the engagement he was very jealous and so are all men. When we came to this country I said to my husband, "You are not to do anything without consulting me. I bring money into this house and we will do these things together in the open without hiding it. If I am not here, then write it down and leave it for me to read. But if you do these things by yourself, I'll walk out of here and I'll never come back and you know that in Australia I can do it and get along fine by myself."

Sicilian men for the first time begin to see clearly the worth of their wives while at the same time they realize their own ambitions to be steady breadwinners and truly the "man in the family." The old ideal of male "command" begins to fade as both husband and wife come to the surface as capable and interesting persons. There were many statements from all the respondents about commanding and making decisions:

1. *Husband commands*

The husband commands and he makes the decisions though he asks her advice. She has equal authority with the husband but he administers.

The final decision is always mine, I lay down the general policy and she carries it out. I command because in Sicilian families the man lays down the general policy, not bothering about details, and within that area the others have freedom to move. She is the first executive officer, like a ship, she is number one. The father is the captain who maps the course and if the mother doesn't agree then she manages to let him think it's his course being followed.

2. *Husband and wife equal*
Both do everything and no one commands, there is give and take, not like Sicilians.

No one commands, that's a stupid idea, you talk things over. For decisions neither of us do anything without completely discussing it together. Like my father always said, "I'm the boss but I do what the wife says."

We both agree for decisions, it's the only way. No one commands, I'm not a general in the army. No one commands anything, what do you mean by that question?

Since it is so frequently stated by Sicilians in Sicily and in Australia that while the husband has the final authority the wife always has responsibility for children, especially when they are young, two questions were asked about this: (1) who has the responsibility for very young children, and (2) who has the responsibility for children when they are older. I hypothesized that change in the direction of more equality would reveal itself in this area of responsibility as well.

In the case of young children, 85 percent stated that either the mother or the father have responsibility, while 15 percent declared that both share the task. Four respondents said the father has the responsibility, four said that the father is responsible for the financial security and the mother for love, and the remainder chose the mother as the responsible party. For older children (above twelve or thirteen, although age was not explicitly mentioned), 58 percent said that one of the parents has responsibility while 42 percent said both parents share equally. Sixteen of the first group said the father is the responsible party while the remainder chose the mother. When the responses to these two questions are combined, a significant association appears between responsibility for children and education: well-educated respondents more often share this duty.

Very young children then are primarily the responsibility of the mother, which follows the Sicilian pattern very closely. Parents share the responsibility for older children much more in Australia than in Sicily. It is probably true that in most western societies the mother is much more responsible for very young children than the father, although the formal responsibility might be shared more equally in other groups. The Sicilian tendency for separation of work load and duties is still quite evident here.

When the children are older then both parents share this task and its attendant responsibility whereas in Sicily the pattern is for men to supervise sons and for women to supervise the daughters. The wife in Australia shares much more fully in all the activities of the family and in addition is much more aware of the demands and perils of the world outside the home through her own activities. In Sicily people claimed that women could not supervise older sons because women were innocent or ignorant of what the real world was like. This argument is no longer valid for many women in Australia since most women have a very clear and practical idea of how the world functions. Daughters come in for more direct supervision by the fathers; and sons, who held a very high position in Sicily, have lost much of their authority and must defer to the mother.

Responsibility for the family finances might be assumed to lie with the husband in the majority of cases but in Sicily, while the husband has the final authority and responsibility for the care of money, it is the wife who pays the bills, goes to the bank, and budgets the remainder. In Sydney, in 52 percent of the cases either the husband or wife cares for money coming into the house; in 48 percent of the cases both share this task. These figures agree with the distribution of decision making because this question refers to decisions concerning the disposition of funds rather than actions taken to distribute the funds. This is the budgeting function in which husbands and wives must decide how much of their income shall be spent for special purchases, such as party clothing, wedding presents, or a television set, after the normal running expenses of the household have been deducted. If these figures are broken down even further to show which of the spouses cares for family finances, we find that among those families in which only one of the spouses handles this chore, 61 percent of the husbands and 39 percent of the wives budget.

Going to the bank tends to be a man's job in Sicily, and although many husbands cannot go to the bank since the hours conflict with their work schedules, there are far fewer women to be seen in Sicilian banks than men. This is one job which, because of its supposed complexity and involvement in the male-oriented world of finance, is definitely considered to be the task of the husband or son or even uncle—but always a male if it is feasible.

In Sydney either the husband or the wife handles this task in 60 percent of the cases while both go to the bank in 40 percent of the cases. The distribution reveals, as above, a high number of immigrant women who can and do alternate with their husbands in banking the money. If only the group in which one spouse has the responsibility for this job is considered, then in 55 percent of the cases it is the husband, and in 45 percent the wife, who always takes care of the banking.

Paying bills is another family responsibility which entails much more than simply handing over cash to the telephone company or the furniture store for time payments. A certain amount of bookkeeping is necessary plus an elementary ability to write checks and oversee financial papers. This is usually not the case in Sicily where to begin with there are few bills to pay and those which do exist are paid in person and by cash at the proper office in town. In Australia, however, this chore becomes much more complicated with credit installment buying of furniture, major appliances, and automobiles and postal payments for utilities and other necessities of Australian life. Even caring for the monthly child endowment check (a social welfare benefit due each resident who has one or more children) is rather complicated with legal papers to be filed at the beginning, remembering dates on which the checks are due, going to the local post office to get the check, and then cashing or depositing the money. This is a fairly mundane matter to people who have dealt with such matters since childhood, but for functionally illiterate peasants and artisans it can assume the proportion of balancing the national budget. It was surprising how well, after an initial confusion, most understood some quite complex financial undertakings and how quickly they adapted themselves to a new financial way of life. In 79 percent of the families, one of the two spouses handled the task of paying bills, while in 21 percent the husbands and wives shared this responsibility. There is less sharing on this financial responsibility variable than on the other two. Of those who do not share, 55 percent of the husbands and 45 percent of the wives care for paying bills. Wives, as in banking, have an important role to play in this complex task.

When the responses for the three questions under consideration here are combined, there is a significant association between financial responsibility and time in Australia and between financial responsibility and occupational mobility: those immigrants who have been in Australia a long time do not share financial responsibility while those who are new immigrants share some but not all of the financial tasks; occupationally mobile immigrants do not share this task while nonmobile respondents share some but not all of the financial responsibility of the home. The older immigrants then hold more to the Sicilian pattern of division of tasks by sex while the new immigrants have begun to deviate from the traditional way. But this difference may not simply be a result of number of years in Australia. In some cases it may be a result of the type of employment of the wife. The wives of the prewar immigrants did work for the most part but they, like their husbands, were constrained to labor in the family fruit shop partly because there was no other acceptable work (Sicilian women will not do domestic cleaning in homes) but more because the shop with its very long hours and rush of customers at certain times of the day demands that more than one person be employed. By utilizing the wife for this job the family saved money on salary and assured the owner that only trusted responsibile individuals would be working in the shop. There is even today a decided preference for employing one's own family in preference to other relatives and certainly in preference to Australians. The wives of the very recent immigrants, on the other hand, work in factories and since the husbands generally work overtime in the evenings and on Saturdays, the wife must be the person who cares for many of these financial duties. She is often the only family member who can go to the bank and the shops and offices in the neighborhood to pay bills. This leads to her handling the other bills and budgeting the money that is earned since she knows where the money goes and, if funds are in short supply, she can manipulate the payment of bills.

The occupationally mobile immigrants are more difficult to understand in this respect because there is no obvious reason why these husbands and wives should not share financial tasks. In eight of these families, the husband handles the financial chores, in four families the wife does, and in two families the responsibility is shared. It is possible that in occupationally mobile families there are more tasks for each member of the family to perform and it might be necessary in this case for the chores to be divided between members in order to assure that the work is done on time and that it is carried out properly. The wives in this group are much more involved in women's organizations and in addition are responsible for seeing that their children, especially the girls, carry out their own activities properly. The children in these families are much more involved in lessons after school (music, language, dancing, etc.), and it is the wife or mother who must see to it that the children get to lessons on time. The men are themselves quite active in organizations, and to maintain a good reputation in the community they must appear to be good businessmen and proper, upstanding individuals.

In general we have seen that the husband alone manages the family finances in about one-third of the families; approximately one-fourth of the immigrant wives handle these chores; while over one-third of the immigrant husbands and wives share the responsibility. It is clear that with two-thirds of the wives participating in this activity there has been little change from the Sicilian pattern although the wife's activity is slightly higher in Sicily.

Since the sharing of duties in the financial sphere might be prevented for practical reasons, such as care of children, it was of interest to probe legal ownership of family property, namely, the house and the bank account. In Sicily both items are almost always in the name of the husband, and the wife has no access to either; but in Australia real estate agents and the banks strongly urge buyers and depositors to have joint tenancy. Therefore, if immigrants defied the advice of professionals and registered both house and bank account in the name of the husband, they would be showing the traditional pattern of male ownership. Twenty-seven percent of the families hold a bank account which is registered only in the name of the husband while 73 percent hold a joint bank account. The house is registered in the husband's name in 31 percent of the families while both husband and wife are the legal owners in joint tenancy in 69 percent of the cases. It is again the case that the husband and wife show a high degree of sharing.

A combined index for these two variables is significantly associated only with occupational mobility; in the highly mobile families the husband retains full control of both house and money while in the low mobility families a medium amount of sharing is found. Again, only the occupationally mobile prove to be authoritarian husbands and submissive wives, thus conforming much more to the stereotyped picture of immigrant families. However, the immigrant families in the literature are the uneducated working-class ghetto resident families, and the occupationally mobile, who have attained at least middle-class status, are assumed to be much closer to the American middle-class pattern. This study shows that such is not the case: the "typical" working-class families prove to be quite egalitarian in their sharing of tasks between husband and wife, and the middle-class husbands who have all the outward appearances of the host society middle-class (white-collar occupations, high English language ability, participation in Australian organizations) are, at home, authoritarian and in full charge of the operation of the home while their wives, who may do much of the actual work, do so under the direction of their husbands. Many husbands in the more egalitarian families do not like or approve of egalitarianism but have accepted it as part of the practical necessity of life in Australia:

> In Italy the bank account was all mine though morally it was in part my wife's too. Here both the husband and wife work and it's in both names but the absolute responsibility, even if it is the money of both, is the husband's—mine.

In Sicily household chores are always in the hands of the woman. No man ever helps in the house, and if the wife is ill and the daughters are too young to do the work alone, there are neighbors and relatives to take charge. In Australia, one of the most startling and most pleasing things that immigrant women discover is the amount of help which Australian husbands give their wives. My own impression is that they actually help far less often and less willingly than in the United States, but any help at all appears to be quite a lot to the immigrants. There is, in addition, much more to do in an Australian home than in a home in Sicily because the homes are much larger and there are more things to clean, wash, and polish. Also, many of the immigrant wives work full-time outside the home and their responsibilities are doubled.

The respondents answered four questions about who does the cooking, the dishes, the shopping, and the gardening and then were asked "Does the husband ever help out around the house?" Answers on the gardening question are omitted because while the pattern is interesting the responses to this question were not in line with the other responses. The general answer was that the wife cares for the flowers and perhaps the lawn, while the husband cares for the vegetables and perhaps the lawn. Almost all the home owners have large back yards and approximately half of this area is planted with vegetables—broccoli, tomatoes, artichokes, spinach, and other plants which the Sicilians prize highly. These items are all available in the fruit shops but the Sicilians enjoy working in a small garden and they claim that home-grown vegetables taste

better than those purchased in the store. Even the fruit and vegetable shop owners usually had little garden plots behind the house
or the store.

The answers to the questions concerning specified household
chores have been divided into two groups: those which the wife
(with the occasional assistance of children) does alone and those
in which the husband and wife share the work, sometimes together, sometimes alternating: in 93 percent of the families, wives
cook, while in 17 percent, the husbands and wives together do
this. Most of the husbands in this group cook on weekends or
when a special Italian meal is being prepared, although several
men stated that they regularly help out with the more pedestrian
tasks such as peeling potatoes or setting the table. Only one man
does all the cooking but he had worked as a chef for over thirty
years. Eighty-five percent of the wives do the dishes alone while
15 percent get assistance from their husbands. More of the men
help out regularly with this chore. Shopping for groceries is done
by 77 percent of the wives and by 23 percent of both husbands
and wives; this is usually a shared activity and refers primarily
to the big weekly shopping by car.

A certain amount of change is apparent and although it is not
great any departure from the Sicilian norm is important because
a man's entire role image is tied in with his "lord and master"
stance in the house. It is simply inconceivable that a Sicilian
husband would help out regularly or even sporadically with
"woman's work." A good expression of the immigrant husbands
attitude is:

> Sure I help and I have ever since the kids were tiny, I even changed
> diapers. I helped with everything. I didn't want to at first but then
> I did it willingly when I realized that I was still the husband even
> if I helped around the house.

The men who most often help out regularly around the house are
the very old respondents who have retired from their own jobs:

> She always helped me in the shop and now I always help her in
> the house. Especially since my operation I don't go to the shop so
> I stay home and do the housework, I'm very good at that.

> I can do everything around the house and I do it better than my
> wife too.

> My husband has always helped me out around the house and
> in the past few years he's gotten even better that way. He sends
> me off to mass on Sunday and gets the whole dinner himself or he

says "You go see your friend" and when I come back he's cleaned the house and has the dinner on the table. He's wonderful that way.

But to find out the pattern of help given by the husband the respondents were asked if the husband ever helped out in the house and were forced to specify how often or at what times. A clear pattern emerged: men who never help, 25 percent; those who help when it is necessary (as when the wife is ill), 46 percent; and those who help out often and willingly, 29 percent. The difference between the Sicilians in Sicily and the Sicilians in Sydney is very great. Husbands, in Sicily, refuse to touch anything which will diminish in any way their stance as commanders who deal only with policy decisions and leave the grubby details to the wife and children. This may be expected perhaps in a land where the economic base is so insecure and where so few men are able to maintain a manly role on the basis of steady work and an income adequate to maintain the family well. In Australia, however, not only do both husbands and wives see the example of Australian couples but, more significantly, the husband is the legitimate support of the family, even if his income is supplemented by his wife's earnings. This sureness in his abilities as a provider allows him to help in the home without being considered an incompetent and henpecked husband whose wife has him doing woman's work. He can prove himself competent not only in the work place but also in the home. Housework undertaken with this attitude increases the prestige of the male and, incidentally, makes him a much nicer person to live with. The rigid sex role boundaries found in Sicily begin to bend and alter in Australia— a sign of real change.

Taking all the husband-wife dependent variables together we can say that, in general, subtle yet complex changes are taking place which tend to do away with the surface command of the husband and the subsurface authority of the wife. New sex role orientations bring to the surface those egalitarian tendencies which were present but hidden in Sicily and do away with much of the phony authoritarianism of the husband. Nothing new has really been injected into the picture. Rather, old habits which are retained in Sicily because of public pressure are allowed to fall away and the easier and often preferred form of relationship which always operated under the surface in Europe is allowed to emerge and develop. There are other Sicilians in Sydney to be sure and the pressure of this public can be and often is intense and important, but they too are being influenced by the new environment and are much less critical of husbands and wives who begin to abandon their traditional poses. As several immigrant respondents said, "life is just so much easier in Australia."

Turning now to the four independent variables some very interesting patterns emerge:

Time in Australia. Prewar immigrants retain the traditional pattern of male control of the financial resources of the family; immediate postwar immigrants tend to marry Australian-born women; and new immigrants marry Sicilian women and then show a moderate amount of change toward egalitarianism in financial responsibility. These findings are rather scattered and while some are interesting, when investigated in detail it is clear that length of time in Australia, as an independent variable, is not terribly significant toward understanding changes in the marital relationship.

Age at emigration. Immigrants who were old at emigration tend to view female independence very negatively, but they tend to marry Australian-born women; individuals who were of middle age at emigration tend to have a positive attitude toward female independence but they tend to marry Sicilian-born women; young emigrants tend to marry Australian-born women. There is a strange association here between negative evaluation of independent women and marriage to Australian-born women, who tend to be more independent; and between a positive view of independent women and marriage to Sicilian-born women, who are generally less independent. It could be hypothesized that the former dislike the independence of their Australian-born wives while this appeared more favorable during the courtship period and that men who are married to Sicilian-born women can allow themselves to say that female independence is a good thing because it will never touch them personally. However, these are merely ideas pulled from results of other studies and are not drawn from data in this study. The riddle must be left to the reader. Aside from this association, age at emigration, like time in Australia, is not significantly associated with enough dependent variables for a pattern to be seen. This independent variable is not highly associated with changes in the marital relationship and is therefore not a useful indicator of change or assimilation.

Education. Highly educated immigrants are very egalitarian in their relationships with spouses concerning authority and responsibility (commanding and decision-making) and responsibility for children. Uneducated immigrants show a medium level of sharing authority and responsibility. Although very few dependent variables are significantly associated with education, those that are are extremely important, particularly authority and responsibility. This set of principles sets the guidelines for the actions of the performers in other spheres of married life. A public admission of egalitarianism in commanding and in making decisions will tend to produce more joint activities between the spouses than the traditional Sicilian practice of revering one ideal but practicing another. Therefore the secure, knowledgable, sophisticated educated individuals in this sample reject the notion of command in the home, and even the uneducated, who are or were more involved with other Sicilians, show a much higher degree of sharing and much less male posing than do similarly placed couples in Sicily.

Occupational mobility. Highly mobile immigrants are found in families in which the husband is in full charge of the financial undertakings and of household property whereas the nonmobile respondents are more egalitarian than either the mobile immigrants or married couples in Sicily. There is a high degree of sex role differentiation in the mobile families, and husbands, wives, and children are more involved in activities such as Rotary, PTA, and lessons after school than are members of the other families. The nonmobile immigrants therefore reveal themselves to be somewhat more egalitarian than couples in Sicily while occupationally mobile immigrants have changed in the direction of greater sex division of duties and male prominence. It cannot be said that these husbands are authoritarian because normally they are not; the difference lies not in statements about the man commanding and making decisions but rather in facts about who is actually controlling the organization of the home and who is carrying out the activities which make the home a smoothly functioning organization. This independent variable is then an accurate and important indicator of change.

SERVICE TO THE FAMILY

The phrase "service to the family" epitomizes the underlying ethic on which relationships within the Sicilian nuclear family and its socialization of children rest. Other studies on Italian immigrants are in agreement with each other and with my own data from Sicily on this one area of Sicilian life. There is little vagueness among Sicilians anywhere concerning how children should be raised and what obligations they have to their nuclear family of orientation. Children are born to give prestige to the parents and later to serve the family in a selfless, unthinking manner to bring the family as far along the path to prominence as is humanly possible. In Sicily the family is severely restricted in how much prestige it can acquire because of the seriously underdeveloped state of the economy. Small, seemingly petty, acquisitions and glories become enormously important and the competition between families, especially related families, is intense. In Australia there is much more opportunity for the immigrants and especially for their children to advance themselves financially, occupationally, and materially; so it was possible that the rivalry between families would lessen and the children would be freer to pursue their own desires. However, as described earlier in this chapter competition, envy, and jealousy between relatives actually increased in Australia and so it is of interest to see how members of nuclear families fare under this circumstance.

SOCIALIZATION OF CHILDREN

The basic difference between Australian and Sicilian ideas of child rearing can be expressed by the word "control." This concept was used before in discussing women who must be controlled, but it is even more obtrusive in the realm of parent-child relationships with the addition of generation and age factors. Control from outside is the traditional Sicilian way and it is neither good nor desirable that an individual be free to follow the dictates of his own mind and conscience. It becomes impossible for the growing child or the young adult to leave his home because he feels that he cannot get along by himself. The following statement by a new immigrant is typical of this philosophy:

> My daughter works after school and her money she must bring to me, and all that happens to her I must do and take care of because I have the responsibility. If she makes a mistake I too make that mistake, we take the road that the parents have. A boy of twenty-one with the parents stays under the parents. They must obey until they marry, otherwise it is an abandoned house.

It is difficult for outsiders to realize all the implications of this traditional socialization technique. The following story told by a second-generation adult expresses beautifully the attitude and actions of immigrant parents, the response of their son, and also the very different attitude of the speaker, whose parents had followed an Australian method in their child-rearing:

219

I have a cousin who is about my age, thirty. His mother took all his money and put it in the bank for him. Then he drew it all out and went off on a toot with some mates, paying for them all the way. No one knew where he was for months and he finally turned up with a beard and flat broke. So I loaned him some money to get started and after a year he still hadn't repaid me so I called him and he said he'd pay me £5 a week and he has ever since. But just last week, and this is typical of the Sicilian thinking about the whole thing, his father asked me if his son had repaid me and if not he, the father, would. I was wild. I said I wouldn't take the money from him, it was up to his son and for the love of heaven let the kid, and he's not such a kid, do something on his own once in his life.

Self-control, which encompasses words like personal freedom, self-reliance, and independence, is the result of training the growing child to be a person in his own right, to hold his own values and ideas, and to cope alone with the demands of life. It is his parents with the help of peers and authorities who accomplish this task:

> They must make some decisions on their own, even if these are wrong, they can learn from that experience and they must learn these things before they are grown. So we start them slowly and increase their own responsibility. It forms character.

One question in a series of questions about the degree to which each respondent family is family centered has proved to be the key to understanding the basic difference between those families which adhere to Sicilian tradition and those who have moved toward the Australian pattern. The question is "When you and your wife go to a party or out visiting, do the children always come with you?" If the respondent replied yes, he was asked, "Is this true even when they don't want to or when they have plans of their own?" The replies outline two vastly different life styles. If the reply is yes, the family is perceived as an indissoluble unit which must make all public appearances together. Therefore children, including adult unmarried children, are required to attend all social functions which interest the parents, and the parents participate in all the children's activities. There is, as in Sicily, no separation of the world of adults and the world of children, and any interests which the child might develop on his own are always subservient to the demands of the family.

The other life style is represented by families which follow the Australian or American middle-class pattern of separating the worlds of children and of adults. They are strict in their rules about bedtime and homework assignments. They never take their children out in the evening or to any social gathering which is not explicitly for children. They associate socially with other adults whose social life is centered about adult dinners, parties, and occasions such as weddings. These people will not associate with other people who insist on bringing children to parties, because they feel that children have no place in these gatherings: if it is evening, then the children should be home in bed with a babysitter.

Sixty-two percent of the married respondents do take their children with them whenever they go out of the house while 38 percent never take their children to social gatherings. It is obvious that there has been a fair amount of change. Even more interesting are the three groups which are most significantly associated with this dependent variable: highly educated persons do not take children to parties while uneducated immigrants always do; occupationally mobile immigrants also do not take children to parties while the nonmobile respondents do; both old and new immigrants take children to all social activities while the middle or immediate postwar immigrants do not (this reflects the fact that a high proportion of the educated and occupationally mobile respondents are in the middle time group). The two most sophisticated groups which have the greatest amount of contact with Australians are the only two which live in a social world which does not include children. This point, contact with non-Sicilians, is extremely important in understanding these associations, because if parties are attended and visits are made in the company of middle-class Australians, then one's own children will not be welcome additions. But there is a strong suggestion in the comments of the respondents that their reasons for leaving children at home are different. The educated immigrants often commented that children have their own lives, their own friends, and their own interests and should not be dragged around to parties and visits which are inherently boring to them. The mobile immigrants, however, mentioned that they could not take children to social affairs at which other mobile immigrants or Australians would be present because the children are not wanted, but they feel it is a good idea for the family to be together as much as possible; very few respondents in this group mentioned the fact that children might have their own interests. Therefore the latter group is adhering to Australian patterns in their life style, not because they value independence in itself or in their children as do the educated immigrants, but rather because it is the expedient thing to do if one wishes to associate with middle-class Australians. There were not enough of these comments from either group to make a definite conclusion; but they suggest a totally different orientation between two groups of immigrants who, on the surface, appear to be very similar.

Many of the Australian-like couples noted the importance of time for husband and wife to be alone together. This point is indicative of a profound change in the marital relationship. Traditional Sicilian husbands and wives are virtually never alone together, do not desire such intimacy, and it is doubtful that they would know what to do with it if offered. An outsider often has the feeling with the traditional couples both in Sicily and in Sydney that each spouse would rather spend his or her free time with others of the same sex and the inclusion of children into the social life ensures they will not be alone.

There are two major ways in which children are socialized to the Sicilian family way of life: one is to make the child physically dependent and bound to the adults in the family; the other is to make the child emotionally dependent upon the others. Both are necessary. The question asked of the respondents was, "Should children listen to their parents in everything or is it good for them to make some decisions on their own?" The words "everything" and "some" were emphasized to heighten the contrast between the two child socialization techniques: 46 percent said that the child should listen to the parents in everything; 23 percent said that it is good for both together to make the decisions; and 31 percent said that children should be taught to make their own decisions. Combining the first two categories in which the parent is very influential in making decisions for the child: 69 percent believe in the traditional way while 31 percent have changed. Most of the immigrants have not changed in their belief that children must be deferent to parents and this percentage agrees with the percentage of immigrants who take their children to parties with them. Agreement between the two questions show how closely linked the two concepts are and how important it is that both be operative in producing Sicilian children or Australian children.

Who are the respondents who favor children making their own decisions? The highly educated are very much in agreement with this method of raising children while the uneducated are very much against it. None of the other independent variables are significantly associated with this practice. The occupationally mobile are conspicuous by their absence since they were associated with the Australian practice of leaving children at home. However, as noted above they leave children home because it is necessary to their social prestige and not because they think it is a good thing. Inside the home they follow the traditional practice because it does not conflict with their social achievement motivations. This group is, in its own way, quite consistent. The educated immigrants on the other hand much more readily change their traditional way of raising children, although there is always the probability that these individuals were never quite as traditional in their belief as the uneducated. However, their comments about their own lives as children in Sicily confirm that while child dependency was not so extreme in their families as in the families of peasants and artisans, they still deviated far from the Anglo-Saxon tradition of independence and self-reliance. Comments from both sides of the fence follow:

1. *Pro parents*

   It is necessary to listen to the parents for the reason that the parents don't give a mistaken road to the children and want them to grow up as they must. They may consent to what the children say but the parents have the greatest responsibility and the greatest importance.

   To take the advice of the parents is always good, they are older and they always give good advice. If the child is older, an adult, he can do some things on his own, but the parents' advice is always good.

2. *Pro children*

   Oh, it's very good to make their own decisions because even now in little things I see my son, for instance, doing something the wrong way. I point it out to him and explain why but I let him do it his own way and he then finds out for himself, and doesn't forget the next time. Experience is the best teacher.

   They are raised to make decisions and take the consequences of those decisions as soon as possible and as much as possible—it's important, that.

Not apparent in these comments is the fact that the parents may be ignorant and unlettered while the children are educated and actually know more than the father. Those Sicilians who believe in the traditional custom base much of their argument on the ignorance and inexperience of the child but several of the respondents, usually older men with adult children, have taken account of the fact that the situation is often reversed in Australia. The father has to depend on his children. Many children from a very early age become go-betweens for their parents and the outside world since their English is often much better and they do not have that instinctive fear of Australian society which is quite common among the immigrants. As these children mature they assume more and more of the responsibilities for running the family, and quite often when the father makes a decision based on Sicilian values and ideas the son or daughter can prove him wrong. This does not change the belief that the traditional way is best, but it does considerably alter the practice.

There is an almost universal Sicilian belief, directed towards Australians and Americans, that non-Sicilian or non-Italian families are "wicked and bad" because the children are allowed too much freedom and the parents therefore do not care about their families enough. If children are allowed to make their own decisions and have their own interests, it is assumed that the parents are indifferent to the children and these practices are evidence of the children "running wild." The normal assumption of non-Sicilians would be that Sicilian parents take much more interest in their children and give them much more attention and love than do other parents. However, such is not the case. Children are objects designed to further the interests of the family and their personal needs and wishes are ignored. Anne Parsons (1967) documents this with data from lower-class Neapolitan families and my own data from Sicily show a complete agreement. The situation is not different in Australia as shown through comments of second-generation children who frequently react with bitterness:

> I'm much closer to my children than my parents ever were to me. Sicilians are not interested in children. It's stressed that Italians are close but I don't think that's true. My father never talked to me, he was only concerned about what *gli altri* [the others] think.

> I wasn't particularly close to my mother and my father never really seemed to care about me. He never showed his affection and he never played with us as I do with my children. I always felt out of things, out of affection. I was nothing in that house, I never had a say.

The only immigrant, a woman, to comment on this said as we watched a group of Australians playing with their children in a picnic ground:

That's one of the reasons I came to Sydney. I want to be able to be close to my children, to have that kind of intimacy that just isn't possible in Sicily. There, the children don't really count although they seem to, but it's just to make the parents look better. Here, these Australians that we think don't care, are very involved in their children. Look at the fun that crowd is having with those silly games, you'll never see a Sicilian doing that with his kids.

The Sicilian pattern is being perpetuated by most of the immigrant parents; only the educated as a group and a few individuals plus most of the second-generation adults have absorbed the Australian idea that children should be trained to independence and self-sufficiency while at the same time a much more personal interest is taken in the child as an individual.

Sicilian children, and in particular daughters, are very protected by the family from real and imagined dangers which lie outside the home. The pattern changes somewhat for all the immigrants in Australia because school attendance is strictly enforced, and every girl was allowed to leave the home to work. School is not such a problem because it is usually nearby and it is possible for family members to deposit and collect the girl at school, although this is rare. The hour of dismissal is well-known and the girl is expected to be home in the shortest time possible or there will be a family crisis of dramatic proportions. Work is allowed because "everyone does it," but even more because: (1) the pay is rather good and can always be used, and (2) the dowry custom has been done away with. Even the oldest immigrants said they had no remembrance of the custom of dowry as ever carrying over to Australia. The dowry in Sicily always consists of hand-embroidered linens, which the girl works on for years, and money or land when the family can afford such an outlay. It may be that in the early days of Sicilian immigration to Sydney their services were so badly needed in the fruit shops that there simply was not time to work on linen, and excess cash or land was practically nonexistent. In any case none of the women in Sydney continued embroidering; in fact, women never do any sort of handwork except utilitarian sewing. Women in Sicily did not enjoy sewing, embroidering, or knitting since they complained constantly about having every moment of leisure time taken up with "doing something," but it was surprising that after immigration they dropped it completely. The same women who enjoy working over a sewing machine in a factory will not touch handwork at home.

The Sicilian ability to change partially or completely is quite evident in the matter of protection of unmarried females. In Sicily almost everyone claimed that if a girl went to school too long and especially if she worked outside the home she would be *disgraziata* and could never marry. They went even further in insisting that this would not change for Sicilians in any part of the world. In Sydney, however, all the young girls go to high school and then to work with no loss of reputation but what they do with their time outside the house is another matter for many immigrants. To test just how far some immigrants would go in retaining old customs or in accepting Australian practice, all respondents were asked if they would allow a daughter to go out alone in four progressively "dangerous" situations (see table 9).

TABLE 9

PROTECTION OF FEMALES

(In Percent)

	Yes	No
Daughter allowed to go out alone:		
during the day with other girls...........	73	27
at night with other girls, to the movies		
for instance.........................	65	35
to a club like the YMCA or the CYO		
with boys and girls..................	50	50
with a boy...........................	29	71

The figures on the table reveal a rather uneven progression from permissiveness in the first situation to strictness on the last. The 73 percent affirmative is actually higher than would be expected for allowing girls out alone during the day and so is 29 percent on the most prohibited custom of going out with a boy. In other words, there was more change than I predicted for this set of variables. While the change is not great in most cases and the 27 percent who will not allow girls out during the day may appear medieval, any liberty at all is noteworthy. It may seem contradictory to allow a girl to work all day in a factory or office full of men, yet at the same time to forbid her to go outside the house by herself. But there is no basic inconsistency in this for traditional Sicilians. A few comments follow:

> My wife and I never went out alone when we were engaged and I wouldn't have married her or gone there if she had. It's the old system but I think it's right. You have more respect for the girl that way and any boy who is sincere will be willing to respect her that

way. I tell my girls all the time that in the fruit shop you don't take the bunch of spinach that's hanging out in the street all tired and dusty, no, you go inside and get the fresh bunch.

No, she [sixteen-year-old daughter] never goes out alone. She goes to tennis, we take her, or sometimes to a girl's house, we take her, and we know the girl and her parents. But the other day a school mate asked her to go downtown and buy some books. She told me and I said I was sorry but I couldn't arrange my day to take them. Well, a couple of days later, because the girl was depending on my daughter to go with her, I took them after school and only then did I find out that had they taken the bus the girl would have gotten off at Lane Cove and left my daughter to go the rest of the way by herself. It's not far, about five blocks, but even so. I said to her later, "You see how it would have been," and she understood and agreed not to take on such a responsibility again in the future.

Education and occupational mobility are the two variables which are significantly associated with protection of females; highly educated immigrants allow their daughters a great deal of freedom while uneducated immigrants hold to tradition; occupationally mobile immigrants permit their daughters to go out alone under all varieties of experience while nonmobile immigrants do not. The educated, who have been associated with change on all of the parent-child indices, are again in the forefront as exhibiting change. In accordance with their belief that children should be free and independent, they allow the daughter to go out alone, even with boys, assuming that the training she receives at home will protect her as no amount of physical enclosement can. They trust their girls to do as their consciences dictate and they are not swayed by the highly critical comments of other Italians in Sydney.

In allowing freedom to their daughters, the occupationally mobile follow their pattern. They want to "get somewhere" and are therefore concerned that their children are not different from Australian children as this might prevent acceptance. As noted before, these sons and daughters are involved in a great many after-school activities and most daughters attend select convent schools where they meet Australian girls from upper middle-class families. Many of the Australian-born wives in this group themselves attended these expensive schools. The girls are not allowed to roam the streets at will (and neither are the children of the educated immigrants) but instead are given a "normal" amount of supervision and then are permitted to lead their own lives as do the girls with whom they associate. There was a great deal of emphasis on knowing the families of the girls they are friendly with, and though this is often mentioned as a safety feature for the daughter there is an underlying sense of knowing only the "right" families.

It is clear there has been a change in protection of unmarried girls, with most evidence of change in those areas of life which are the least dangerous, as in going to the store alone, and least when a man is involved. The greatest change occurs among those groups which permit their children to have interests of their own and to make some of their own decisions: the educated and the occupationally mobile.

FINANCIAL OBLIGATIONS TO THE FAMILY

In Sicily children are always subject to the demands of the family and any assets such as money or talents are the sole property of the group and are to be employed in advancing the prestige and material situation of the family. To examine this area of family life, three questions were asked which tap the differences between those families which subsume the child under "family" and those families which view the child as a distinct individual with his own personality and rights: first, "Should sons and daughters work in a family business rather than hire an outsider, even if they want to do something else?" Sixty-two percent of the respondents declared that children should work for the family while 38 percent stated that they should not. The fruit shops were in mind when this question was written, but there was no difference in the distribution of responses between the fruit shop owners and those who work in industry. The only independent variable significantly associated with this question is education: highly educated immigrants do not favor working in a family business whereas uneducated respondents are in favor of the practice. This is still in line with the over-all pattern developing for the educated and for the uneducated immigrants. But the occupationally mobile are conspicuously absent in this test of significant association, again fitting into a very different pattern. However, a fair number of working-class respondents were definitely against the common Sicilian custom of whole families working together. They have seen too many examples of the problems which result, and they determined years ago that they would never follow this practice even if it meant spending hard-earned money on a salaried employee. The practice in the families which do have children working in the business, following Sicilian custom, is not to pay anyone more than a small weekly amount for miscellaneous expenses but at the time of marriage to give each child a share of the banked profits of the business.

The one variable which enters in the Australian setting that is not a factor in Sicily is opportunity for mobility—educational, occupational, and social. Most respondents were thinking of the small family-owned fruit shop or grocery store when they replied to this question, and many of these replied that they are not in favor of it because if the child has an opportunity to "do something better" he should be allowed to take it. It does not mean that these same people, in principle, do not favor family enterprises, but they realize only too well that it is more rewarding to have a doctor son or a teacher daughter than it is to have a child working in the fruit shop, even if this means a loss of income during the years that the child is out of the work force. Many immigrants have not themselves been occupationally mobile, but the great majority are extremely ambitious for their children. Mobility is an important intervening variable which becomes even more important than the immediate welfare of the nuclear family.

The second question, "Does a son or daughter whose parents sacrificed to send them to school have the right to marry immediately after graduation and thus not contribute any money to the family?" touches upon a burning issue in the Sicilian community in Sydney. Traditional Sicilians everywhere send their children to school so that the family may at some later time enjoy increased income and prestige. Several young second-generation people had recently completed their university course and married immediately; their families were desolate and complained bitterly that after all their sacrifices they were not going to be able to enjoy the fruits of their labors. They stated that the child should have deferred his own selfish gratification and helped the family establish itself firmly since the other members of the family had deferred their own gratification for years. The parents made the point that they could have done as other Sicilians do and pulled the son or daughter out of school at fifteen and set him to work. The entire problem refers to the two ways to mobility discussed below; these disappointed parents chose the Australian road to success by denying themselves the house, the car, and the prestige which they could have acquired years earlier if they had not sent their children to the university.

Fifty-six percent of the respondents believe that children have an obligation to care for the family first; 44 percent feel that no such obligation exists. The number of Sicilians in the former category would be much higher in Sicily, but in Australia where the assistance of children is not so urgent or even necessary the immigrants can let this duty to the family lapse. Many who do not believe in this custom stated that "it's not necessary, I don't have to take from my children," while eight of the twenty-eight who do in fact agree with this practice stated that "it's better to marry but if there is need in the family they must wait and help."

Education is the only independent variable which is associated with this question. Highly educated immigrants do not believe that children have an obligation to repay parents for an education while uneducated immigrants believe they do. Here again, as in every index in this section, the educated respondents are liberal and Australian-like in their ideas about children. These men, of course, are themselves educated as were many of their parents; so it is perhaps logical that they would see education in a light different from the other immigrants. However, not all the educated immigrants held to the more individual-oriented idea, and the concept in Sicily is not confined solely to the working-class families. More to the point is the fact that child socialization beliefs and ideas regarding the nuclear family and service to that family are, for the educated, consistent throughout and as a pattern reveal a very different outlook on all things pertaining to the family and its members. The question of need arises for some of the immigrants; for others it is not relevant, and regardless of the state of the family finances, the child has an obligation to repay the family before he thinks of himself:

> No, if she wants him to marry her, it's better to leave her. He must think, "My parents sent me to the university and I have the obligation to give them some help, at least half." He must help, it is necessary.

The changed group replied:

> It has nothing to do with the sacrificing of the mother and father. You are not sending them to school as an investment. If I want money I'll buy flats.

The responses of these individuals are very much to the point and they often make the important distinction that traditional Sicilians send their children on in school as a form of investment. They could have bought property but instead they bought an education; if property fails to produce an income the investment is a failure and the same reasoning applies to the education which does not pay off. Here, as in other places in this study, we see the importance of finding out why people take certain actions: some immigrants send their children to university for their own profit while others send them so that the children may eventually profit, and it would be a serious mistake to lump both groups together and say that all are changing to Australian values because they have mobility aspirations for their children.

Almost all of the other studies about southern Italian immigrants mention the fact that working children of immigrants must give all their pay to the parents, who then return a small sum for weekly expenses. In Sicily children are put to work so that their earnings may be added to the family income and thus enable the family to buy a house or pay off other debts. Even if the parents are not needy most children must still give all their pay to the family because no child is "capable" of handling his own money; the parents "save" it for him, often by spending it on household furnishings. In response to the third question, "Do you think working children should give all their pay to the parents?" only 38 percent in this Australian sample insist that children turn over all their pay while 62 percent allow children to keep and handle their own money. This is a very real change. Part of the change occurs because parents in Sydney are not so needy today and since many immigrants were quite young on arrival they have had a period of five to fifteen years to establish themselves before their children leave school. But this does not explain why so many Sicilian parents in Australia are willing to give up the principle that children are not to be trusted with their own money. There is not a concrete reason for this change but from the comments of immigrants and their children it is possible that immigrant parents realize that their children are capable, and since they know personally of so many "horror stories" resulting from the traditional practice, they are willing here to permit a degree of autonomy to the children. Most of these stories, which are confirmed by attorneys and by the daily newspaper, concern boys (girls rarely) who have so little spending money in comparison to their friends that they steal and rob in order to keep up with their friends; it is impossible to appeal to their parents, most try it but to no avail. Other boys rob the family kitty and run off to "blow" the money in one glorious fling. A Sydney barrister who handles many of the cases involving immigrants explains to the parents that it is their fault for taking the boy's money and keeping him on such a short rein; he added that parents from northern and central Italy understand quite quickly what the problem is and are willing to change their custom but southern Italian parents often never understand what the barrister, the social worker, and the judge say because "it is my son's obligation to give his money to us, we are buying the house with it." No amount of argument will convince the parents that their seventeen-year-old son is not interested in buying a house for the family: he would much prefer to have enough money to keep up with his friends. Very few parents bank the child's money since the purpose of taking his pay envelope is to help the family. The money given should be returned to the child at marriage and while some of it is, all of it never comes back and this again is a point of contention between parents and child. Most people are quite emphatic about this matter as the following comments show:

1. *For giving pay to family*
   It's better to give it to the father and divide it when the father dies. We do this. It's a very good idea here, if you don't the father doesn't interest himself in the children who will then become delinquents.

   Yes, if they give to the parents then the parents must pay for the marriage, if not the parents can't pay. The sons give me all their pay and when they marry I prepare the house, etc. If they didn't how could I do it.

2. *Against*
   No, they work for it and they should spend it. My boys paid me board and then they managed the rest for themselves. That's how it should be.

   The child has to have something for himself, although if the parents are paying off debts they can contribute board. I don't believe in paying it all and when they marry they don't have anything. I definitely don't agree, and they have to scrape and ask for their own money.

Again the elements of "being controlled" or "self-control" enters; the traditional parents must control the children and their money because children (often adults) are wastrels and ignorant and will spend the money foolishly. Many of these young people are quite foolish with their money because they have never learned not to be. Another factor, noted by several of the more liberal respondents, is having to ask and beg for the use of one's own funds. If a child hands his money to his parents and later wishes to buy something, he must explain and justify his expense. This is far different from the child who manages his own money and who can buy something and then simply explain why he did so. Constant dependency on the parents and on their decisions is fostered by this practice.

Because of the change in attitudes toward financial obligations the unity of the family has been affected. Some responses to the general question, "For this family inside the house, do you think it is as united here as it is in Sicily?" suggest this. Fifty-three percent of the immigrants replied no and 47 percent said yes.

> For Sicilians no. More members of the family have financial independence. It's the influence of the environment, they see and understand that they are individuals in their own right and not just members of the family. The example is supplied by the Australians.

> It [the family] can't be so tight here. There is time here and there is more money and entertainments here. That's true between brothers and sisters here too. For work here you don't depend on anyone, they don't help as often here. And an older brother here can't tell younger brothers to stop smoking and expect to be obeyed as he is in Sicily.

Those who think the family has changed almost unanimously feel that this change is for the worse: the family members go their own ways under the influence of money and the Australian environment. The others feel that there is no change in their own families and little or none in the families of most other Sicilians; the tone of family life depends on the family and not on outside influences.

MOBILITY ASPIRATIONS

"Would you let your daughter go away from Sydney to Teachers College if that was the only opening?" This question was originally asked as the last in the series of queries regarding female protection but the most unexpected answers revealed that the subject was instead tapping mobility aspirations. In Italy girls are not allowed to leave home, and if a girl has the opportunity to attend a university away from home, she is ordinarily permitted to go only if there are relatives in the other city with whom she can live. In Australia, teachers colleges are very crowded and it is becoming increasingly necessary for young people to leave home and attend school in another city. Thirty-eight percent of the respondents replied that they would not permit their daughters to leave home while 62 percent said they would. Following the conservative answers regarding letting the girl out of the house this is astonishing unless the comments of the respondents are analyzed. Mobility aspirations enter here to permit daughters a degree of freedom which would otherwise be unthinkable. Those who replied no to this question made very few comments but the others ordinarily added these statements: "Yes, it's logical if that's the only place"; "Yes, for school but not for holiday"; "If I had to, yes." This then brings us to the entire question of mobility aspirations for the children of immigrants.

Often the immigrant himself cannot progress occupationally and socially because of age, language, lack of education, or family responsibilities—less than 30 percent of the respondents in Sydney were occupationally mobile (see chapter 7)—but almost all the Sicilian immigrants would like their children to be occupationally and socially mobile. However, only a minority of the second-generation adults are in higher status positions. Why should this be? There are two reasons: (1) parents place a higher value on acquiring property than on allowing children the opportunity to continue in school; and (2) children who do go on in school are unable to compete successfully because of family demands. One of the few reseachers to apply himself to this question in any cultural context is the social historian Stephen Thernstrom, who through the skillful use of historical documents studied the mobility patterns of a group of Irish immigrants in Newburyport, Massachusetts, during one period in the nineteenth century. He proposed two determinants of social status: occupational mobility and possession of property, the latter being "a dimension of social mobility which has received too little attention in the literature of social stratification" (1964, p. 115). The Irish immigrants were poor, unskilled laborers who settled into the bottom rung of Newburyport's occupational and social ranks. With time some began to advance themselves either by (1) becoming skilled factory operatives or merchants or (2) by buying property. None did both. Others did not advance at all but were able to see their sons move into the middle class through virtue of education and subsequent middle-class occupations. To move from the working to the middle class it was necessary for the sons of immigrants to go to high school and this necessitated fantastic sacrifices on the part of other family members who had not only to support the child while in school but also to do without the earnings he would have brought home had he been working. This route of social mobility is and has been the American way from the earliest times to the present.

The other way to gain some sense of social status in the community was to prove oneself hard-working, frugal, and respectable. This was possible through the acquisition of property and did not necessarily involve any increase in occupational status; in fact, it actively prevented it. Children were taken out of school after the few years considered sufficient to teach them to read and do arithmetic and put to work as factory operatives. Then, over a period of years, the family, by means of "ruthless under-consumption" (p. 136) saved enough money to buy a small house in the city or more usually a small farm on the edge of town. They were still unskilled factory workers but they were men of property and as such took their place in Newburyport society. However, the effect of this road to increased social status was to keep the children and their children in the working class because their education, the only way to middle-class status, had been sacrificed to the immediate demands of advancing the entire family. These families were still working class but they had moved up within the class and commanded a certain respect in the city. By normal measures of social mobility, and occupational mobility, they had not advanced but they had accomplished something important to them.

The Thernstrom argument is as important for Sicilian immigrants today in Australia as it is for Irish immigrants of 1860 in Massachusetts. Sicilian immigrants can defer prestige aspirations and send their children to the university, or they can take their children out of school at fourteen, put them to work and buy a house and then other pieces of property, thus gaining immediate prestige in the Italian and in the Australian community. These Sicilians, like Newburyport Irish, are able to buy houses only by putting each and every member of the family out to work. Often today, wages are good enough that the wife can stay home, another very important Sicilian value, while the children, male and female, work. The aspirations of the children are disregarded because the family and its needs come first in Australia as in Sicily.

Families which allow children to stay in school scrimp and save just as much as home-buying families, but they receive no tangible reward; they are looked down upon by other Italians as being superficial and putting on airs. Relatives and friends very often apply pressure to take the children out of school. This was often mentioned by the educated second-generation adults:

> My aunts and uncles were terrible. They were pretty well-off and they tried to discourage me. They said we couldn't afford it, that I should help my father in the fruit shop, things like that. But my father opposed them.

Oh, the relatives had a lot to say about college, not so much finishing the four-year high school. For college, my aunts said "Why bother, she's a girl," and that my parents "lost five years of money." They told me I was ungrateful but my parents made up their minds and they encouraged me and they didn't care what the relatives said.

These mothers and fathers who sacrifice so much to keep their children in school are following what they think to be the best road to success in life, because learning will bring prestige and increased social standing to the educated child and to all the members of his nuclear family. However, this prestige does not come until the child has finished school—until the whole family has proven that he can do it. At that point the prestige of a family with a professional son or daughter soars far beyond that of the others who took their children out of school, and it is only a short time before they too have a house, a car, and other status symbols. This is not an easy road to take. There are constant sacrifices for ten years or more and there is the general feeling in the community that the parents are being foolish and "uppity." But the determination to put a child through school is so strong that nothing deters them, and their own feelings about the families who don't are strong indeed:

> They must go to the university, that is the only place for them here in Australia—there is nothing to stop them. But so many Italians take their children out of school at fourteen and they do it for the money, they can't see farther than their noses. So I tell them that all the time. They are always coming into the shop complaining to me, "My boy pays no attention to me, I have lost him, he is always running around," and I tell them, "Sure he is, you sold him for $10 a week and now he pays you $4 for living expenses and he is free of you—you sold him. You dragged him out of school, to put him to work. Well, you're getting the money so what are you complaining about." I've lost more customers than I can count because of that. They have to buy the house. I don't own a house because I spend the money for education and so what! What can I do with a house? We still live in a nice place and if I never own a house I still have two sons who are university graduates. But not for them, ignorant people they are.

Even school teachers have made it difficult for those seeking the route of education to higher status:

> I remember when I was in school, in about the fourth or fifth grade, the teacher went around asking everybody what they wanted to be when they grew up and I said I wanted to be a doctor. The teacher looked at me and said, "You're going to have to sell a lot of bananas to do that." So I went home and told my father about it and he said,

"We will sell just as many bananas as is necessary to put you all the way through medical school." [Second-generation physician.]

These sons and daughters who finally become teachers, pharmacists, and dentists enter the ranks of the middle class and embark on the escalator of social mobility which alone will ensure for them a continued high standard of living in Australia.

Why do some Sicilian immigrants value houses and others education? The difference does not lie in traditional versus acquired values because in Sicily education and professional positions are equally valued with land ownership. The latter normally precedes the former but there is little difference in the weight attached to each. Why then did men from the same small town, who emigrated at the same time, and are the same age choose different paths for their families to follow in Australia—the land where everything is possible? Considered logically the path to money and prestige is better followed through education of children because the financial rewards are greater and so is the prestige. Why then did most of the immigrants take the logically least sound path?

One factor might be operative: family background. Those men who had strong aspirations for their children's education are the men who speak of their fathers and their grandfathers, their mothers and their uncles and aunts in terms of culture—here used in the sense of refinement and love of beauty. Men commented that their fathers bought books for the family to read instead of buying bread; others mused about their relatives who could converse about the beauties of Italian culture and who inculcated in them a love of and appreciation for art and music; still others recounted tales of how their mothers and fathers, who could not send them to school, insisted that they grow up with a feeling for learning and knowledge, insisted that they too could perceive as educated people even though education had been denied to them. There is a real, though unrealized, cultural tradition in many working-class families which came to fruition only when emigration allowed them or their children to become officially educated, or "literate" as they would put it. Education is valued for the money it brings and for the prestige it gives, but it is also appreciated for the sense of confidence it bestows on the person who now knows how to "present himself" to the world, and who understands fully the wonders of this world:

My father taught us to look and to really see the things all around us. We weren't educated and we couldn't read very well but he said that was no excuse to be ignorant. I love to go out into the country and look and think. I can walk all day by myself and come back full of ideas. The first thing I made here was a wireless in the shape of a mountain I had seen. I was out walking and I noticed the shape the mountain had with the smaller hills in front of it and I went on thinking about its form and its beauty and I came back and I re-created it. I remember too, when I was a little boy, we used to go fishing and I'd throw a stone in the water and watch the rings move out. I used to wonder about that, think about it, why and how, and we would all talk about it. And now look, they have found out about those rings, they know they are in the air too and they use them so that we can hear and see things from other countries. We have television beams bouncing off stars and planets. Now those bodies have always been there in the sky but we were ignorant before. And so many people are ignorant, not because they don't have schooling but because they don't look at what they see. On a picnic in the country they sit and listen to the radio and play cards, and so never see and hear the things that are all around them. Those are the ignorant ones. [Three years of school.]

Study carries the man and the woman to be perfect gentlemen. I wanted her [respondent's daughter] to have a profession, not a craft. The educated person is always educated: with culture he can go anywhere in any group and always have pride and confidence in himself or herself. Otherwise they are rough. My father and mother tried to give us that sense of culture: we read books in my house and we discussed things but it was hard because none of us had any schooling. But our daughter is something today—she is the realization of all the dreams of my father and my grandfather and his father. The others who take their children out of school are stupid, they think only of themselves and not of their children. [Five years of school.]

The men who do not value education never spoke this way and never mentioned their families in connection with learning or culture. Those who are satisfied with a house are men who think it would be nice if their child had a better job than themselves, but if the child has a good factory job or is a hairdresser that is fine too because the wages are good and steady and there is plenty of overtime. The others, those who brought dreams of learning and culture with them from Sicily, are insistent that their children should be educated. Many children have not made the grade at the university but this does not invalidate the parents' wishes to actualize a dream which was passed from generation to generation and kept alive in the minds of over-worked, half-starved peasants and craftsmen. White-collar workers who were middle class in Sicily never speak in this way. Their families certainly had a tradition of education and were able to act upon the wish, but the respondents in this group see education as a fact of life which will enable one to live well, buy a good house, and remain in the middle class. Never did they speak of the advantages of learning and perceiving as did the uneducated to whom education is a living reality.

The second reason for the failure of second-generation children to advance occupationally and socially is their inability to complete a course of higher education. Superficially the reason for this lies with the child himself, but in most cases there is an underlying and much more important cause which stems from the demands of the family on the time and resources of the child; and this is frequently compounded by the inability of parents to understand the requirements of higher education. Many respondents and their relatives had very high aspirations for their children, but the children are today employed in lower white-collar positions or in blue-collar jobs. Their families had been eager and anxious for them to continue in the university and never considered taking them out of school in order to have their wages. They were given all the opportunities possible to succeed in school and yet the majority failed.

First of all, there is an unshakable obligation to be at home as much as possible, to attend all family visits and parties, and to be available to help out in the house. This means, for instance, that if the son wishes to study in the university library he is accused of being a wastrel and of not appreciating his room with desk and bookcase which the parents and siblings have sacrificed to provide. If the family is close to the relatives then the house is filled with people at all times of the day or night, and in families of this type there are many relatives and friends who need help with documents and papers, and the best person to ask is the cousin or nephew who is at the university. If the family pays a visit or goes to a party (and there is a great deal of socializing) or if others visit them then the children, all the children, are expected to be with the parents. The student who pleads exam study as an excuse is told, "Just once in a while couldn't you do something for us, who have done so much for you. How will it look if always you are somewhere else? What will the others think of us?" A noisy house and a study-bedroom constantly filled with relatives is not conductive to study or to good grades.

In addition to a nonstudious atmosphere there is the attitude of parents who do not understand what is involved in preparing a child to compete successfully at the university. Practical subjects in high school are preferred and nothing from school is ever discussed in the home. Facts are learned at school and questions to the parents are discouraged—"You should ask your teacher," or "What do you do all day in school, I have no time for that kind of nonsense." One evening at dinner a first-grader asked her father why a Chianti bottle had a raffia covering. He glowered and said: "Why do you ask me such questions, I'm not the teacher." When asked by an adult if he knew why the raffia was there, he explained its purpose, but added "school is for learning, home is for obedience and working." He, and many others, had no conception of how to provide a learning situation at home which would augment or even surpass what the school was able to provide.

Students are pushed from the day they begin school, they are overwhelmed with charges to do well in school because "we have sacrificed so much to come to this country to give you the opportunity," they are threatened with expulsion from the house if they do badly in their courses, and they are expected to maintain their heavy obligations to work and serve the family at the same time. If they do manage to get to university, and many do, and then fail or drop out because it is too difficult or too uninteresting, they are berated on all sides and made to feel guilty over their failure to the family for the rest of their lives. "What do you think people will say about us. You let us down. You failed us. You could have been out working all these years and the house would be paid for but no, big deal, you went to school and you couldn't even manage to succeed there. Now what do we have for our years of scrimping and working?—a failure for a son." No matter what this child does in his adult life, no matter how successful he is in other lines of work, he will never be allowed to forget that he has let the family down.

Reviewing the distribution of answers to the questions asked about service to the family, it is clear that roughly one-third of the immigrants have moved away from the Sicilian norm, and on two particular issues even more have changed. Taking children to parties, making decisions, protecting females, working in a family business, repaying parents for an education—all these areas of family life remain Sicilian for about two-thirds of the immigrants. The rest have changed drastically in their notions of child-rearing and approach Australian values in these regards. On two issues, giving pay to parents and unmarried girls going away to school, more than one-third have changed toward leniency. The reason for the first change is largely inexplicable, the second is simply a result of mobility aspirations on the part of many immigrants. Most of the questions under service to the family reflect changes primarily due to mobility aspirations: a not surprising conclusion when one recalls the reasons for which the majority of the respondents emigrated.

The combined index for six of the dependent variables is associated with education and occupational mobility: highly educated immigrants exhibit great change while uneducated immigrants do not change; occupationally mobile immigrants show high change while nonmobile immigrants do not.

Time in Australia. This independent variable is associated only with taking children to parties and out visiting; old and new immigrants do not change the Sicilian pattern whereas those who immigrated just after the war do change. This finding is partly a result of the many educated and occupationally mobile immigrants who are included in the immediate postwar group and shows that these, not time, are the relevant factors associated with change. Otherwise time in the host country is not a valid or useful index of change.

Age at emigration. None of the dependent variables are significantly associated with this index and, as above, it is therefore not useful in discovering or measuring change.

Occupational mobility. Two of the five tested variables are highly associated with this independent variable and three are not. The two are protection of females and child attendance at parties and visits: in both cases occupationally mobile individuals have changed from Sicilian practice to Australian while the nonmobile have not changed. The former have changed in those areas of nuclear family life which impinge on the outside world and are connected with mobility. These individuals follow a way of life with Australians and other mobile immigrants which does not include the presence of children at social affairs. In order to foster the child's activities it is necessary that Sicilian beliefs in female protection be relaxed or dropped entirely and this the occupationally mobile do. The three other indices which relate to the nuclear family value of service to the family and which are not intrusive in the public sphere of life are not associated with occupational mobility. In these areas the mobile immigrants distribute themselves in quite the same way as do the nonmobile individuals: some change and some do not. Therefore, the mobile immigrants change in their values toward the nuclear family when mobility is an added factor and retention of Sicilian values and practices might serve to retard mobility; when mobility is not a factor, inside the home, then these individuals retain or change their ideas and customs in precisely the same way as the nonmobile immigrants. The occupationally mobile, in these areas of life as well as in others discussed earlier, have manipulated the Australian environment, picking and choosing those factors which are congruent with their ideas of the good life and rejecting those other changes which they deem unnecessary to their advancement in Australia. This independent variable then is an extremely important index of change which reveals not only the amount and direction of change but also why some changes are made and others are not.

Education. All five of the nuclear family variables are associated with this independent variable indicating in all cases that highly educated immigrants change their values and their practices while uneducated immigrants tend not to change. The educated individuals now live in families which are like Australian middle-class families in that they separate the worlds of adults and children, allow children to have their own lives, and teach them to make their own decisions. They do not protect unmarried females, they consider education a right belonging to the child which need not be repaid, and they believe that children should work away from the family since it teaches independence and good work habits. The entire focus of family life has shifted from an adult family-service orientation in which the child must be controlled by others to one which is child-centered and individual-oriented and the child is taught from his earliest years to rely on himself. Educated individuals do not have a base, as do the occupationally mobile, on which they discriminate between those factors which it is expedient to change and those which can safely be allowed to remain unchanged. Instead, they have committed themselves to a totally new family way of life. The educated have, in a sense, been quite consistent in the changes which have occurred or which they have allowed to occur. It seems almost that they have been passive actors who permitted the new customs and ideals to come in and take over without any active resistance by them. This total shift to new values and new customs, which are very similar to those found in middle-class families in all the major English-speaking Anglo-Saxon countries, is an extremely important finding and shows that this variable is most valuable in studying patterns of change.

12

PUBLIC SATISFACTION AND PRIVATE SATISFACTION

When asked what things they most disliked about Australian life Dutch persons generally stated that they disliked the Australian habits of drinking, gambling, lack of home life and sexual customs.
Ronald Taft

EISENSTADT (1954) has written of the importance of measuring the immigrant's satisfaction with the new country while Gordon (1964) makes identification with the people of the host society one of the most important steps in his typology of assimilation. The former notes that personal adjustment is used by other researchers as an index of full absorption and that it is concerned

> with the point of view of the individual immigrant and the ways in which the new country affects his personality, his satisfaction, his ability to cope with the various problems arising out of his new situation. It is assumed that migration entails many frustrations and difficulties for the migrant, and that it is mainly the degree of of his adaptation to the situation that determines the success of the process as a whole. [1954, p. 12]

Gordon states that "identificational assimilation" occurs when the immigrants have developed a sense of peoplehood or ethnicity with those in the host society (1964, p. 70). It is not clear in any of the culture change literature just exactly how various divisions of the process of assimilation, acculturation, or absorption are integrated with one another, nor is it easy to find out what terms such as "success" mean (see Eisenstadt above). However, one comes away from these studies with a strong feeling that if an immigrant is satisfied he will begin to assimilate, and if he begins this part of the process then he will eventually identify with the local people and actually become one himself, thus losing all sign and sense of his former identity. I personally feel that these are exceedingly simplistic views, and since they are seldom backed up by actual field data the reader is left to ask questions regarding exact meanings of terms and to wonder how it all fits together.

243

My own data make it clear that it is essential to specify what is meant by the terms "satisfaction" and "identification" and then look at what the immigrants themselves mean by the same words. It is entirely possible that an immigrant may be totally satisfied with his new country, the public sector, and completely disenchanted with the people and with their way of life, the private sector. The opposite, of course, is also possible though not quite so likely; and there may be disillusionment with everything. What these various manifestations of satisfaction and identification have to do with change is still a question. Are they to be used as measures of change, or do they merely encourage or inhibit change? Let us first look at the present data and then examine the total picture for Sicilian immigrants in Sydney, Australia.

PUBLIC SATISFACTION

The world, for most people, is divided into public and private areas of life, and while there is some natural connection between the two they are not the same. Public satisfaction refers to the approval given by individuals to the public institutions of a society. Some of these are housing, occupation, and government (the latter includes the legal system, the political system, social benefits, international policies, etc.). Although these are factors of great importance to native-born citizens, they are often taken for granted. Immigrants, however, are keenly aware of the pros and cons of the new society's institutions precisely because they are new and fresh and because the immigrants have other institutions, now left behind, with which to compare them. Immigrants, at least in the beginning years, are rarely indifferent to things they see about them; they are much like religious converts to whom every part of the new belief is curious and must be examined, analyzed, and finally accepted or rejected. How satisfied are these immigrants with Australia?

Housing is very important to most people and in particular to adults with growing families. Sicilian immigrants are especially sensitive because their housing situation in Sicily was usually not good and also because ownership of a house is a matter of such importance both for security and for prestige. Seventy-seven percent of the respondents are satisfied with their houses while 23 percent are not satisfied. Five of the eleven immigrants who are dissatisfied are renting their present homes and for this reason alone they wish to change quarters; the remainder are rather neutral saying they would change if they happened to see a better house at a good price. No one is anxious to move except for those who rent. There are many comments about neighbors, almost all Australians, who have proved to be considerate and helpful in times of emergency but for the most part leave the immigrants alone to live their lives as they see fit, which accords perfectly with the Sicilian definition of a good neighbor. Respondents commented on the availability of housing in Sydney and how wonderful it is that even a factory worker can own his own home. They appreciate spacious rooms and large backyards, which no one, not even the wealthy, has in Sicily. A great many immigrants commented on the banks in Australia stating that everyone, rich and poor, receives equal treatment and that even a salaried immigrant is treated well by the banks and can quickly establish a good credit rating, which is important in financing a business venture. This emphasis on the equal treatment is understandable since in Sicily peasants usually had no dealings with the bank and when they did they were treated with condescension or scorn. Peasants wait hours to be seen in Sicilian banks and if one of the local *pezzi grossi* (big shots) walks in he is immediately seated and served. This would be unthinkable in an Australian bank, and the feelings of pride and self-esteem which this democratic treatment fosters are immeasurable. It is widely known in many parts of Australia today that Italian immigrants are very good credit risks, and in one rural immigration area the local bank manager stated that they lend to Italians on more advantageous terms than they do to Australians because the Italians have proven themselves, over the past twenty years, to be trustworthy and super prompt in repayment. A source of great wonder to Australians is the fact that immigrants can buy a house two or three years after arrival. It is managed, of course, by a strict regime of sacrifice, self-denial and hard work.

Time in Australia alone is significantly associated with housing satisfaction. Old immigrants and immediate postwar immigrants are satisfied while the new immigrants are dissatisfied. This finding is in line with the statements above because it is the newest immigrants who are still, for the most part, living in rental housing in neighborhoods that they do not like because there are too many factories and the air is not good.

In sum then, everything about the housing situation in Sydney is to the immigrants' satisfaction since they can after a few years, with hard work and stringent saving plus the aid of helpful banks, buy the house they desire. No one ever has to live in American-style slums where large families are crowded together in tenement apartments.

All of the respondents when asked whether they are satisfied with their present jobs replied that they are, but 23 percent stated that they would change their jobs if they could; 77 percent said they would not change their jobs. There is, first of all, an extremely high rate of job satisfaction. Secondly, of the eleven people who would change jobs, three came in the immediate postwar period and eight are very recent arrivals. Of the eleven, two are occupationally mobile and are planning to change their jobs for better, more prestigious positions, and nine would change their jobs if they were offered more money. Therefore, it is not the job itself which is unpleasant to them but rather the wages, and since all of these individuals emigrated to make money to buy material possessions they are simply being consistent in their aims. In addition, most of the people in this group of nine are living in rented houses and are desperate for more money to make a down payment on a house.

Most immigrant studies in anthropology, sociology, and history assume, as do many economists and political scientists, that factory work is a demeaning, stultifying occupation which places man on the level of an animal-robot. However, many of these writers are middle-class professionals who look down on the working class and project their own feelings on factory work. It is true that many factory workers do find their jobs boring and tiresome, but this is no reason to assume that most or even many find them so. With no one is this cautionary note more important than with immigrants. By extension, researchers assume a wide-reaching dissatisfaction with the host country for forcing them to suffer and sacrifice to this extent. Handlin, for example, makes the following point many times:

> In all matters, the New World made the peasant less a man. . . .
> Bound to the monotony of a minute task, endlessly repeated, the
> worker sometimes could not envisage the whole of which his bit
> would be a part. . . . Such labor was labor for its own sake and
> meaningless [1952, p. 79].

However, another researcher makes the following point:

> For Handlin, "the history of immigration is a history of alienation
> and it's consequences." . . . While there is no desire here to belittle
> the hardships, fears and anxieties to which the immigrant was sub-
> ject, there are good reasons for contending that Handlin overstates
> the disorganizing effects of emigration. [Vecoli 1964, p. 407]

And Lewis notes for Puerto Rican immigrants:

> Almost all of the migrants expressed satisfaction with the higher standard of living in New York despite the fact that they were almost at the bottom of the income level in the city [1966, p. xli].

Sicilian factory workers in Australia show total satisfaction with jobs:

> Yes, I like my job. The people are good, the wages are good and the work is interesting. [radiator assembler]

> I worked in a sugar refinery, I did all kinds of work there. I was a general worker, just unskilled labor, but it was a nice clean place and people were good to me.

> Now I've learned to do spot welding and I do that on air-conditioners. It's a good job, though it could pay more; it's easy, clean and I just generally like it.

> Now I am sewing lingerie in a factory and it's very sympathetic there. I like it very much, and I'm still there after five years. I hardly ever sewed in Italy, but I have an inclination for the machines and I got on fine with the work. [female operative]

Several points emerge from these comments: first, the workers have often learned to operate machines while on the job and have advanced from unskilled to semiskilled workers; second, many had what is considered interesting work in Italy, such as being a tailor or chauffeur, but are much happier now with Australian factory jobs; third, the factories are clean and the Australian employees are good to work with. It is important to consider that most did not have nice clean work in Sicily and what work there was did not pay well. Work was not steady, there were no raises, no paid holidays, no pensions, and no opportunity for advancement. By comparison with their former employment the Australian factory jobs are indeed, in their terms, "deluxe." Most of the factory operatives do not see the entire manufacturing process of the air conditioner or plastic plates, but they do know the value of their own job in the operation and they take pride in their ability to do it well. The radiator assembler quoted above often told people about his job and described how he passed hours every day thinking about all the foreign countries where his trucks go and of all the different kinds of people who will use the result of his and his fellow workers' skills. The two mobile individuals who wish to advance further did find their repetitive factory jobs boring and uninteresting. This attitude may well be a psychological mechanism for pushing an individual to make greater efforts at training or education so he can get out of this kind of work. How many college and high school students in the United States have returned to school in the fall with renewed vigor and enthusiasm after a summer spent stamping coils in a hot factory?

Another source of enormous satisfaction is their fellow workers. For most respondents the majority of their work mates are Australians, although some factories have a large number of Italians, Greeks, and Yugoslavs. When asked "Do you prefer to work with Australians or Italians?" 19 percent said they prefer to work with Italians, 19 percent have no preference, and 62 percent prefer to work with Australians. Why?

> With Italians there are always fights. And an Italian boss, never! He makes them work too hard and is never nice about it. In Italy when the worker says "good morning," the boss doesn't answer. The bosses here think the workers are men not beasts.

> If we in the factory are five or six Italians each one tries to do more than the others, they get into everyone else's work. The Australians do their own work and that's enough, and it's good with the boss too. The Australians work regularly in a calm way. We don't, there is always movement with the Italians.

> They command better, the Australians. They say "please" and "thank you" and "would you." An Italian says, "eh, va, va, porco di dio" [eh, go on, go on, for Christ's sake get going]. I remember the work in Italy with its antique atmosphere, like the days of hundreds of years ago when there were masters and slaves and it is still that way there. With Australians it is fine, there is some respect. At work give me Australians every time.

The main note struck in these, and other, comments is the difference between an aristocratically based and a democratically based work place. Workers are beasts in Sicily who are afraid for their jobs because there are so few. They work more than is necessary and are treated like slaves by the bosses. In Australia all men are equal and the boss is over you only because he has more experience, not because he is better than you. Italians try to raise their own positions by downgrading everyone else, and if this involves fights and reporting to the boss then one does that. But Australians do their own work in a calm manner and try to help their workmates. Work is plentiful, well paid, and interesting so there is reason to be satisfied.

One of the most frequently used indices of change is naturalization since it is believed or assumed that becoming a citizen of the new country indicates a satisfaction with a new life and a sense of identification with the people of the host society. The Sicilians in Sidney answered two questions concerning naturalization: one to measure the extent of naturalization and the other to find out the feelings of the immigrants about naturalization.

Two respondents are employed by the Italian government and are not eligible to be naturalized; so from a total of forty-six respondents, 11 percent are not naturalized, 8 percent have not yet decided whether they will become Australian citizens, and 81 percent are naturalized citizens of Australia. These figures represent those who have been in the country more than five years and are therefore eligible for naturalization plus those who arrived less than five years ago who gave their proable course of action for the future. All five respondents who are not naturalized are eligible but two refuse to take out citizenship papers as long as Australia is part of the British Commonwealth (they have no objection to being Australian citizens but want no part of England); two others say they just have not gotten around to it; and one claims there is "no profit" in being a citizen until age sixty-five when you can collect a government pension. The four who are undecided are all new arrivals; two of these said that if things continue going along well in the new country they will undoubtedly become naturalized after five years; the other two are dissatisfied with Australia and are not sure they will remain there. Most immigrants were naturalized very soon after the waiting period elapsed. Time in Australia is the only independent variable which is significantly associated with naturalization. The old and immediate postwar immigrants are naturalized while the new arrivals are not. Time then seems to be a somewhat relevant factor towards naturalization, but we cannot be sure that time alone is responsible because we cannot accurately judge how many new immigrants would become citizens if the legal five-year waiting period did not exist.

It is legal to remain in Australia for all of one's life without ever renouncing the citizenship acquired at birth. The only benefit which is denied noncitizens in Australia is the old-age pension. Child endowment payments and government scholarships are also awarded to holders of immigrant visas. No penalty attaches to the person who remains a legal citizen of another country and no force is exerted upon the immigrants by the local government to change their legal status. I therefore hypothesized that some immigrants would take out citizenship papers because they felt a sense of belonging or loyalty to the new country and some because it is expedient and profitable. The immigrants were asked, "Do you think that becoming naturalized is just a legal formality or does it mean changing your loyalty?" Thirty-seven percent feel that the change is strictly a legal formality while 63 percent definitely think it means a change of loyalty. None of the independent variables are significantly associated with this measure. The comments of naturalized immigrants illuminate the thinking which lies behind the figures:

1. *Negative toward Australian citizenship*
   It's just a formality, you don't renounce your origin. It's like a woman with her name changed after marriage. You would still think of yourself by your father's name.

   I am loyal to Italy because I'm Italian and to Australia because my children were born here. I am a foreigner in my own family because my wife was born here too, but I'm a real Italian, I'm not one of them. I had to sacrifice. But if I had to choose it would be Italian of course.

2. *Positive*
   It's a change. We are Australians and that means to live like them and we do.

   It's in your heart to change. This is my land. I didn't leave Italy completely but I'm here and I belong here and I'm a good Australian.

   You gotta do it otherwise they don't think you are sincere. After all when you adopt this land for your country you should change your citizenship and to a great extent that means changing your loyalty.

Although only five of the forty-two eligible immigrants are not naturalized, eighteen of the total group consider it simply a formality which allows them equal rights with Australians and in their hearts they are still Italians. Well over half of the respondents in this sample, however, feel that they owe their loyalty to Australia—a high proportion. It was anticipated that the distribution would be reversed with the majority holding on to their ethnicity while they changed nationality to have social welfare benefits. Obvious satisfaction with Australia, its jobs, houses, and government is responsible for the large number of people who no longer feel they are part of Italy and who have "become very attached to this new land." Many immigrants left Italy with feelings of bitterness and cynicism hoping to find a better life in

Australia; by their own terms the majority have found the good life in Sydney and they are therefore loyal and trustworthy citizens of their new home.

As another test of the immigrant's satisfaction with Australia, two questions were asked which probed their feelings about any deep or lingering desire to visit or to return to Italy. The first was "Have you ever visited Sicily and (a) if so, did you like it, (b) if not, would you like to?" Forty-six percent showed a positive orientation toward visiting Sicily while 54 percent were negatively oriented. A total of eighteen immigrants had returned to visit Sicily: four liked it and fourteen did not; thirty immigrants had not visited Sicily since emigration, but sixteen would like to and fourteen would not like to. A much higher proportion of people who visited did not like it, and conversely a higher proportion who have not visited would like to. A test of significant association reveals that time in Australia is the only independent variable which is associated with attitudes about visiting Sicily. Old immigrants and immediate postwar immigrants do not wish to visit Sicily, and if they have done so they did not like it; whereas new immigrants all want to visit. Therefore, time is, in this case, an extremely important variable in lessening the desire to return for a visit or in making Sicily seem drab if a visit is made. Those who have returned have this to say:

> I've been back twice on business, the first time about ten years ago and I was shocked how dirty and poor and underdeveloped it was. The boredom and routineness of life were appalling—they're still talking about the same things they talked about when I left forty years ago. I didn't like it.

> I went back for a visit about six years ago when I still thought of going back to live there for good. Oh, Italy is beautiful but it was different than I had thought. When I was young nothing was right here. The difficulty of the language and the difficulty of assimilation give you a push to go back where you can defend yourself, where you can demand your rights. But the mind all by itself forms a different opinion than the reality. When I came here at twenty-one, I kept repeating Italy, Italy, Italy and so just by repeating that the mind formed the concept that it was marvelous. And so it is, but after so long here I found that they think and act differently than in my dream. There are things like the push to get on a bus, to get into a store, even to walk down the street. I had forgotten that. No, it isn't really forgetting, it's just that when I was there it was the normal natural thing and that was one of the ordinary things that was not included in my dream. And waiting for everything and nothing being

easy. You know we have a proverb in Sicily which says that in a country of blind people a man with one eye is king. Well, here in Australia one eye is not enough. If you were to spend all your life with sick people and you were sick too you wouldn't know what it was to be in good health. It's only when you go to live with healthy people and you become healthy too that you know you cannot go back to living with the sick ones.

The second question in this section was designed to tap several areas of life in Australia, one of which was whether the immigrants would return to live in Sicily or Italy if they had the chance and the money. Australia has a much used national lottery system and the largest of the prizes is £100,000. When asked "If you were to win the big lottery, say for £100,000, what would you do with the money?" ten percent said they would return to live in Italy, though not Sicily (three of these five respondents are not naturalized). About half the respondents said they would spend all or part of the money on a world trip, and most of these specifically included Italy but excluded Sicily—"What would I do there?"

In sum, a very low percentage of people are so dissatisfied with Australia that they would like to return (one had returned and then re-emigrated to Australia several years ago). About half of the respondents, including all of the recent immigrants, would like to visit Sicily or have done so and did like it. The rest are quite satisfied with their lives in Australia and would not dream of returning to live in Italy and if trips are planned prefer to see Australia and the South Seas, or, farther afield, America and the Soviet Union rather than Italy.

The question "Did you plan to stay permanently in Australia before emigration?" was discussed, but the second part of this question—"What made you change your mind?"—has been deferred until the present section since it more properly belongs to an analysis of satisfaction than immigration. Fifteen respondents replied to the first question that they did plan to remain in Australia permanently and this group is accordingly omitted from the following discussion. Of the remaining thirty-three respondents, 34 percent stayed because they were "forced to" (five of these are still undecided whether to remain or return), 7 percent made the final decision after a trip back to Italy, and 59 percent slowly changed their minds over time. The majority of those in the first group are still dissatisfied with many aspects of their lives in Australia and have never completely committed themselves to adjusting to their new lives, although several of these are prewar immigrants. The largest group are fairly optimistic and show that though they may have been very unhappy at the beginning they changed or became accustomed to new customs and new ideas. The Sydney Sicilians often spoke with contempt of other immigrants who come out for a year or so and then return. I was present at a Sicilian home once when a man and his adult daughter who had been in Australia about fifteen months came by to say their farewells since they had decided to return to Sicily. The group in the house were most outspoken in their comments, going so far as to call the man a "quitter," a "coward," and a "malcontent," though these terms were used only after they had reasoned with him for about two hours, describing their own problems in the beginning and relating how things change and get better. Only when he, with bitterness, had rejected their arguments, did they attack him and say finally, "You, you'll never be happy anywhere." When the man left there was a heated discussion about such types who haven't the guts to hold on until they learn and like the ways of the new country.

Another man who had been in Sydney about sixteen years and had done well financially decided to return to his home and build a hotel for the rapidly expanding tourist industry. He met with approval everywhere, and even those who did not know him personally knew of the man and applauded his idea. He had stuck it out, he had adjusted to Australia, and he had profited by Australia. Therefore, he was free to leave in order to capitalize on his Australian experience.

No one is as aware of the problems of emigration as the immigrants themselves. A nonimmigrant cannot appreciate how difficult the early period is, nor how satisfying it is to overcome seemingly insuperable problems and begin to live a full life—fuller and better than it had ever been in Sicily. Needless to say this study does not touch those immigrants who did return dissatisfied and disgruntled, but unpublished figures at the Italian Consulate in Sydney show that southern Italian immigrants (mainly Calabrese and Sicilians) have a much lower rate of return than the largely government-assisted immigrants from northern Italy. However, the difference in outlook between the immigrants who were "forced" to remain and those who gradually adjusted themselves to Australia after an initial period of feeling forced is shown in the answers to "Did you plan to stay permanently?" and "What made you change your mind?"

1. *Negative*

   I expected much more here and expected to make £50–60 a week, instead I worked for £14. So I wasn't able to go back, I had to stay here. There was no choice.

   No, I wanted to go back at first and then again after the war but my wife wrote me about how bad things were in Italy so I just had to stay, and after the way they treated me during the war!

2. *Negative at first but changed later*

   No, it was just for a year. But my pride was involved because I didn't do well in the beginning so I had to stay more. And then I began to get used to a new environment and by the time I met my wife I was about half-and-half settled in here. So then I decided definitely to stay.

   No, I only came for three or four years. At first it was very hard, there was no progress, I was better off in Italy. But with security I become more confident, I could talk to Australians and you like them then and it's like living in your own country.

All of the indices in this chapter show a very high degree of satisfaction with specific areas of the public sector of life. Even those who do not like some aspects of their present life still say that Australia is a good place to live, and the five respondents who are considering a return to Italy admit they are happy enough in Australia. General testaments to Australia were scattered throughout the interviews:

> I can tell you that everything here is better than it was in Sicily and that says it all. Here I work all week, every week. I take the money and I can buy what I want, what is in my heart, and I can do what I want to do. Today here, with work and sacrifices they have what they never had in their own country—life.

> I hated Australia, I never wanted to come but there was no other place. Only fifteen years ago it was a terrible place but it was better than Sicily. I went back once for two years but I just couldn't live there and so now I'm back here again. It's still not so good here, but it's somewhat different than before and always it's better than Sicily.

> I began to forget right away. I like everything. Australia has been a marvelous thing for me. This land has taken me by the heart. There is no difference between me and an Australian. I like every single thing they like.

There are several items which are mentioned over and over by almost all the immigrants as being among the main things that they like in Australia: steady work for all; housing; democratic relations between men, even officials and higher-ups; justice administered equally to all men irrespective of position; money to buy the material possessions which make life pleasant; money and opportunity to afford children an interesting and profitable life. No one, least of all these immigrants, claims that life in Australia is easy. Hard work and sacrifices are part of a normal existence, but the difference in Australia is:

> that here sacrifices are possible; in Sicily the whole of life is a sacrifice. You know there you must make the hardest sacrifices just to stay alive and so there is nothing left over to sacrifice to get extras, if you call education and decent housing extras. Yes, that's the difference—in Sicily life itself is a sacrifice.

PRIVATE SATISFACTION

Private satisfaction is intended to include all those feelings, ideas, and reactions which deal with the Australian people and with their way of life. In the preceding section we looked at Australian institutions and mentioned Australians only as they functioned in the public sector work roles. This section is intended to clarify the immigrants' ideas about the native people with whom they live and with their conceptions of the Australians' way of life. The ideas presented here are those of the immigrants and may or may not reflect reality. If the immigrants have misconstrued the real facts, if they have selected from reality some things and ignored others, it is of interest to us because it reveals very clearly those things which are important to the immigrants and how they restructure fact to fit a Sicilian-based value and normative structure. For instance, the immigrants showed they were very satisfied with the Australian form of democratic government and justice and many specified the Sydney police force as a model of fair play and equality. The fact is that at that time the police force was rocked by a series of scandals which drew the highly critical attention of all Australian newspapers, local government, and civic groups. When this was mentioned to the Sicilians (none except the educated ever brought it up) they brushed it off as being of no consequence. They read newspapers, saw television, and were well aware of the facts, but they deliberately ignored the unsavory side of the police department because it did not touch them directly, and it was still better, they claimed, than the Italian police department "where there are so many scandals the papers don't even bother with them any more."

The expressed attitude of Sicilians is that there is little basic difference between Italians and Australians: 71 percent of the respondents think that an Australian can be as intimate as an Italian. However, only 44 percent of the respondents actually have Australian friends and these are mainly the educated and the occupationally mobile. In theory many do not object to a marriage between their children and Australians, but 40 percent prefer Italian or Italo-Australian spouses, 56 percent express no preference, and only 4 percent actually favor an Australian. There are many statements to the effect that "Australians are good and bad, just as Italians," or "they are no more wicked than us," but there is very little first-hand social contact with Australians and as the previous chapter on the family revealed over two-thirds of the immigrants retain their traditional Sicilian ways in the home.

Three very broad questions elicited responses so broad and lengthy that it was necessary to break the answers into several more discreet units. The questions are: (1) What do you think of the Australian people and the way they live? (2) What do you think are the main differences between the Australian way of life and the Sicilian way of life? and (3) What way of life do you have now? Since these were open-ended questions and the respondents were allowed to structure the answers in their own way many responses crossed the lines set in the questions. Therefore, this presentation is in accordance with the main focuses which the immigrants themselves used in their answers. First, note the distinctively "Australian" traits enumerated by the respondents: (1) present orientation—Australians think only of drinking and sports; they do not save their money but spend it on foolish amusements; they never make sacrifices to get ahead; (2) disaffected relationships—each Australian thinks only of himself, he is selfish; the family is disunited; women are too free; children are too independent; they don't have close friends; they are false and superficial; their behavior is inconsistent, they are friendly one day and cool the next; (3) world outlook—they think they know too much; they are ignorant of the world and of others.

These characteristics add up to a way of life in which Australians are self-centered, oriented to present gratification, and feel superior to all others. Australian men work at menial jobs and then relax in the pubs and at sporting events with their mates while women are free to carry out their own activities with other women. Family members are not concerned about one another and each—mother, father, child—does as he or she pleases. There are no ambitions for the future, no work and saving to advance oneself or one's children, because it is enough to have any job which will furnish enough money to permit amusements, and in any case, who wants to kill himself working or going to school. There is some evidence in the literature, mainly descriptive and impressionistic, that this view is not completely wrong. Australians do spend vast sums of money on beer, horse racing, and slot machines, and they do not value education very much beyond the lower high school level; nor do they value jobs which demand too much of the worker. This is a more valid picture of working-class Australians than of other classes, although even the urban middle class follows these lines to a much greater extent than do other middle-class groups in England or in the United States. Most of the immigrants, however, see and know only working-class Australians; so their ideas of the Australian way of life are drawn entirely from this group.

Almost none of the immigrants had anything good to say about Australians or their way of life because it is the absolute antithesis of the Sicilian way of life. However, there is a curious incongruity in the data. The qualities which make Australians admirable work-mates, policemen, judges, and politicians are the very same qualities, under different names, which make them most undesirable as friends, parents, and children. At work Australians mind their own business, while at home they are selfish; they are democratic in the world and indifferent in personal relationships. The Australian attitude which allows workers to labor unbothered by others is the same attitude which makes them cold and selfish friends. If a man is brought up to respect the legal and personal rights of others, then he is usually consistent in applying the principle and, in this case, respect means independence for oneself and for others in all contexts. It is very doubtful if Australians are cold as friends, but a friend who does not make it his personal business to draw out of another all his problems and interests would appear self-centered and cold to most Sicilians. Sicilians do recognize that the peculiarly Sicilian quality of concerned interest in others can sometimes be a comforting and warm thing which fosters feelings of security and being wanted and that at other times it can be annoying—and then it is called snooping or gossiping. This is recognized by Sicilians about Sicilians because they know Sicilian habits and ideas. However, their contact with

Australians is limited, for the majority, to the work place and they never learn that a friend who may appear standoffish is in fact very concerned and interested. As one respondent, who does know Australians commented:

> Australians are much freer in their way of life. They often board away from home when they are working and are completely free. I used to wonder if the families cared, it seemed not, they just let the children go off and that was that. Now I know that they do, I have met some of them.

Sicilians, of course, are seen as warm, interested, selfless, and hard working. The Sicilian way of life revolves around the family, which in turn is oriented to the future and its rewards; for these each member of the united family works today. The Puritan ethic of hard work and saving is a guiding principle of the Sicilian way of life, and while amusements and having fun are not vetoed, they take place always in the company of family, relatives, and old friends. Sicilians do not drink or go to pubs, their gambling is limited to penny-ante card games at home, and soccer is the only sport to which some are addicted and which they attend with relatives and friends.

Forty-six percent of the respondents think that the majority of Australians and their traits are bad, 35 percent think they have good and bad traits, and only 19 percent think that the Australian people and their way of life is good. Some comments from each group are illustrative:

1. *Australians bad*
   They take the pay envelope Friday and Sunday night, then there is nothing left because they don't have control. We have control. They don't think of the future; they think of horses, sport, amusements, drinking. I don't trust them very much, they say one thing today, another to-morrow. With an Italian or a Sicilian I can know what he is like, know all about him without knowing him. But with an Australian I can't know or indicate with precision who or what he is.

   They have no respect, even in the family, not for the father like among us. They are independent people and I don't like them. They think they have the world in their hands and want to know nothing about the rest of the world, ignorant people they are.

2. *Australians good and bad*
   The Australians, from some points of view, I like, the

liberty, earning, spending, amusements. On the other side there are things I don't like—the cheap girls—they are also in Italy of course but they are more liberal here. I don't say they are worse than us because we do hidden what they do openly.

I would say I don't like the Australian way of life. But neither do I like the very possessive way of Sicilian families with the girls and the children, chaperones and such. It's better to educate them more and give them their freedom, yet the Australian goes the other way. They are the two extremes. Up to a point I am more Australian, I have tried to accept what is good on both sides. I have been selective. Assimilation comes from both sides, neither is all good or all bad.

3. *Australians good*
People here have been very good to me. There is little difference between us today. Before there was a lot of difference, eating, all things. Today Italians go to the pub after work, yesterday no. I go to boxing now, wrestling. The Sicilian is like the Australian today. But they have changed too, like eating, they eat spaghetti and rabbit.

The Sicilians are very strict with their children, their way of life in the home. Children don't come in conversation with parents. Girls, children born here, it's very hard for them. Some assimilate and some of the immigrants don't. Those carry on the tradition of the old mum, they won't mix, they hold themselves all in one group, they even all live together out in Leichardt. That's wrong. We are here and we must assimilate and live among the people of the country in every way as I do.

After citing the differences between the two ways of life the respondents were asked to say what way of life they followed: 58 percent said Sicilian, 19 percent said both Australian and Sicilian, and 23 percent said Australian. There were no significant associations with any of the four independent variables on this index. However, bearing in mind the perceived and, to a large extent, real differences between the two life styles, a cursory examination of the individuals who followed an Australian way of life reveals that only two of the eleven have anything remotely resembling the life Australians lead; one is a highly educated professional and the other is a working-class man who early in his time in Australia cut himself off from Italians and from that day,

259

before the war, to this has had no contact with Sicilians. The other nine immigrants are uneducated working-class individuals who are very Sicilian in their way of life, attitudes, and ideas. However, they are extremely happy in Australia and are willing to admit that much of the Australian environment which seems negative to them may be merely a reflection of their own ignorance of Australians.

The other 77 percent who wholly or partially retain a Sicilian way of life because they still think it is the best way of life are completely and utterly satisfied with Australia—because they have jobs, money, opportunity, and the freedom to live like Sicilians. Their satisfaction does not stem from a change in their way of living, as so much of the literature indicates, but instead from the freedom to live as one pleases, that is, as loyal citizens and good workers outside the home and traditional Sicilians inside the home. They may dislike intensely the Australian way of life, but since they are not forced or coerced to follow this road, they can pick the things they like from the Australian environment and ignore the rest:

> Life here is beautiful, it's better here. You can work, you can do anything you want. The Australians spend, enjoy themselves, don't think of the future, go to pubs every night. But here we are free to do as we please, to live in our own way, they do what they want, we do what we want, and there is a chance for everyone.

Many respondents then are stating and living the principle of cultural pluralism which posits that some societies may be so structured as to permit a number of subsocieties to coexist at any one time. An individual may choose any life style which is not in direct opposition to the laws of the country and yet enjoy the same chances, opportunities, and rights of all other individuals. This explains how some respondents could claim an Australian way of life; for them, all ways of life are included under this generic term. Other immigrants of course chose to use the phrase in its specific sense. In sum those features of Australia which are relatively universal and public, such as occupation, housing, voting, and legal justice, are viewed positively by this sample of Sicilian immigrants, and those features which are personal and private, such as personal relationships, are generally disliked.

One index of change which is often noted in the writings of sociologists as being of utmost importance is the attitude of natives of the host society toward the newcomers. While very few researchers have actually done fieldwork connected with this subject, all agree that its importance cannot be overestimated. I did not work with Australians and there are no studies of Australian attitudes toward immigrants, but I did get some impressions of their attitude and my own respondents made a few statements which bear on the subject. Their general impression is that Australians are highly discriminatory and prejudicial toward non-British immigrants, but I feel that this is a gross over-simplification which does injustice both to the Australians and to the European immigrants. It seems that as a result of the history of immigration to Australia and the democratic mateship myth which pervades Australian society, Australians are willing to accept and make friends with European immigrants if the immigrants are willing to change themselves completely and become Australians and lead an Australian way of life.

There is today little bitterness toward the immigrants though this surely existed in the past. Until the end of World War II, Australians knew only British customs, ideas, and peoples. They did not have a history of accepting new and diverse peoples and so they had no experience of living with people different from themselves. The United States and Canada have both formed unique characters and customs as a result of the constant flow of immigrants from all parts of Europe and Asia. Australia, which for most of its history made it government policy only to accept British immigrants, was not prepared for the emotional accommodation necessary to meet mass immigration from hitherto untapped areas of Europe. Australia has known some violent periods in its history when the native-born felt themselves threatened by foreign-born citizens, especially during periods of economic depression. However, since the end of the last war the country has experienced an unparalleled expansion and no threat to Australian-held jobs is in sight. The immigrants have proved themselves to be hard workers and law abiding citizens and most Australians admit these facts readily. They have learned some things about the curious newcomers and have even adopted some of their customs, mainly in food and clothing. But the Aussies have not learned to interact on a personal level with people whose ideas and customs are different from the majority. Foreign (non-British names) are funny, non-Australian accents are ugly, pierced ears are deformities, and anyone who does not eat meat pies is insane.

Thus a non-Australian will be accepted socially if and when he becomes or demonstrates that he is trying to become a "dinkum

Aussie." If, on the other hand, the outsider maintains his own traditions, he is tolerated and ignored but he can never become "one of the mob." An extremely popular fiction book which has now been made into a film deals with the adventures of an Italian immigrant (northern Italian) as he enters Australian society and gradually becomes changed until, with the exception of some speech peculiarities, he is indistinguishable from his Aussie mates. The book is entitled *They're A Weird Mob* (1963), which refers in a jokingly affectionate way to Australians, and the author, Nino Culotta, is in reality a native-born Australian named John O'Grady. This book embodies the fondest hopes and dreams of most Australians—that the immigrants, who are really weird, will change themselves into Australians and become only nicely weird.

Working-class immigrants who encounter only working-class Australians in the factory reported that they were often asked to go to the pub with their mates after work, a dearly loved ritual in Australia. They all refused because Sicilians do not drink, pubs are dirty and uncomfortable, and the family is waiting for father. No Sicilian in his right mind would dream of going to stand up in a pub drinking beer with friends when he could be home with his family where he can also have a drink if he wishes. Because of this basic incompatibility on the first level of male social intercourse, none of these immigrants will ever get to know Australians outside the work place or see them at home with their families. The refusal of both groups to change their ways of living or even to accept differences means that each will continue to misunderstand the other.

This is a situation in which the values and norms of each group are so totally different that, coupled with an inability to adjust to differences, communication is impossible—which in turn perpetuates two incompatible ways of life. One immigrant who said that immigrants are more like rich Australians than lower-class Australians put his finger on the problem. If the Sicilians could live with and interact with middle-class Australians, they would find much more understanding because these two groups share very similar values concerning work, mobility, and soberness. The educated immigrants who do live, work, and socialize with middle-class Australians have few difficulties because there are few differences, and this exposure to a slightly different but basically similar way of life leads to changes in those areas of life which are different, mainly in husband-wife and parent-child relationships.

13

SUMMARY OF THE DATA

CONCERNING pre-emigration attitudes, it is apparent that over half of the immigrants were somewhat ambivalent about emigrating and about Australia as the site of residence. Most decided to come to Australia because it was the only country open to them and they planned to stay for only a period of years and then return to Sicily. After arrival a little over one-half were displeased with Australia and had real difficulties with language, status, or work in their first year. Today, in the public sector, half speak excellent English, live in high status suburbs and in neighborhoods which are high in number of Italians.

In the private sector over half still eat Italian food; one-third speak only Sicilian at home and almost half use both languages; over half do not have any Australian friends and the majority of the rest know Australians only as acquaintances; only one-fourth belong to Australian organizations while over half do not even belong to one Italian organization.

There has been virtually no change in relations with members of the extended family although a clumping together for a few years after immigration is common. There has been some change toward egalitarianism in the husband-wife relationship which does not involve the addition of new features so much as it represents a shift in the constituent factors of this relationship. The major difference lies in the increased status as individuals of males and of females in Australia which results in greater responsibilities for the husband and a diminution of responsibilities for the wife. At the same time each is more cooperative with the other and the traditional layering principle which masks the real responsibilities of each spouse is greatly diminished. Within the nuclear family about one-third of the families have changed from a system which is based on being controlled to one of self-control in which there are separate worlds for adults and for children and the latter are treated as children though they are, at the same time, given a much greater degree of personal freedom and independence.

There is high satisfaction with all the public institutions of

Australia—occupation, residence, and judicial system—and there is a correspondingly low level of satisfaction with the Australian people and their life style. So although there are changes in the public sector and an expressed satisfaction with this area of life, there is not a significant number of changes in the private sector since the Sicilian way of life continues to be positively evaluated while the Australian life style is devalued for the majority of immigrants in this sample.

The four independent variables which are often cited as important catalysts of change were examined separately to determine precisely what effect these variables have on the change patterns of individuals who are so categorized. The chi-square test of significance was used to determine which dependent variables show a meaningful association with each of the independent variables. Results are shown in Appendix B.

Age at emigration is significantly associated with dependent variables in only three of the eight major divisions of the data. There is no association whatsoever with the public sector, the extended family, nuclear family, public satisfaction, or private satisfaction. In the remaining three divisions there is an association with only one variable in each division, a number one would expect to find by chance. Therefore, in this study, the age at which a person emigrates appears to have no important bearing on later changes, and the hypothesis that those things which are learned early in life will be hardest to change cannot, by extension, be used with youth or maturity at emigration. A young person or an older person does not, as a member of such groups, show any change which distinguishes him from other immigrants. However, one cannot simply rule out this variable because neither the present study nor any others have systematically investigated the importance of age at emigration upon change. A detailed study focusing on this variable would surely uncover many differences in the patterning of change variables.

Time in Australia is associated with dependent variables in seven of the eight divisions; the only one which is absent is private satisfaction. Time is associated with only one of the emigration variables which shows that the prewar immigrants were able to emigrate the moment they decided to make the move while the second, postwar group had to wait from two to ten years to leave. This difference reflects the historical fact that emigration to Australia before the war was much freer and more open while several years after the war the Australian government had placed restrictions on emigration. This dependent variable is not itself a measure of change but it may have some bearing on change.

Long-time immigrants speak good English, live in high status suburbs, own their own homes, and display satisfaction with their jobs. New immigrants, on the other hand, do not speak English well, live in low status suburbs, rent their homes and, while they are satisfied with their jobs, would change if more money were offered. Many variables in the public sector of life are strongly associated with number of years in the new country, but there are confounding factors in each case which explain the reasons for the differences. The most important factor is the condition which prevailed during the historical period in which the immigrant entered the country. Tied in with this are considerations such as number of like-nationality individuals present, occupational opportunities, and type of job which the immigrant takes. The role of the fruit shops has been detailed already but it is best to point out once again that employment in these shops affected language capacity and residence. Home ownership is extremely important to the prestige and mobility of the immigrants as Thernstrom's material and my own data reveal but it is difficult for very new immigrants to amass the cash needed for a down payment on their own homes and this fact is reflected in the data. In sum, there are changes over time and there are differences between immigrants who have been in the country for varying lengths of time, but it is the historical period which is of prime importance in most cases, not years in themselves. These changes are not necessarily assimilative in themselves: they may be for certain individuals but this must be ascertained by examining yet other variables because the changes which occur in the public sector of life are descriptive. They are not measures of change from similar Sicilian variables.

In the private sector of life, the old immigrants eat Australian food and speak or allow the use of English at home while the new immigrants retain Sicilian food habits and dialect in the home. Changes in both categories appear to be significantly affected by the pressure of school-age children, and although the prestige of the woman in the family seems to be an additional factor in the preparation of Australian food, its weight cannot be ascertained at this time.

Turning now to the kinship variables, I found that the old immigrants retain the over-all Sicilian pattern of relationships with members of the extended family and in regard to helping kin.

New immigrants display a medium level of change indicating that while there is a clumping effect in the period just after immigration this soon wears off for the majority of immigrants who then revert back to the strife-ridden, envy-inspired pattern of little contact with kinfolk and even less interest in their affairs. Of the variables in the husband-wife relationship only one, financial responsibility, is associated with time: it is held by the old immigrant men while the new immigrant husbands tend to share it more. All but the immediate postwar group take children to parties and out visiting. This association is highly correlated with the fact that the middle time group is largely composed of educated and occupationally mobile immigrants which tends to skew the results of the variable.

In the divisions of the private sector there has been remarkably little change associated with time in Australia and changes in this sector, which would be value changes, are simply not there. Generally speaking, all three time groups display the same inner distribution. Time then cannot be used as an independent variable in measuring change: it makes no difference how long the immigrant has been in the country when matters concerning his private life are involved.

As might be expected five of the seven public satisfaction variables are highly associated with time: in every case the old immigrants are more satisfied with Australia and its institutions than are the newer immigrants. This is quite a logical conclusion and might have been predicted from the associations in the public sector of life because the older immigrants, who are established and secure, have more to be satisfied with. They have jobs they like which furnish them an adequate income, they own their own homes in suburbs, they are citizens of the country, and they have, by now, lost any lingering desire to visit Sicily. The new immigrants however are still struggling financially, have not yet been able to settle down in their own homes, and still think of Sicily as a place they would like to see again.

None of the private satisfaction variables are associated with time in Australia.

A combination of years in the new country and the conditions in the country when the individual emigrated serve to form an index of change in the public sector, but it does not have a direct correlation with change in the private sector. Long-time immigrants are highly satisfied with the public institutions of Australia but they retain their Sicilian way of life at home; newer immigrants are not so satisfied with the jobs and houses they find in Australia, the jobs and houses they have are not so good, and they retain their Sicilian way of life. In other words, public sector factors such as occupation and language ability have no bearing on the changes of these Sicilian immigrants. The old and the new live like Sicilians, raise their families according to traditional Sicilian ideas, and associate only with other Sicilians. English language ability, job, or type of neighborhood are quite irrelevant factors in determining how they live their lives in private. They conform to Australian laws, customs, and rules when they must associate with Australians outside the house, but inside the house they are Sicilians who continue to think that their way of life is best as long as it is enhanced by the greater earning power and increased opportunities for advancement found in Australia.

Occupational mobility. Immigrants who are occupationally mobile display a change pattern which is internally consistent and congruent with the road to successful social mobility. These are the manipulators who use the system to advance their own ends and since the ends are definite and attainable they display a remarkable ability, conscious or unconscious, to do the right thing. These are individuals who left Sicily to advance themselves and their families (whereas the nonmobile left to acquire material possessions). To achieve this goal they, first of all, advance occupationally, speak beautiful English which they practice at home, and associate with Australians and professional Italians in organizations of all kinds. Their friends are usually Sicilians. They are family-oriented; within the confines of the nuclear family there is a strong tendency toward sex role and age differentiation. They are willing to move away from traditional patterns of the husband-wife relationship and service to the nuclear family when, and only when, it is expedient to do so. They allow their daughters and sons freedom unheard of in Sicily but they do not believe that children should be trained to independence. They are goal- and achievement-oriented individuals who have, by their own terms, been highly successful in using to their own ends the system they found in Australia. These are the immigrants who speak of wearing Australian masks to hide their real identity. They are so successful that Australians never guess that underneath the polished Anglo-Saxon exterior lies a real Sicilian who jeers and scorns the Australian people and their private way of life.

Have they changed? It is not really a difficult question because the respondents themselves answered it. In the public sector they are Australians and so they appear, but in private they are the Sicilians they have always been, living a Sicilian way of life and holding intact those Sicilian values, norms, and behavior patterns which perpetuate their way of life in the face of intrusions from the outside. This is the second instance of changes in the public sector which are not accompanied by changes in the private sector; both long-time immigrants and the occupationally mobile are essentially unassimilated, though for very different reasons.

Education. The educated, like the occupationally mobile, display a pattern which is internally consistent but, unlike the mobile immigrants, there is no sense of conscious direction or goal. Instead, for all their sophistication, they appear passive—accepting that which comes to them and allowing their old values and behavior patterns to alter. They are not unaware of the changes, and many respondents in the group spoke of their difficulties in initially accepting some Australian ideals; but they valued the ideals and changes positively and made themselves accept them because of a deep-seated belief in assimilation. It may have been easier for these immigrants to change because through their education in Sicily they were already aware of differences in patterns of belief and custom in the world, and many stated that they arrived with the intention of becoming Australian. They believe that one should not and must not live in a country for the majority of one's life as a foreigner and therefore they, as foreigners, must change and fit into the Australian society. Many were disenchanted with Italy—its social system, mores, customs, and people —and were prepared to try a new system which appeared to offer more rewards than their homeland.

Educated immigrants left Sicily for personal reasons and they left immediately when they once decided. Their first impression of Australia was negative because they so keenly felt their own loss of status which was due to inability to speak the language and their consequent employment at physical labor. They experienced feelings of inferiority and loneliness based more on lack of recognition of their own capabilities than on an absence of people around them. But they quickly improved their English and today eat Australian food, associate with Australians as friends and as co-members of organizations, and run their homes and families on Australian rules. They have changed little in regard to relatives but their reason is that they prefer to see friends and that they have nothing in common with brothers, cousins, and aunts. Inside the house the husband and wife share decision making and responsibility for children, and no one commands. Their nuclear families have become individual-oriented; children are taught to control themselves, to be independent, are allowed to make their own decisions, and owe nothing in the way of service to their parents. The parents and children, while they form a close-knit group and are loving toward one another, have their own worlds which do not overlap except in the house.

The educated immigrants have made great changes in the public sector, have been successful occupationally and socially, and in addition, have made sweeping changes in the private sector so that they are now like Australians or are becoming like Australians.

Evaluation. This study was based on the hypothesis that first-generation individuals would show habit changes in the public sector of life and value changes in the private sector of life. I believe that the data, drawn from a diversified sample of immigrants, have borne out the validity and the usefulness of such an approach. The conclusions reveal that it is not necessary to become embroiled in arguments about whether what happens is called acculturation or assimilation; if we simply follow life as it happens—public versus private—patterns and trends emerge which are clear, logical, consistent with the pre-emigration social organization and the effect of education, mobility and time upon individuals. This study shows that there are areas of change and areas which resist change; there are groups or subgroups which change and subgroups which do not change. Some of the changes merely contribute to securing a better but not essentially different life, while other changes involve alterations in Sicilian values, norms, and ideals.

The Sicilians arrived in Australia with a set of values, some of which closely approximate like Australian values, especially when advancement, mobility, or any kind of movement is involved. The correlation between the two national value-sets here makes it possible for immigrants to realize their ambitions without alterations in their traditional means of attaining these ends. Caudill (1952), in a thesis on first- and second-generation Japanese in the United States, makes this point the basis of his entire study; he shows that Japanese values of hard work, cleanliness, and advancement are congruent with like American values, and therefore Japanese immigrants and their children are praised by Americans for their "American" virtues. But Caudill also shows that many other facets of Japanese social structure, especially in and about the family,

269

are alien to the American society, and although these are not evident to Americans, they are the source of endless and severe personal and emotional difficulties for the adult second-generation children. The same duality is present in the situation of Sicilian immigrants in Australia (and obviously in the United States and Canada as well): many Sicilian values, such as occupational and social mobility, university education, hard work, saving, and property ownership are congruent with Australian values, but other Sicilian values such as service to the family, unconcern with the demands of tertiary educational institutions, and prestige as seen in the eyes of other Sicilians are at odds with the Australian society.

The picture is not all black and white—it is mainly shades of grey. These shadings taken in conjunction with a detailed analysis of the traditional society are usually the logically predictable result of known influences on the traditional pattern. There are no wildly deviant patterns nor are there any patterns which are inconsistent with our knowledge of Sicily. We have seen that there are two kinds of change—habit change and value change—and by using this division we can begin to understand why and how it is possible for immigrants to change their habits in the public sector and develop a deep commitment to the new country while at the same time many continue to hold their traditional values in the private sector. The separate examination of the four subgroups has enabled us to see the patterns of change followed by certain individuals who by virtue of their years in the new country, their superior education, or their aspirations to advance occupationally and socially are different from other immigrants.

The basic questions of sociologists in the past have been "How do the immigrants assimilate?" and "Do the immigrants acculturate?" These are misleading questions and will never lead to an organized body of data from which cross-cultural comparisons can be made and from which hypotheses and untimately theory can be abstracted. Instead we must ask: what changes? who changes? how do they change? when do they change? These are simple clear questions unencumbered by terminology, jargon or value judgments. Allowing for the validity of cultural pluralism, which is itself based on a public sector-private sector distinction, it is time to ask basic questions in order to find basic answers and then go on to the higher levels of abstraction which are our ultimate goal. Until those elementary questions can be answered there is danger in even speculating about broad trends because we simply do not now have the data on which to base such wonderings. We already know that when someone asks the question "Do they change and become like us?" we must answer yes and no, because there are enough studies to show that most immigrants and their descendants become like us in habit and custom but not necessarily in value and ideal. This is specific and definite information and with the use of the present formulation we can detail precisely how and why such a situation exists. The advantage of the present formulation is that it is simple, easy to use, broad enough to cover all important life areas, and is applicable to all social scientists and to all immigrant groups. By avoiding an a priori division of data by discipline or by theory and by using a division based on a habit-value (or "real-ideal", or "behavior-norm") duality that has already proved useful in traditional anthropological studies, we avoid any judgments about how change will proceed.

Some definite findings emerge from the data while other ideas are only suggested by this study. One of the latter is the agreement with the finding of Thernstrom that social mobility is closely tied in with traditional values relating to land ownership and occupational mobility for the immigrant and for his children. This is an extremely important hypothesis which must be tested on other immigrants in the future because it serves to explain not only why immigrants opted for one road or the other (in the case of the Italians both ways are highly valued) but also why their children and grandchildren continue on the road set by the immigrants. In addition, the present study reveals the enormous importance of family values which overide and supersede other values in the majority of cases. Southern Italians who respect and value education and the prestige and mobility associated with the educated person value even more the family and the particular form it takes among them.

Another suggestion which emerges from this study is the importance of knowing family background and the precise reasons why individuals emigrated. Two studies, McDonald (1958) and Lopreato (1960), show that for at least two regions of southern Italy it was not the very poorest who emigrated; rather the bulk of the immigrants came from the group just above the bottom—poor but managing. These individuals were not starving to death and they left their homes to advance themselves and their children, whatever advancement may mean to the person. My own data bear out this finding which has received no recognition in the rest of the immigrant literature. Instead there is an assumption that these admittedly poor immigrants were drawn from the very lowest level of society, and there appears to be no knowledge of the fact that there are many levels below the middle-class which show a great deal of variation in income, life style, and aspirations. This assumption then "explains" why the immigrants have not been mobile in their new country and why they have not taken full advantage of the educational and occupational opportunities offered to them. I believe that for many immigrants the truth lies elsewhere: traditional values relating to family solidarity or to life style prevented the utilization of the opportunities offered. This is another area of immigrant change which must be investigated in the future.

Another area of research concerns the utmost importance of knowing the pre-emigration social organization. To my knowledge, all studies of immigrant change stress "culture shock" and the inability of the immigrant generation to change their language, their customs and their values. But there is another study of Sicilian immigrants (or more correctly migrants) who moved from the village of Belmonte Mezzagno to the city of Palermo—a distance of fifteen kilometers (Romano 1961). The author's conclusions are:

> The Belmontese family represents a closed, solid ethnocentric group which does not admit from outside itself or with the "citizens" relations other than those based upon simple cordiality. . . . Friendships maintained are with people known for a long time. The families do not participate in any association and no clubs or associations have been formed among the villagers. . . . The Belmontese, according to the unanimous reply in the interviews, accept only the work of Palermo which remains, however, an isolated factor in the day. After work, and above it, is the family. An abyss seems to separate the Belmontese from the Palermitani, almost as if a deep inborn hostility keeps them far apart.

> The nearness of the community of emigration to Palermo and a long and continual exchange between Belmonte and the capital is believed to have created a familiarity with the city that should have rendered this entry easy. It has been possible to ascertain, on the contrary, that the difficulty of acculturation remains considerable. Also, if the repudiation of the Palermo mentality and customs is not mentioned in precise accusations it still occurs. . . . [pp. 72–74, 81, my translation]

The results of this study are extremely interesting because we have here a situation in which culture shock should not have occurred since the immigrants moved only fifteen kilometers to a town they were already familiar with and where they were not "foreigners." They knew the language and the dialect, the political system, the religious system, food habits, the educational system, and in addition, had for years been familiar with the occupational structure of the city which is after all what drew them to make their homes in the city. The way to assimilation or acculturation should have been easy and quick but it has not been so. The Sicilians in Palermo exhibit the same pattern of change as the Sicilians in Sydney (and very probably as in New York and Toronto) maintaining the values which support the family as the center of existence and rejecting anyone or anything, other than work and means to mobility, which comes from the outside. These findings substantiate the hypothesis based on my own data that changes are based on and flow directly from the original social organization. In addition, the Palermo study notes the difference between public and private sectors (the terminology is mine) and shows once again that habit change, which involves nonvaluative alterations that are new and must be learned, are not directly linked to value change.

Although the methodology of this study could be more sophisticated and the sample size enlarged, it still illustrates the usefulness and workability of the ideas which guided the analysis. The hypotheses and methods used here are simple and logical; the two kinds of change are separated and can be examined, analyzed, and then recombined into total patterns of change on the group, subgroup or individual level.

One improvement I would like to see added to future studies is the analysis of individual patterns of change. This type of detailed and extremely complex analysis requires the use of a computer and a researcher or his assistant who is competent to handle such tools. But some of the individual patterns in my own data are so interesting and so intriguing that I feel this area of analysis must be attempted in the future. I have written of groups and subgroups and I have used individuals only as they are representative of those groups, but I have not mentioned some of the patterns which the individuals exhibited as individuals. For example, one of the university graduates is the most liberal and the most Australian in his relations with his children, but in the husband-wife relationship he is the most Sicilian of all the respondents, educated and uneducated. Another man, a prewar immigrant, is the only person who has completely cut himself off from all Europeans, who served in the Australian army in the last war, who belongs to and is active in the Australian equivalent of the American Legion, who will not speak Italian, who could not answer many questions about Italians because "I don't know anything about those people," and who, alone, refers to Italians as "them" and Australians as "us."

Personality differences do not come through in this study because it was not my intention to attempt such a task, but a mere perusal of the interviews themselves reveals that these differences are enormous and there can be no doubt that they play an extremely important part in change patterns. Individuals from the same village who arrived at the same time and were both immediately put in internment camps for many long years have totally different perceptions of this experience. One man became, or perhaps already was, disgruntled and bitter toward Australians to the point that today his life is taken up with a seething hatred of the people among whom he lives; the other saw the experience as unjust but understandable and is today anxious for immigrants to become "assimilated," to move more in the Australian community so that the native-born may know them and thereby understand that all men are the same. Even among closely related kin there are extraordinary differences: one set of four brothers are so different from one another that it is often difficult to believe that they are indeed siblings, but their mother and relatives spoke often of these differences which, of course, manifested themselves in early childhood. One brother is surly and cranky and likes nothing, another is the "life of the party," another is serious and withdrawn, and the fourth is today a "dinkum Aussie" and very probably was so even in Sicily. It is impossible to deny that such differing personality assemblages have an effect on patterns of individual changes, but it is impossible at this point in our knowledge to do more than speculate on how important they are and in what ways they manifest themselves.

The ideas used in this study have been fruitful for an analysis of the change patterns manifested by a sample of Sicilian immigrants in Australia; yet it remains to be seen whether this is a unique situation or whether the theoretical and methodological innovations proposed here can be duplicated with another immigrant sample and so reveal their distinctive patterns. Little advanced work has ever been done on other large immigrant populations in the United States or elsewhere (though Australian sociologists are moving ahead quickly); Poles, Bohemians, Germans, Irish, Mexicans, and Cubans all wait for researchers. A few studies such as the Padilla monograph on New York Puerto Ricans (1958) reveal certain patterns which are very like those of Sicilians, but a concentrated effort to examine all these peoples before the first generation is completely lost is necessary now if we are ever to know of the various change patterns possible and begin to construct a theory of social change. There appears to be a growing interest or perhaps a reawakening of interest in the study of change in all the social science disciplines, and the opportunity to use this world-wide phenomenon as a natural laboratory should not be missed.

APPENDIX A
Australian Interview 1

1. Name
   Nome

2. Address
   Indirizzo

3. Age
   Età

4. Birthplace in Sicily
   Luogo di nascita in Sicilia

5. How many are there in your family here?
   Quanti siete nella vostra famiglia qua?

Name	Age	Relationship	Occupation
Nome	*Età*	*Parentela*	*Occupazione*

6. Who lives in this house?
   Chi abita in questa casa?

7. Do you have relatives in Australia?
   Ha parenti qua in Australia?

8. Were they here before you?
   Erano qua prima di lei?

9. When did you arrive in Australia?
   Quando è arrivato in Australia?

10. Did you come directly from Sicily?
    È venuto direttamente dalla Sicilia?

11. Why did you migrate to Australia?
    Perchè è emigrato in Australia?

12. Did someone help you to come here?
    Qualcuno lo ha chiamato qua?

13. What did he do for you?
    Cosa ha fatto lui per lei?

14. Was Australia your first choice as country of emigration?
    L'Australia era la sua prima scelta come paese d'emigrazione?

15. Why did you decide to come here _____ years ago? Why not before?
    Perchè ha deciso di venire _____ anni fa? Perchè non prima?

16. Did you talk to other people in Sicily about making this decision?
    Ha parlato con altre persone in Sicilia per fare questa decisione?

NOTE: The Italian in these interviews is conversational rather than formal and follows Sicilian usage.

17. Did you plan to stay permanently in Australia?
    Ha pensato di stare permanente in Australia?

18. Do you remember what impression this country and its people made on you when you first arrived?
    Ricorda i suoi pensieri sul paese e la gente nei primi giorni d'arrivo qua?

19. How did you find the life during your first year here?
    Come era sua vita durante il primo anno qua?

20. What was your greatest difficulty in settling down in Australia?
    Cosa era la più grande difficoltà per ambientarsi in Australia?

21. What do you think are the main differences between the Australia way of life and the Sicilian way of life?
    Quali sono le maggiori differenze tra lo stile di vita australiano e lo stile di vita siciliano?

22. Do you think you have a Sicilian or an Australian way of life now?
    Pensa di avere lo stile siciliano o lo stile australiano ora?

23. Are you a naturalized Australian?
    È naturalizzato Australiano?

24. Will you become naturalized?
    Pensa di fare la naturalizzazione?

25. Do you think that becoming naturalized is just a legal formality or does it mean changing your loyalty?
    Pensa che fare la naturalizzazione è solamente una formalità legale o significa un cambiamento di lealtà (fedeltà)?

26. What do you think of the Australian people and the way they live?
    Cosa pensa del popolo australiano e del loro modo di vivere?

27. What is the attitude of the Australian man-in-the-street toward the New Australians?
    Come è l'attitudine dell'Australiano verso i "New Australians"?

28. Do you think this is a land of opportunity?
    Pensa che questo è un paese d'opportunità?

WORK

29. What kind of work did you do in Sicily?
    Quale lavoro faceva in Sicilia?

30. What was your first job in Australia?
    Cosa era il suo primo lavoro qua?

31. How did you find that job?
    Come ha trovato quel lavoro?

32. Were you trained for that work?
    Ha fatto un apprendistato per quel lavoro?

33. Were most of your fellow workers Sicilians or Australians?
    Per la maggior parte, i suoi compagni di lavoro erano Australiani o Siciliani?

34. Do you prefer to work with Italians or Australians?
    Preferisce lavorare con Italiani o Australiani?

35. Was the pay good?
Era buono lo stipendio?

36. How long did you work there?
Per quanto tempo ha lavorato là?

37. And then where did you go?
E poi, dove è andato?

Job	Pay	Training	How found
Lavoro	*Soldi*	*Apprendistato*	*Come trovato*
Others	Time	Why left	
Altri	*Tempo*	*Perchè lasciato*	

38. Are you satisfied with your present job? With the pay?
È soddisfato con il lavoro attuale? Con i soldi?

39. If you had a choice would you stay in this job or would you change?
Se avesse una scelta, cambiarebbe questo lavoro o starebbe qua?

40. Do you have any long-range plans for the future?
Ha un programma per il futuro in questo campo di lavoro?

41. Have you taken any special job training here?
Ha fatto qualcosa per imparare una specializzazione?

42. Do you expect to?
Pensa di farlo nel futuro?

43. For you, what is a successful man?
Per lei, come è un uomo di successo?

RESIDENCE

44. Where did you live when you first arrived in Australia?
Dove ha abitato quando è arrivato qua all'inizio?

45. With whom?
Con chi?

46. Where did you go then? How long? Why did you move?
E poi, dove è andato? Per quanto tempo? Perchè ha cambiato?

Place	How found	With whom	Time	Why changed
Posto	*Come trovato*	*Con chi*	*Tempo*	*Perchè cambiato*

47. Have you lived with relatives in Australia?
Ha abitato con parenti in Australia?

48. Do you own this house?
Lei è il proprietario di questa casa?

49. (if yes) When did you come here?
(se si) Quando è venuto qua?

50. Why did you buy in this part of Sydney?
Perchè ha comprato in questa parte di Sydney?

51. How did you finance the purchase?
Come ha finanziato la casa?

52. Did any relatives or friends help you?
C'erano parenti o amici che le hanno dato aiuto?

53. Are there other Sicilians around here? On this block? Neighbors?
Ci sono altri Siciliani qua? Su questa strada? I vicini?

54. Do you think it is important to be near other Sicilians?
Pensa che è importante di stare vicino ad altri Siciliani?

55. Are any of your relatives living nearby?
Ci sono alcuni parenti che abitano vicino?

56. Are you planning to stay here?
Pensa di stare qua?

57. (If no) Are you planning to buy a house?
(se no) Voi pensate di comprare una casa?

58. What kind of house do you want?
Quale tipo di casa volete?

59. In what section of Sydney would you prefer to settle?
Quale parte di Sydney preferite per la casa vostra?

60. How will you finance your house?
Quali mezzi pensate di usare per finanziare la casa?

61. Do you think it is important to live near relatives?
Pensa che è importante abitare vicino ai parenti?

62. Have you ever lived with relatives?
Ha abitato mai con parenti?

63. Do you think it is important to live near Italians?
Pensa che è importante abitare vicino agli Italiani?

LANGUAGE

64. What languages do you speak?
Quali lingue parla?

65. What language is used at home?
Quale lingua è usata a casa?

66. Did you know any English before coming here?
Sapeva inglese prima di venire qui?

67. Have you studied English in Australia?
Ha studiato inglese in Australia?

68. Do you plan to?
Pensa di farlo?

69. How have you learned to speak English?
Come ha imparato l'inglese?

70. Do you think it is important to know how to speak the language of the country?
Pensa che è importante potere parlare la lingua del paese?

71. Would you like to speak English better? Why?
Le piacerebbe parlare inglese meglio? Perchè?

72. Would you like to speak better Italian?
Le piacerebbe parlare meglio l'italiano?

73. What languages do your children speak?
Quali lingue parlano i suoi figli?

74. Do you prefer that they speak English, Italian, or dialect?
Preferisce che loro parlino inglese, italiano, o dialetto?

75. I have heard that there are *doposcuole* [after-school programs] here for children to learn Italian. Do you think this is a good idea?
Ho sentito che ci sono dei doposculoa qua per ragazzi imparare l'italiano. Pensa che questa è una buona idea?

FOOD

76. What type of food do you eat at home?
Quale tipo di cibo mangiate a casa?

77. Has your food or style of eating changed since coming here?
Il vostro cibo o stile di mangiare ha cambiato da quando siete venuti qua?

78. What kind of food do your children prefer?
Quale tipo di mangiare preferiscono i suoi figli?

79. Do you ever go out to restaurants? What kind?
Andate mai ai ristoranti? Di quale tipo?

EDUCATION

80. Did you attend school in Sicily?
Ha fatto la scuola in Sicilia?

81. How many years?
Per quanti anni?

82. Why did you stop?
Perchè ha smesso di andarci?

83. Did you want to continue?
Voleva continuare?

84. Have you attended school in Australia?
Ha fatto la scuola in Australia?

85. What school do your children attend?
A quale scuola vanno i suoi figli?

86. What grades are they in?
In quale classe?

87. Do they like school?
A loro piace la scuola?

88. How long do they plan to go to school?
Per quanto tempo vogliono andare a scuola?

89. What do you want them to do when they have finished school?
Cosa vuole che loro facciano quando avranno finito la scuola?

90. Do you think it is important for parents to push their children?
Pensa che è importante per genitori spingere i loro figli?

91. Do you think it is important in Australia for a person to go on in school?
Pensa che è importante in Australia per una persona andare avanti nella scuola?

92. Is this true for both boys and girls?
È vero per i maschi e le femmine ugualmente?

93. Have any of your relatives been to the university?
Ha qualche parente laureato dall'università?

94. What church do you attend?
    A quale chiesa andate?

95. Do you attend any functions there other than religious services?
    Andate là per altre occasioni oltre che per la messa?

96. Do you belong to any Italian clubs?
    È membro di qualche club italiano?

97. Do you belong to any Australian clubs?
    È membro di qualche club australiano?

98. Do you belong to a union?
    È membro di un sindacato?

99. Do you participate in political activity?
    Partecipa alla vita politica?

100. Is there any organization for parents at your children's school?
     C'è un'organizzazione per genitori alla scuola dei suoi figli?

101. Do you participate in any club or organization?
     Fa un participazione in qualsiasi club o associazione?

SOCIAL

102. What do you usually do for entertainment? With whom?
     Cosa fa di solito per divertimento? Con chi?

103. Movies?
     Cinema?

104. Television
     Televisione

105. Sports
     Sport

106. Dancing
     Ballare

107. Theatre, music
     Teatro, musica

108. What newspapers do you read?
     Quali giornali legge?

109. Where do you go on your yearly holiday? With whom?
     Dove va per il holiday annuale? Con chi?

110. What about holidays—what do you do on:
     E per i giorni di festa—cosa fa:
     Easter?
     Pasqua?

111. Christmas
     Natale

112. New Year's Day
     Capodanno

113. San Giuseppe

114. National holidays
     Feste nazionali, come Anzac Day

115. Are the church holidays here as they were in Sicily?
I giorni santi della chiesa, sono qua come in Sicilia?

116. If you were to win the big prize in the lottery, say one hundred thousand pounds, what would you do with the money?
Se vince la grande lotteria, come dire cento mila sterline, cosa farebbe con i soldi?

Australian Interview 2

1. Who are you named after?
Da chi ha preso lei il suo nome?

2. And who are your brothers and sisters named after?
E i suoi fratelli e le sue sorelle?

3. Who are your children named after?
Da chi prendono i loro nome i suoi figli?

4. And what about your grandchildren?
E i suoi nipoti?

5. Is there a rule in your family for naming babies?
C'è nella sua famiglia una regola per dare il nome ai bambini?

6. Who are your children's godparents?
Chi sono i padrini e le madrine dei suoi figli?

7. Who are your godparents?
Chi sono i suoi padrini (madrine)?

8. Are godparents more often relatives or friends?
I padrini e le madrine sono più sovente parenti o amici?

9. Do friends become relatives when they are godparents?
Quando gli amici sono compari o comari diventano parenti?

10. Who would you say is your best friend?
Chi considererebbe lei il suo migliore amico?

11. Are most of your friends Sicilians, Italians, or Australians?
Sono i suoi amici per la maggior parte Siciliani, Italiani, o Australiani?

12. Do you have different friends now than when you first came to Australia?
Ha amici differenti adesso da quelli che lei aveva quando è arrivato in Australia?

13. Do you have any Australian friends?
Ha degli amici australiani?

14. Can an Australian be as intimate a friend as an Italian?
Può un Australiano essere amico così intimo come un Italiano?
I mean really intimate friends who come to your house?
Voglio dire, amico veramente intimo che viene a casa sua?

15. Would you like to have Australian friends?
Le piacerebbe avere amici australiani?

16. Do your children have more Australian or Italian friends?
I suoi figli hanno più amici australiani o più amici italiani?

17. Do you have friends who are not also friends of your wife?
Ha degli amici che non sono anche amici di sua moglie?

18. Can one trust a friend as much as a relative?
Ci si può fidare di un amico come di un parente?

19. Among those you left behind in Sicily do you miss your friends or your relatives more?
Delle persone che lei ha lasciato in Sicilia di chi sente di più la mancanza, degli amici o dei parenti?

20. How did you meet your wife (husband)?
Come ha incontrato sua moglie (o suo marito)?

21. How did you become engaged?
Come vi siete fidanzati?

22. Who else had to be consulted?
Chi dovette essere consultato sul fidanzamento?
A. Parents (*genitori*)
B. Sibs (*fratelli e sorelle*)
C. Relatives (*parenti*)

23. Have your children followed the same procedure?
I suoi figli hanno seguito (seguiranno) la stessa procedura?

24. Do you agree with the saying that a marriage is with all the family?
È d'accordo lei col proverbio che dice: un matrimonio è con tutta la famiglia?

25. (If yes) Then do the parents and all the relatives have a responsibility to approve or disapprove of this marriage?
Se è così i genitori e tutti i parenti hanno la responsabilità di approvare o disapprovare il matrimonio, non è vero?

26. (If no) Then who has the responsibility to approve or disapprove of this marriage?
Se no, chi ha la responsabilità di approvare o disapprovare il matrimonio?

27. What would happen to a young person who went against their parents' wishes in this matter?
Cosa succederebbe a un giovane che andasse contro i desideri dei suoi genitori in questa faccenda?

28. Do you know of any such cases?
Sa lei di casi simili?

29. Would you prefer your children to marry Sicilians, Italians, or Australians?
Preferirebbe lei che i suoi figli si sposassero con siciliani, italiani, o australiani?

30. I often heard a proverb in Sicily which says: the real relatives are those inside the house. Do you agree?
Ho sentito spesso un proverbio in Sicilia che dice: i veru parenti sunnu chiddi dintra la casa. È d'accordo lei con questo proverbio?

31. What exactly does this proverb mean?
Che cosa significa esattamente questo proverbio?

32. Who are those "inside the house"?
    Chi sono quelli "dintra la casa"?

33. What about the married children?
    E i figli sposati?

34. For this family inside the house, do you think it is as united here as in Sicily?
    Questa famiglia che è dentro la casa, crede lei che sia unita qui come in Sicilia?

35. Would you say that you spend more or less time with your family in Australia than you would have done in Sicily?
    Crede che in Australia lei passa con la sua famiglia più tempo o meno tempo di quello che lei non avrebbe fatto in Sicilia?

36. In your house, who does:
    A casa sua chi fa:
    A. The cooking (*il cucinare*)
    B. Washing the dishes (*il lavare i piatti*)
    C. Caring for the yard (*il badare al giardino*)
    D. The shopping (*la spesa*)
    E. When someone wants a cup of tea while watching TV
       Il tè quando qualcuno vuole una tazza di tè mentre la famiglia guarda la televisione
    F. Gets up at night when the children cry
       Chi si alza di notte quando i bambini piangono

37. Do you ever under any circumstances do any of these?
    Ci sono delle circostanze in cui lei fa alcune di queste cose?

38. In your family:
    Nella sua famiglia:

    A. Who chose this house?
       Chi ha scelto questa casa?

    B. Who picked out the furniture?
       Chi ha scelto la mobilia?

    C. Who decided to buy:
       Chi decise di comprare:
       1. the car (*la macchina*)
       2. the fridge (*il fridge*)
       3. clothing (*il vestiario*)

    D. Who actually went out to buy:
       Chi in effetti è andato a comprare:
       1. the car (*la macchina*)
       2. the fridge (*il fridge*)
       3. clothing (*il vestiario*)

    E. Who decides about the children's school?
       Chi decide a proposito dell'educazione scolastica dei figli?

    F. Who keeps up the most contact with relatives?
       Chi mantiene il maggior contatto coi parenti
       1. Here, *Qui*
       2. In Sicily, *in Sicilia*

G. Who takes care of money coming in the house (business)?
Chi si prende cura del denaro che entra nella casa ("business")?
1. banking (in whose name is the bank account)?
Chi va alla banca (a nome di chi è il conto bancario)?
2. budgeting?
Chi tiene i conti?
3. paying the rent, utility bills, hire purchase accounts?
Chi paga l'affitto, il conto della luce e del gas, le rate mensili per gli acquisti a credito?

39. Is the eldest son consulted in these matters?
Il figlio maggiore viene mai consultato in alcune di queste faccende?

40. Do you think the children of a widowed mother have the right to leave her to live alone on a pension?
Crede lei che i figli di una madre vedova hanno il diritto di lasciarla vivere sola con la pensione?
A. What should they do?
Che cosa dovrebbero fare?
B. Is it the same for sons and daughters?
È lo stesso per i figli maschi e per le figlie femmine?

41. Does a son or daughter whose parents sacrificed to send them to school have the right to marry immediately after graduation and thus not contribute any money to the family?
Crede lei che un figlio o una figlia, i cui genitori si sono sacrificati per mandarli a scuola, hanno il diritto di sposarsi immediatamente dopo la laurea di modo che essi non contribuiscono con denaro alla famiglia?

42. Who has the major responsibility for young children?
Chi ha la responsabilità maggiore per i bambini piccoli?

43. Who has this responsibility when the children are older?
Chi ha questa responsabilità quando i figli sono più grandi?

44. Who commands inside the house?
Chi comanda dentro la casa?
A. (If husband) Does that mean the wife has no authority?
Vuol dire questo, che la moglie non ha autorità?
B. (If both) Does that mean their authority is equal for all things?
Vuol dire questo, che la loro autorità è uguale in tutto e per tutto?

45. Do you think women have more freedom in Australia? Is this freedom a good thing (for the women, for the family)?
Crede lei che le donne hanno più libertà qui in Australia? È una cosa buona questa libertà (per le donne, per la famiglia)?

46. If a woman has independence and ability and strength of character does that mean her husband is weaker than she?
Se una donna ha indipendenza, abilità e forza di carattere, significa questo che suo marito è più debole di essa?

47. Are you glad your children are growing up in Australia?
È contento lei che i suoi figli crescono in Australia?

48. Do children respect and obey their parents more or less here in Australia?
    I figli rispettano ed ubbidiscono di più o di meno qui in Australia?

49. To what age must children obey their parents?
    Fin' a qual'età i figli devono ubbidire ai loro genitori?

50. Should children listen to their parents in everything or is it good for them to make decisions on their own?
    I figli dovrebbero ascoltare i loro genitori in ogni cosa o è bene per essi prendere decisioni da soli?

51. Do (did) your children always have to obey you and your wife about:
    I vostri figli devono sempre ubbidire lei e sua moglie riguardo:
    A. Whether they can go out
       Se possono uscire
    B. What time they should be home
       A che ora devono essere a casa
    C. Who their friends are
       Chi sono i loro amici
    D. How far they will go in school
       Fin' a che punto devono andare a scuola
    E. What job they will take
       Che lavoro devono prendere

52. Do you allow your children to stay up at night? A set hour?
    Permette lei ai suoi bambini piccoli di rimanere alzati di sera tardi? Un'ora fissa?

53. When you and your wife go to a party or out visiting, do the children always come with you? From thirteen, fourteen, and up?
    Quando lei e sua moglie vanno fuori ad una festa o a far visita, i figli vengono sempre con voi, voglio dire quelli di quattordici anni o più?
    A. Is this true even when they don't want to or when they have plans of their own?
       Devono venire con voi anche quando non vogliono o quando hanno i loro piani?
    B. Is is true for boys and girls equally?
       È lo stesso per i figli maschi e le figlie femmine?

54. Would you say that your children have their own lives independent of the family?
    Direbbe lei che i suoi figli hanno una loro vita indipendente da quella della famiglia?

55. Do you think children should be trained to be independent or is it better for them to refer all their problems to the family?
    Crede lei che i figli dovrebbero essere educati ad essere indipendenti o meglio per essi riportare i loro problemi alla famiglia?

56. Do you think you are closer to your children than your parents were with you?
    Pensa lei di essere più intimo coi suoi figli di quello che i suoi genitori non erano con lei?

57. Do your children receive a weekly allowance?
    I suoi figli ricevono una somma settimanale per le loro spese?

58. Do you think working children should give all their pay to the parents?
Crede lei che i figli che lavorano debbono dare tutta la loro paga ai genitori?

    A. What do your children do?
    Cosa fanno i suoi figli?

    B. (If yes) Australian children keep their own money—have you ever thought of changing your mind about this?
    I figli australiani tengono i loro soldi—ha pensato mai di cambiare la sua idea in questo campo?

      1) How do your children feel about this?
      Che cosa ne pensono i suoi figli?

    C. (If no) Most Sicilian families do this—have you changed your mind about this since coming to Australia?
    La maggior parte delle famiglie siciliane fanno così. Ha cambiato idea lei su questa faccenda da quando è venuto in Australia?

59. Do you allow your daughter to go out alone:
Permette lei a sua figlia di uscire sola:

    A. During the day with other girls
    Durante il giorno con altre ragazze

    B. At night with other girls
    Di sera tardi con altre ragazze

    C. To a club with boys and girls
    A un club con ragazzi e ragazze

    D. With a boy
    Con un ragazzo

60. Would you let your daughter go away from Sydney to Teachers College if that was the only opening?
Lascerebbe andare lei sua figlia lontano da Sydney alla scuola magistrale se quella fosse la sola via aperta?

61. Should sons and daughters work in a family business rather than hire an outsider, even if they want to do something else?
I figli e le figlie devono lavorare nell'impresa di famiglia piuttosto che impiegare un estraneo, anche se essi vogliono fare qualcos'altro?
    A. Do you know of any cases of this?
    Sa lei di casi simili?

62. Now, getting back to that proverb, the relatives are those outside the house right? Well, within that group of your relatives is there a head of the family?
E adesso, per tornare a quel proverbio, i parenti sono quelli che stanno fuori di casa, non è vero? Ebbene, dentro quel gruppo di vostri parenti c'è un capofamiglia?

63. Is there anyone who most of the others go to when they want advice or help?
C'è qualcuno da cui la maggior parte degli altri vanno quando essi vogliono consigli o aiuto?

64. Who do you go to when you need advice?
Che cosa fa lei quando ha bisogno di consigli?

65. Who do you go to when you want to borrow money?
   Da chi va lei quando lei vuole prendere denaro in prestito?

66. Have you ever tried to borrow money from a relative?
   Ha mai tentato lei di farsi prestare soldi da un parente?

67. Have you ever gone to a friend to borrow money?
   È mai andato da un amico a farsi prestare soldi?

68. Has a relative or friend ever come to borrow money from you?
   È mai venuto da lei un parente o un amico per farsi prestare soldi?

69. Do you or have you ever sent money to people in Italy?
   Ha mai mandato lei o manda adesso denaro a qualche persona in Italia?

70. Do you think relatives help each other as much as they should?
   Crede lei che i parenti si aiutano l'uno con l'altro quanto dovrebbero?

71. Do relatives change when they come to Australia?
   Crede lei che i parenti cambiano quando vengono in Australia?

72. Are the relatives as united here as in Italy?
   I parenti qui sono così uniti come in Italia?

73. If a youngster does something shameful, such as a boy stealing a car or a girl going to live with a man of ill repute, is the whole family and all the relatives dishonored by this action?
   Se un giovane fa qualche cosa vergognosa, per esempio, un ragazzo che ruba una macchina o una ragazza che vive insieme a un uomo di cattiva fama (uno spregiudicato), crede lei che tutta la famiglia e tutti i parenti sono disonorati da quella cattiva azione?

   A. Do they all have responsibility?
      Crede lei che in quel caso tutti sono responsabili?

74. Suppose a sister or brother is well established here and the others are struggling—must that one help the others?
   Supponiamo, per esempio, che un fratello o una sorella sono ben sistemati qui mentre gli altri vanno avanti alla meglio—crede lei che quello che è ben sistemato ha il dovere di aiutare gli altri?

75. If a man lost everything in a fire and he must have help to get started again, would it be best if he:
   Se per esempio un uomo ha perduto tutto in un incendio e ha bisogno di aiuto per ricominciare da capo, quale è la cosa migliore da fare per lui:

   A. Depended on his brothers and sisters or other relatives to help him as much as each one could, or
      Dipendere dai suoi fratelli e sorelle o altri parenti per farsi aiutare da ognuno nella misura del possibile, o

   B. Would it be better for him to try to raise money on his own, without depending on anybody?
      Sarebbe meglio che egli cercasse di ottenere del denaro da solo senza dipendere da nessuno?

76. As a youngster did you have one favorite relative?
   Quando lei era ragazzo aveva un parente favorito?

77. Did any of your children have a favorite relative?
    I suoi figli hanno un parente favorito ognuno?

78. Now this is your family tree—I'd like to complete this with you to see where people in a family live and what they do.
    Adesso, questo è il suo albero di famiglia. Vorrei che lei lo completasse per vedere dove la gente vive in una famiglia e che cosa fa per lavorare.

APPENDIX B
Chi-Square Results

CHI-SQUARE RESULTS

	Time in Australia		Age at Emigration		Occupational Mobility		Education	
	χ^2	p	χ^2	p	χ^2	p	χ^2	p
Emigration								
Why emigrate	.43	$p > .98$	4.50	$.50 > p > .30$	7.02	$0.5 > p > .02^*$	7.03	$.05 > p > .02^*$
Was Australia first choice	3.98	$.20 > p > .10$	1.48	$.50 > p > .30$	.03	$.90 > p > .80$	.33	$.70 > p > .50$
Why emigrate x years ago	13.33	$p < .01^*$	5.22	$.10 > p > .05$	.33	$.70 > p > .50$	5.58	$.02 > p > .01^*$
Plan to stay permanently	3.40	$.50 > p > .30$	4.40	$.50 > p > .30$	.81	$.70 > p > .50$	.38	$.90 > p > .80$
Immigration								
First impressions	.92	$.95 > p > .90$	2.18	$.50 > p > .30$	.33	$.70 > p > .50$	3.05	$.10 > p > .05$
First year	4.79	$.50 > p > .30$	5.29	$.30 > p > .20$	1.67	$.50 > p > .30$	3.46	$.20 > p > .10$
Greatest difficulty	2.38	$.70 > p > .50$	10.40	$0.5 > p > .02^*$	1.63	$.50 > p > .30$	1.54	$.50 > p > .30$
Public sector								
English language capacity	4.74	$.10 > p > .05$	2.68	$.30 > p > .20$	14.67	$p < .01^*$	5.58	$.02 > p > .01^*$
Suburban status	8.56	$.02 > p > .01^*$	1.51	$.50 > p > .30$	2.02	$.20 > p > .10$	.09	$.80 > p > .70$
Neighborhood ethnicity	4.17	$.20 > p > .10$	1.25	$.70 > p > .50$	3.46	$.10 > p > .05$	.27	$.70 > p > .50$
Spouse nationality	5.52	$.10 > p > .05$	4.57	$.10 > p > .05$	1.56	$.30 > p > .20$	2.62	$.20 > p > .10$
Private sector								
Food habits	11.63	$p < .01^*$	4.89	$.10 > p > .05$	.39	$.70 > p > .50$	3.94	$p < .05^*$
Home language	28.60	$p < .01^*$	1.66	$.50 > p > .30$	2.99	$.10 > p > .05$	4.15	$.20 > p > .10$
Friends	1.47	$.50 > p > .30$	3.56	$.20 > p > .10$	2.32	$.20 > p > .10$	11.58	$p < .01^*$
Australian associations	.60	$.80 > p > .70$	.35	$.99 > p > .98$	6.19	$.02 > p > .01^*$	12.45	$p < .01^*$

	Value	p	Value	p	Value	p	Value	p
Extended family								
Naming	7.65	p > .10	.63	.98 > p > .95	1.99	.50 > p > .30	8.13	p < .01*
Who really counts	.84	.70 > p > .50	.24	.90 > p > .80	.24	.70 > p > .50	.02	.90 > p > .80
Do relatives help	12.24	.02 > p > .01*	7.82	p > .10	.21	p > .90	3.95	.20 > p > .10
Relatives vs. friends	3.96	.50 > p > .30	3.06	p > .30	.25	p > .90	4.85	.20 > p > .10
Do relatives live near	.56	.80 > p > .70	1.97	.50 > p > .30	.38	.70 > p > .50	.01	.95 > p > .90
Husband-wife relationship								
Authority-responsibility	1.84	.80 > p > .70	2.85	.70 > p > .50	3.04	.30 > p > .20	6.36	.05 > p > .02*
Female independence	.04	p > .98	4.80	.10 > p > .05	1.38	.30 > p > .20	2.51	.20 > p > .10
Responsibility for children	4.25	.50 > p > .30	2.51	.70 > p > .50	1.29	.70 > p > .50	7.01	.05 > p > .02*
Financial responsibility	11.80	p < .02*	2.83	.70 > p > .50	6.40	.05 > p > .02*	2.18	.50 > p > .30
Household property	2.39	.70 > p > .50	6.79	.20 > p > .10	6.04	.05 > p > .02*	.11	.95 > p > .90
Household chores	4.83	p > .30	5.50	.30 > p > .20	.52	.80 > p > .70	1.29	.70 > p > .50
Nuclear family								
Responsibility for marriage	1.68	.50 > p > .30	.66	.80 > p > .70	0	p > .99	.05	.90 > p > .80
Female protection	6.38	.20 > p > .10	2.38	.70 > p > .50	6.41	.05 > p > .02*	6.64	.05 > p > .02*
Service to the family	3.49	.50 > p > .30	0	p > .99	2.45	p > .30	9.05	.02 > p > .01*
Decision making	2.59	.70 > p > .50	.76	.98 > p > .95	.95	.70 > p > .50	7.28	.05 > p > .02*
Going to parties	9.18	.02 > p > .01*	0	p > .99	11.83	p < .01*	4.92	.05 > p > .02*
Marry after graduation	4.94	.30 > p > .20	1.35	.90 > p > .80	3.34	.50 > p > .30	9.22	.05 > p > .02*
Public satisfaction								
Job satisfaction	12.09	p < .01*	2.10	.30 > p > .20	.70	.50 > p > .30	6.75	p < .01*
House satisfaction	29.59	p < .01*	1.82	.50 > p > .30	2.53	.20 > p > .10	1.30	.30 > p > .20

CHI-SQUARE RESULTS (Continued)

	Time in Australia		Age at Emigration		Occupational Mobility		Education	
	x^2	p	x^2	p	x^2	p	x^2	p
Public satisfaction (cont.)								
Naturalized	15.53	$p < .01$*	.65	$.98 > p > .95$	4.56	$.30 > p > .20$	2.86	$.30 > p > .20$
Meaning of naturalization	1.92	$.50 > p > .30$	.54	$.80 > p > .70$	.02	$p > .99$	1.60	$.30 > p > .20$
Visit Sicily	21.13	$p < .01$*	.68	$.80 > p > .70$	0	$p > .99$	1.28	$.30 > p > .20$
Return to Sicily	4.20	$.20 > p > .10$	1.81	$.50 > p > .30$	0	$p > .99$	.03	$.90 > p > .80$
Private satisfaction								
Freedom for women	.04	$p > .98$	4.80	$.10 > p > .05$	1.38	$.30 > p > .20$	2.51	$.20 > p > .10$
Australian vs. Italian friends	.02	$p > .99$	2.63	$.30 > p > .20$	.40	$p > .70$	.01	$.90 > p > .80$
Important live with Italians	.79	$.70 > p > .50$	2.12	$.50 > p > .30$	1.17	$.30 > p > .20$	.02	$.90 > p > .80$
Child's spouse	.82	$.70 > p > .50$	1.23	$.70 > p > .50$	.45	$p > .50$	3.16	$.10 > p > .05$
Australian way of life	9.18	$.10 > p > .05$	5.43	$.30 > p > .20$	.11	$.95 > p > .90$	2.62	$.30 > p > .20$
Own way of life	3.40	$.50 > p > .30$	6.36	$.20 > p > .10$	3.85	$.20 > p > .10$	1.72	$.50 > p > .30$

NOTE: Significance levels of .05 and less are starred.

REFERENCES

Adler, Dan L.
   1965   Matriduxy in the Australian family. In *Australian society,* ed.
         A. F. Davies and S. Encel. New York: Atherton Press.

Anfossi, A.; Talmo, M.; and Indovina, F.
   1959   *Ragusa: Comunità in transizione.* Turin: Taylor.

Australia
   1961   *Census of the Commonwealth of Australia.* Commonwealth
         Bureau of Census and Statistics. Canberra, A.C.T.
   various Yearly bulletins. Commonwealth Bureau of Census and
   years Statistics. Canberra, A.C.T.

Banfield, Edward
   1958   *The moral basis of a backward society.* Glencoe: Free Press.

Barker, George C.
   1947   Social functions of language in a Mexican-American com-
         munity. Ph.D. dissertation, University of Chicago.

Barnard, Marjorie
   1962   *A history of Australia.* Sydney: Angus and Robertson.

Barnett, H. G. et al.
   1954   Acculturation: an exploratory formulation. Social Science Re-
         search Council summer seminar on acculturation, 1953. *Ameri-
         can Anthropologist* 56:973—95.

Barrabee, Paul and Van Mering, Otto
   1953   Ethnic variations in mental stress in families with psychotic
         children. *Social Problems* 1:48–53.

Barzini, Luigi
   1964   *The Italians.* London: Hamish Hamilton.

Beaglehole, Ernest
   1937   *Some modern Hawaiians.* University of Hawaii Research
         Publications, no. 19.

Boissevain, Jeremy
   1966   Poverty and politics in a Sicilian agro-town. *International
         Archives of Ethnography* 1:198–236.

Borrie, W. D.
   1954   *Italians and Germans in Australia.* Melbourne: F. W. Cheshire.
   1957   Australian family structure: demographic observations. In
         Marriage and the Family in Australia, ed. A. P. Elkin. Sydney:
         Angus and Robertson.

Borrie, W. D. et al.
1959 *The cultural integration of immigrants.* Survey based upon the Papers and Proceedings of the UNESCO Conference held in Havana, April, 1956. Paris: UNESCO.

Borruso, Vincenzo
1966 *Pratiche abortive e controllo delle nascite in Sicilia.* Palermo: Libri Siciliani.

Bromley, J. E.
1955 The Italians of Port Pirie. Master's thesis, Australian National University.

Broom, L. and Kitsuse, J. I.
1955 The validation of acculturation: a condition to ethnic assimilation. *American Anthropologist* 57:44–58.

Bruner, Edward M.
1954 A study of cultural change and persistence in a Mandan-Hidatsa Indian village. Ph.D. dissertation, University of Chicago.

Campbell, J. K.
1964 *Honour, family, and patronage.* Oxford: Clarendon Press.

Caudill, William
1952 *Japanese-American personality and acculturation.* Provincetown: Journal Press.

Child, Irvin
1943 *Italian or American?* New Haven: Yale University Press.

Congalton, Athol A.
1961 *Status ranking of Sydney suburbs.* Studies in Sociology, no. 1. Sydney: University of New South Wales.
1962 *Social standing of occupations in Sydney.* Studies in Sociology, no. 2. Sydney: University of New South Wales.

Covello, Leonard
1944 Social background of the Italo-American school child. Ph.D. dissertation, New York University.
1958 *The heart is the teacher.* New York: McGraw-Hill.

Crichton, Robert
1966 *The secret of Santa Vittoria.* New York: Simon and Schuster.

Culotta, Nino
1963 *They're a weird mob.* London: Kaye.

Davies, A. F. and Encel, S.
1965 *Australian society.* New York: Atherton Press.

Day, Helen A.
1929 Sicilian traits. In *Gold coast and slum: a sociological study of Chicago's near north side,* ed. H. W. Zorbaugh. Chicago: University of Chicago Press.

References

Dickinson, Robert E.
1955   *The population problem of southern Italy.* Syracuse: Syracuse University Press.

Dolci, Danilo
1960   *Spreco.* Turin: G. Einaudi.
1964   *Waste.* Translated by R. Munroe. New York: Monthly Review Press.

Douglas, Norman
1915   *Old Calabria.* Boston: Houghton Mifflin Co.

Eggleston, Sir Frederic
1953   The Australian nation. In *The Australian way of life,* ed. G. Caiger. New York: Columbia University Press.

Eisenstadt, S. N.
1954   *The absorption of immigrants.* London: Routledge and Kegan Paul.

Elkin, A. P., ed.
1957   *Marriage and the family in Australia.* Sydney: Angus and Robertson.

Embree, John
1941   *Acculturation among the Japanese of Kona, Hawaii.* Menasha: American Anthropological Association.

Fairchild, Henry Pratt
1926   *Immigration: a world movement and its American significance.* New York: Macmillan Company.

Fallding, Harold
1957   Inside the Australian family. In *Marriage and the family in Australia,* ed. A. P. Elkin. Sydney: Angus and Robertson.

Firth, Raymond
1956   *Two studies of kinship in London.* London: Athlone Press.

Foerster, Robert F.
1919   *The Italian emigration of our times.* Cambridge: Harvard University Press.

Franco, Francesca
1960   Il problema della preparazione al matrimonio visto da ragazze dai 14 ai 18 anni e da madre che frequentono i gruppi di un centro sociale E. Si. S. Diploma thesis, Scuola di Servizio Sociale E. Si. S., Palermo.

Freeman, J. D.
1961   On the concept of the kindred. *Journal of the Royal Anthropological Institute* 91:192–220.

Gamba, Charles
1952   The Italian fishermen of Fremantle: a preliminary study in sociology and economics. University of Western Australia, Department of Economics Publications, ser. A (Economics), no. 2.

REFERENCES

Gans, Herbert
1962   *The urban villagers.* Glencoe: Free Press.

Glazer, Nathan and Moynihan, Daniel
1963   *Beyond the melting pot.* Cambridge: M.I.T. Press.

Goffman, Erving
1959   *The presentation of self in everyday life.* Garden City: Double-day & Co.

Gordon, Milton
1964   *Assimilation in American life.* New York: Oxford University Press.

Gower, Charlotte
1930   [Untitled manuscript.] Anthropology Department, University of Chicago.

Handlin, Oscar
1952   *The uprooted.* Boston: Little, Brown and Co.

Hempel, J. A.
1959   Italians in Queensland: some aspects of the post-war settlement of Italian immigrants. Unpublished report, Australian National University.

Herskovits, Melville J.
1958   *Acculturation: the study of culture contact.* Gloucester, Mass.: P. Smith.

Honigmann, John
1941   *Ethnography and acculturation of the Fort Nelson Slave.* New Haven: Yale University Press.

Horne, Donald
1964   *The lucky country.* Ringwood: Penguin Books.

Italy
1882   *Censimento della popolazione del regno d'Italia, 31 Dicembre 1881.* Ministero di Agricoltura, Industria e Commercio, Direzione della Statistica Generale. Rome.
1947   *La distribuzione della proprietà fondiaria in Italia: Sicilia.* Istituto Nazionale di Economia Agraria. Rome.
1962   *Primo censimento generale dell'agricoltura, Aprile 1961.* Istituto Centrale di Statistica, vol. 2, no. 82. Rome.
1963   *10° censimento generale della popolazione, 15 Ottobre 1961.* Istituto Centrale di Statistica. Rome.
1964   *Risultati economici di aziende agrarie: Sicilia, 1962.* Istituto Nazionale di Economia Agraria. Rome.

Jones, Frank Lancaster
1962   The Italian population of Carlton: a demographic and sociological survey. Ph.D. dissertation, Australian National University.

References

Kluckholn, Florence
 1958   Variations in the basic values of family systems. *Social Casework*
         39:63–72.

Komarovsky, Mirra
 1967   *Blue collar marriage.* New York: Random House, Vintage
         Books.

Lampedusa, Giuseppe
 1958   *Il Gattopardo.* Milan: Giangiacomo Feltrinelli.
 1961   *The leopard.* New York: Signet Books.

Lee, Rose Hum
 1960   *The Chinese in the United States of America.* Hong Kong and
         Oxford: Hong Kong University Press and Oxford University
         Press.

Levi, Carlo
 1947   *Christo si è fermato ad Eboli.* Turin: G. Einaudi.
 1963   *Christ stopped at Eboli.* New York: Farrar Strauss and Co.

Lewis, Oscar
 1966   *La vida.* New York: Random House.

Lopreato, Joseph
 1960   Effects of emigration on the social structure of a Calabrian
         community. Ph.D. dissertation, Yale University. (Revised and
         published as *Peasants no more.*)
 1967   *Peasants no more.* San Francisco: Chandler.

McDonald, Joseph S.
 1958   Migration from Italy to Australia. Ph.D. dissertation, Australian
         National University.

McGregor, Craig
 1966   *Profile of Australia.* London: Hodder and Stoughton.

McNeish, James
 1965   *Fire under the ashes.* Boston: Beacon Press.

Marello, Gabriele
 1960   *Aspetti socio-economici della comunità di Gela.* Banco di
         Sicilia, booklet 4. Palermo.

Mariano, John H.
 1921   *The second generation of Italians in New York City.* Boston:
         Christopher Publishing House.

Martin, Jean I.
 1965   *Refugee settlers.* Canberra: Australian National University
         Press.

Moss, Leonard and Thompson, Walter H.
 1959   The south Italian family: literature and observation. *Human
         Organization* 18:35–41.

References

Neiva, A. H. and Diegus, M.
1959   The cultural assimilation of immigrants in Brazil. In *The cultural integration of immigrants,* ed. W. D. Borrie. Paris: UNESCO.

Padilla, Elena
1958   *Up from Puerto Rico.* New York: Columbia University Press.

Pampilone, Silvio
1964   Inchiesta igienico-sanitaria a Palma di Montechiaro. Monograph printed in Danilo Dolci, *Spreco.* Turin: G. Einaudi.

Parca, Gabriella
1959   *Le Italiane si confessano.* Florence: Parenti.
1963   *Italian women confess.* Translated by Carolyn Gaiser. New York: Farrar, Strauss.
1965   *I sultani: mentalità e comportamento del maschio Italiano.* Milan: Rizzoli.
1966   *Love Italian style.* Englewood Cliffs: Prentice-Hall.

Park, Robert E. and Miller, Herbert A.
1925   *Old world traits transplanted.* Chicago: University of Chicago Press.

Parsons, Anne
1960   Patriarchal and matriarchal authority in the Neapolitan family. Paper delivered at American Anthropological Association meeting, Minneapolis, Minn. 1960, unpublished.
1967   Is the Oedipus complex universal?—a south Italian "nuclear complex." In *Personalities and cultures,* ed. Robert Hunt. American Museum Sourcebooks in Anthropology. Garden City: Natural History Press.

Partridge, P. H.
1955   Depression and war. In *Australia: a social and political history.* Sydney: Angus and Robertson.

Pisani, Lawrence
1959   *The Italian in America: a social study and history.* New York: Exposition Press.

Pitkin, Donald S.
1954   Land tenure and family organization in an Italian village. Ph.D. dissertation, Harvard University.

Pitrè, Giuseppe
1899   *Usi e costumi, crendenze e pregiudize del popolo Siciliano,* vol. 1. Palermo: L. P. Laurill di C. Clausen.
1910   *Proverbi, motti e scongiuri del popolo Siciliano,* vol. 23. Turin: Carlo Clausen.
1913   *La famiglia, la casa, la vita del popolo Siciliano,* vol. 25. Palermo: A. Reber.

Price, Charles
1963   *Southern Europeans in Australia.* Melbourne: Oxford University Press.

References

Radin, Paul
1935   *The Italians of San Francisco, their adjustment and acculturation.* Abstract from the SERA project 2–F2–98 (3–F2–145) : Cultural Anthropology.

Rainwater, Lee; Coleman, Richard P; and Handel, Gerald H.
1959   *Workingman's wife.* New York: Oceana.

Reiss, Albert
1961   *Occupations and social status.* New York: Free Press of Glencoe.

Renda, Francesco
1963   *L'emigrazione in Sicilia.* Palermo: Sicilia al Lavoro.

Romano, Maria
1961   Gli immigranti Belmontesi a Palermo. Diploma thesis, E. Si. S. Scuola di Servizio Sociale, Palermo.

Schiavo, Giovanni
1928   *The Italians in Chicago.* Chicago: Italian American Publishing Co.

Siegel, Bernard J.
1955   *Acculturation: critical abstracts, North America.* Stanford Anthropological Series no. 2. Stanford: Stanford University Press.

Silvani, A. Mariarosa Franco
1965   Un lavoro di sviluppo nella Sicilia occidentale: un'esperienza di lavoro di comunità. Diploma thesis, Scuola di Servizio Sociale, U.N.S.A.S., Milan.

Spicer, Edward et al.
1961   *Perspectives in American Indian culture change.* Chicago: University of Chicago Press.

Spiro, Melford E.
1955   The acculturation of American ethnic groups. *American Anthropologist* 57:1240–51.

Taft, Ronald
1961   The assimilation of Dutch male immigrants in a Western Australian community. *Human Relations* 14:265–82.

Tentori, Tullio
1956   *Matera—il sistema di vita della communità Materana,* vol. 3. Rome: UNRRA-CASAS.

Thernstrom, Stephan
1964   *Poverty and progress: social mobility in a nineteenth century city.* Cambridge: Harvard University Press.

Thomas, William and Znaniecki, Florian
1918   *The Polish peasant in Europe and America.* Chicago: University of Chicago Press.

Vaillant, Roger
1958   *The law.* New York: Alfred A. Knopf.

Vecoli, Rudolph
  1964   Contadini in Chicago: a critique of the uprooted. *American Journal of American History* 51:404–17.

Ware, Caroline
  1935   *Greenwich village.* New York: Houghton, Mifflin.

Warner, William L.
  1941   *The social life of a modern community.* New Haven: Yale University Press.

Whyte, William F.
  1943   *Street corner society.* Chicago: University of Chicago Press.

Williams, Phyllis
  1938   *South Italian folkways in Europe and America.* New Haven: Yale University Press.

Wirth, Louis
  1928   *The ghetto.* Chicago: University of Chicago Press.

Wood, Arthur E.
  1955   *Hamtramck, then and now; a sociological study of a Polish American community.* New York: Bookman Associates.

Young, Michael and Wilmott, Peter
  1962   *Family and kinship in east London.* Baltimore: Penguin Books.

Younger, R. M.
  1963   *The changing world of Australia.* New York: Franklin Watts.

Zurbrzycki, Jerzy
  1960   *Immigrants in Australia: a demographic survey based on the 1954 census.* Melbourne: Melbourne University Press.

INDEX